Reading Skills Handbook

Second Edition

Reading
Skills
Handbook

Harvey S. Wiener

LaGuardia Community College
City University of New York

Charles Bazerman

Baruch College
City University of New York

Houghton Mifflin Company / Boston

Dallas   Geneva, Illinois   Hopewell, New Jersey   Palo Alto   London

Printed in the U.S.A.

Library of Congress Catalog Card Number: 81-82562

ISBN: 0-395-31710-X

LB
1050
.W438
1982
Jan. 1999

Acknowledgment is made to the sources of reprinted materials listed here. The boldface number before each reference refers to the pages of this text on which the work appears.

4   Robert Graves and Alan Hodge, *The Reader over Your Shoulder* (New York: Random House, 1979), pp. 4–5.

21   From "A Shropshire Lad"—Authorised Edition—from *The Collected Poems of A. E. Housman.* Copyright 1939, 1940, © by Holt, Rinehart and Winston. Copyright © 1967, 1968 by Robert E. Symons. Reprinted by permission of Holt, Rinehart and Winston, Publishers; and The Society of Authors as the literary representative of the Estate of A. E. Housman; and Jonathan Cape, Ltd., publishers of A. E. Housman's Collected Poems.

29   © 1979 by Houghton Mifflin Company. Reprinted by permission from *The American Heritage Dictionary*, Paperback Edition.

42   Jerome Bruner, "Freud and the Image of Man," *Partisan Review,* Summer 1956.

42   Erich Fromm, *Man for Himself* (New York: Holt, Rinehart and Winston, 1947).

43   David McCullough, *New York Sun*, May 25, 1883.

45   George Orwell, *Animal Farm* (New York: Harcourt Brace Jovanovich, 1954).

46   Joanna Clark, "Motherhood," in *The Black Woman,* ed. Toni Cade (New York: New American Library, 1970).

46   William Zelermyer, *The Process of Legal Reasoning* (Englewood Cliffs, N.J.: Prentice-Hall, 1963), p. 1.

47   From *New York Daily News*, July 6, 1980. Reprinted by permission of United Press International.

49   Herbert Hendin, *The Age of Sensation* (New York: Norton, 1975).

50   Isaac Asimov, *A Choice of Catastrophes* (New York: Simon and Schuster, 1979).

51   Thomas J. Cottle, *Time's Children: Impressions of Youth* (Boston: Little, Brown, 1971).

51   James Baldwin, "Life in Harlem," in *Nobody Knows My Name* (New York: Dial Press, 1960).

52   Philip Drucker, *Cultures of the North Pacific Coasts* (New York: Harper, 1965).

52   Paul Ehrlich, "World Population: A Battle Lost?" *Stanford Today,* Winter 1968.

53   Mirra Komarovsky, "The Bright Girl's Dilemma," in *Women in the Modern World* (New York: Irvington, 1971).

53   *Newsday*, "Problem Line" by Anita Richterman, May 5, 1975.

56   Associated Press release reprinted by permission as it appeared in *Newsday,* January 31, 1981.

59   "Graduate School: A Way to Double Your Money." © 1979/80 by The New York Times Company. Reprinted by permission.

63   Peter Berger, *An Invitation to Sociology: A Humanistic Perspective* (New York: Doubleday Anchor, 1963), p. 23.

65   *Wilson Quarterly*, Winter 1980, p. 115.

66   Cheryl Morrison, "Looking for Trouble," *New York Magazine,* March 3, 1980. Copyright © 1980 by News Group Publications, Inc. Reprinted with permission of *New York Magazine.*

71   Excerpts reprinted by permission of *Sports Illustrated* from the July 21, 1980 issue. Copyright © 1980 Time Inc. "A Girl Who's Just One Of The Guys" by Steve Wulf.

78   Reprinted from *A Study of Writing*, rev. ed., by I. J. Gelb, by permission of The University of Chicago Press. Copyright 1952 in the International Copyright Union. All rights reserved.

80   From *Errors and Expectations: A Guide for the Teacher of Basic Writing* by Mina P. Shaughnessy. Copyright © 1977 by Mina P. Shaughnessy. Reprinted by permission of Oxford University Press, Inc.

81   From *How to Buy Stocks: A Guide to Making More Money in the Market*, Fourth Edition, revised by Louis Engel. Copyright 1953, © 1967 by Louis Engel. By permission of Little, Brown and Company.

83   From *The Human Body* by Isaac Asimov. Copyright © 1963 by Isaac Asimov. Reprinted by arrangement with The New American Library, Inc., New York, New York.

88   Adapted from Gerald Carson, "Jefferson Davis's Camel Corps," *Natural History*, May 1980, pp. 70–75.

89   John J. Regan, "My Room at the Lilac Inn," in Don M. Wolfe, *Creative Ways to Teach English* (Indianapolis, Ind.: Bobbs-Merrill, 1966).

94   Murray Rubenstein, "Ancient Wonders," *Science Digest,* 89, No. 1 (January/February 1981) p. 77.

95   Randolph Wolfe, "Alabama." American Express Publishing Corp., 1974.

96   Maxine Hong Kingston, *The Woman Warrior* (New York: Knopf, 1976).

97   John D. Stewart, "Vulture Country," *The Atlantic Monthly,* August 1959.

98   Don M. Wolfe, *The Image of Man in America* (Dallas: Southern Methodist
        University Press, 1957).

99   Henry Miller, *Black Spring* (New York: Grove Press, 1964).

100   Mark Twain, *Autobiography*, ed. by Charles Neider (New York: Harper and
        Row, 1959).

\1   Christopher Morley, "On Doors," in *Mince Pie* (Garden City, N.Y.:
        Doubleday, 1919).

10.   Tania Grossinger, "Growing Up at Grossinger's," *New York Times,*
        January 13, 1974.

105   Margaret Mead and Frances Balgley Kaplan, *American Women: The
        Report* (Washington, D.C.: Zenger Publishing Co., 1976).

106   From *Black Elk Speaks* by John G. Neihardt, copyright John G.
        Neihardt, 1932, 1959, 1961. Published by Simon & Schuster Pocket Books
        d the University of Nebraska Press.

121   R   rto Acuna, in *Working* by Studs Terkel (New York: Avon, 1974), p. 36.

122   Rola   E. Wolseley, "The American Periodical Press and Its Impact,"
        Gazei   International Journal of the Science of the Press, Vol. 15, 1969.

123   From *M   ology* by Edith Hamilton. Copyright 1942 by Edith Hamilton.
        Copyrigh   ) renewed by Dorian Fielding Reid and Doris Fielding Reid,
        executrix   he will of Edith Hamilton. By permission of Little, Brown and
        Company.

125   *The New Yor*   January 19, 1981, p. 30.

128   George Orwell,   Hanging," in *Shooting an Elephant and Other Essays*
        (New York: Harc   t, 1950).

130   William Butler Yeats, "Sailing to Byzantium," in *The Collected Poems*
        (New York: MacMillan, 1956).

130   William Shakespeare, *As You Like It,* Act II, scene 7, 1. 174.

130   Ralph Waldo Emerson, "Voluntaries, III," in *Poetry USA: 105 American
        Poems*, ed. by Paul Molloy (New York: Scholastic Book Services, 1968).

130   From *There's a Trick with a Knife I'm Learning to Do* by Michael Ondaatje.
        W. W. Norton, 1979. By permission of the author.

131   Joseph Campbell, "The Old Woman," from *Oxford Book of Twentieth-
        Century English Verse,* ed. by Phillip Larkin (New York: Oxford, 1973).
        Reprinted by permission of the author.

131   Robert Frost, "Out Out," from the *Complete Poems of Robert Frost* (New
        York: Holt, Rinehart and Winston, 1967).

131   Stephen Crane, "Love Walked Alone," in *Works*, Vol. 10, ed. by Fredson
        Bowers (Charlottesville: University Press of Virginia, 1975).

131   William Shakespeare, *Macbeth*, Act I, scene 5, 1. 62.

131   Emily Dickinson, "Because I could not stop for Death," from *The Poems of Emily Dickinson,* ed. Thomas H. Johnson (Cambridge: The Belknap Press of Harvard University Press).

132   "Dream Deferred," Copyright 1951 by Langston Hughes. Reprinted from *The Panther and the Lash,* by Langston Hughes, by permission of Alfred A. Knopf, Inc.

133   Albert Camus, "The Sea Close By," in *Lyrical and Critical Essays* (New York: Knopf, 1968).

135   James Joyce, "Eveline," in *The Dubliners* (New York: Viking, 1967).

138   Excerpt from page 23 in *Growing Up in New Guinea* by Margaret Mead. Copyright 1930, 1958, 1962 by Margaret Mead. By permission of William Morrow & Company.

141   John Fischer, "Salvaging a City," *Harper's Magazine*, March 1974.

144   C. Northcote Parkinson, *The Law of Delay* (Boston: Houghton Mifflin, 1970).

145   Selma H. Fraiberg, *The Magic Years* (New York: Scribners, 1959).

151   Camille Belolan, "Education's No Lark," *Newsday,* April 30, 1980. Reprinted by permission of the author.

156   Carl Sagan, *The Dragons of Eden* (New York: Ballantine Books, 1977), pp. 114–115.

157   Paul R. Wendt, "The Language of Pictures," in *The Use and Misuse of Language,* ed. S. I. Hayakawa (New York: Fawcett, 1962), p. 175.

161   John Holt, *How Children Fail* (New York: Dell, 1964), p. 103.

163   Edgar Allen Poe, "Shadow," in *Poems,* ed. by Dwight MacDonald (New York: Dell, 1971).

165   Edgar Allen Poe, *Selected Poetry and Prose of Poe,* ed. T. O. Mabbott (New York: Random House, 1951), p. 58.

166   Nikolai Gogol, "The Overcoat," in *The Overcoat and Other Stories,* tr. Constance Garnett (New York: Collins-Knowlton-Wing, 1923).

179   Vine DeLoria, Jr., "This Country Was a Lot Better Off When the Indians Were Running It," in Scott Momaday, *American Indian Authors* (Boston: Houghton Mifflin, 1972).

180   Adapted from William M. Pride and O. C. Ferrell, *Marketing: Basic Concepts and Decisions.* Copyright © 1977 Houghton Mifflin Company. Used by permission.

184   James M. McCrimmon, *Writing with a Purpose,* 7th edition, pp. 206–207. Copyright © 1980 Houghton Mifflin Company. Used by permission.

188   Adapted from Roger P. Wilcox, *Communication at Work: Writing and Speaking,* pp. 448–450. Copyright © 1977 Houghton Mifflin Company. Used by permission.

289   Laureen Mar, "My Mother, Who Came from China, Where She Never Saw Snow," in *The Third Woman: Minority Women Writers of the United States* ed. by Dexter Fisher (Boston: Houghton Mifflin Company, 1980), pp. 521–522. Reprinted by permission of the author.

294   Copyright 1941 by John Collier; copyright renewed 1968 by John Collier. Reprinted by permission of the Harold Matson Company, Inc.

302   From L. Dodge Fernald and Peter S. Fernald, *Basic Psychology,* 4th edition. Copyright © 1979 Houghton Mifflin Company. Used by permission.

313   James J. Berry and William M. Leonard II, "A Different Approach to Classroom Testing," *Today's Education,* November–December 1974. Reprinted with permission.

325   Alan Sherman, Sharon Sherman, and Leonard Russikoff, *Basic Concepts of Chemistry.* © 1980 Houghton Mifflin Company. Used by permission.

333   Malcolm Cowley, from *A Second Flowering* by Malcolm Cowley. Copyright © 1973 by Malcolm Cowley. All rights reserved. Reprinted by permission of Viking Penguin, Inc.

Contents

Reading Selections   203

To the Instructor

In this second edition of the *Reading Skills Handbook*, we have improved and expanded a text that has already helped many students to strengthen their reading abilities. As before, the text is divided into two main parts, a *Handbook* that provides instruction in all basic reading skills and *Reading Selections* that provide longer text passages and related exercises. In both parts, we have updated many reading passages to continue offering lively, provocative selections from books of nonfiction and fiction, from newspapers and magazines, and from collections of essays. To guarantee varied and practical reading experiences, we have also frequently drawn material from texts students typically encounter in course work—texts on sociology, psychology, literature, history, chemistry, and so forth. Throughout both Handbook and Reading Selections, students will find questions to guide their understanding and interpretation of specific passages, and they will find that we have given particular emphasis to vocabulary-building skills, both in the text preceding a given selection and in the exercises after it.

What makes the *Reading Skills Handbook* special is that our book describes and discusses the specific skills good readers need in language that is easy for students to read and understand. We begin with basic techniques for dealing with words and sentences; we next examine important comprehension skills; we then advance to skills that require students to interpret and evaluate what they have read. Finally we deal with basic study skills—techniques for note-taking, outlining, and summarizing—to help students improve their performance in class.

We have expanded many of the topics included in the first edition: material on inference, figurative language, and study skills, for example, is now more comprehensive. A wholly new chapter, "Understanding Exam Questions," presents fundamental strategies that students need for dealing with both short-answer and essay tests in college courses. About half of the reading passages are new in both parts of the book.

Most reading textbooks provide only selections and study questions; here, after a clear explanation of some specific skill, students read a straightforward analysis of how that skill applies to a particular passage. Then they have a chance to test mastery of that skill in an exercise specially chosen because it clarifies the new concept. For this edition we have designed many new exercises for practice and review. The more advanced skills build step by step on the earlier ones so that students move from the simple to the more complex in a nonthreatening manner.

Instructors have several options in deciding how to incorporate the two main parts of the book into a specific course. Some instructors take the early weeks of the term to teach Units 1–4 of the Handbook, postponing the Reading Selections until students know the essential reading skills. Since numerous brief readings throughout the Handbook allow the prompt reinforcement of newly learned concepts, students should be quite ready to apply skills to longer selections by the time they reach the Reading Selections. Other instructors choose to reinforce skills taught in Part 1 by assigning appropriate selections from Part 2 after the class reads a chapter or several chapters from the Handbook. Still others *begin* with the Reading Selections and return to key instructional units in the Handbook as students' specific needs arise in class. Whatever approach you choose, students will appreciate the fact that we have keyed each question in the Reading Selections to sections in the Handbook, so that if students have difficulty finding an answer, they can review the appropriate chapter on that particular skill. Thus a **7** after a question means that a review of Chapter 7, "Inference," will help the student by recalling the techniques that readers can use to make valid inferences.

Our intention in the *Reading Skills Handbook* is to provide a comprehensive guidebook for students required to take basic skills courses in reading before or along with courses in the subject disciplines. Encouraged by the success of the first edition, we are confident that students who use this book will make substantial progress in improving their reading competency.

We have many people to thank for their ideas on revising the book. Scott McPartland's intelligent assistance has helped make this edition stronger than the first. Several colleagues scattered over the country have made thoughtful suggestions and guided many of our revisions, including Ann N. Weisner, Department of English, New York Institute of Technology; Anne G. Phillips, Department of English, Santa Monica College; and Adrienne Perry, Department of Reading, Seminole Community College. To them and to our wives and families, we owe our thanks and appreciation.

H.S.W.
C.B.

Handbook

Unit One

Vocabulary

1 Building a Strong Vocabulary

1a How to Find Out What Words Mean

One basic way to better reading is to build up your vocabulary. The more words you recognize and understand, the easier it will be for you to read without stopping and wondering, "What is going on here?"

Most writers are not trying to be difficult when they use big or unusual words. The best writers are those who can draw on a large vocabulary for variety in their writing. By expanding your own supply of words, you can improve your chances of understanding and appreciating what you read. Besides, a rich vocabulary will keep you from limiting your use of words to a small group of familiar ones.

The first step in improving your vocabulary is, of course, recognizing that it is not possible for you to know the meaning of every word you see. Sometimes you may say to yourself, "I sort of know what this means" or "I can get by without figuring this one out." But often you really need to find out exactly what those words mean. In the short run, not paying attention to words you don't know may save you some work. But in the long run, you just won't know as much as you should. Here are some ways to find the meanings of difficult words.

- Learn to use the *context*—that is, clues that sentences sometimes give about the meanings of new words.

- In a word you don't know, look for parts within the word, parts whose meanings you might know.

- Learn the difference between what a word means and what a word suggests or makes you feel.

- Learn the difference between words that mean close to the same thing but have different shades of meaning.

- Learn to use a dictionary so you can find meanings easily.

- Keep a list of words you want to add to your vocabulary.

Exercises

1. Spotting Problem Words

In the following paragraph, underline twice any words you do not know at all. Underline just once any words you are familiar with but for which you do not know the exact definition.

The general European view is that English is an illogical, chaotic language, unsuited for clear thinking; and it is easy to understand this view, for no other European language admits of such shoddy treatment. Yet, on the other hand, none other admits of such poetic exquisiteness, and often the apparent chaos is only the untidiness of a workshop in which a great deal of repair and other work is in progress: the benches are crowded, the corners piled with lumber, but the old workman can lay his hands on whatever spare parts or accessories he needs or at least on the right tools and materials for improvising them. French is a language of fixed models: it has none of this workshop untidiness and few facilities for improvisation. In French, one chooses the finished phrase nearest to one's purpose and, if there is nothing that can be "made to do," a long time is spent getting the Works—the Academy—to supply or approve a new model. Each method has its own advantages. The English method tends to ambiguity and obscurity of expression in any but the most careful writing; the French to limitation of thought.

—Robert Graves and Alan Hodge

2. Building Your Vocabulary

List what you remember of the ways to learn new words.

_____

_____

_____

_____

_____

1b How to Remember New Words

Once you've learned a new word and you think you understand it, you must try to make sure you don't forget it. Here is how to remember new words:

- Write the word and its definition often, just for practice.

- Try to learn the word and its meaning the first time you see it.

- Use index cards to study vocabulary. Write the word on one side of the card and its definition on the other side.

- Make up a sentence you can understand using the word.

- Change the ending of the word: try to make it plural; try to change the tense; try to add _ly_.

- Use the word when you talk—in class, on the job, at home. Make sure you can pronounce the word correctly. Dictionaries will help you to figure out the pronunciation of a word.

- Use the word whenever you can in your writing assignments.

- Say the word and its meaning over and over again in your mind.

- Don't try to learn long lists of new words. Study just a few words each day for several days so that you can learn by repeating.

Exercises

1. Steps in Remembering New Words
   List the steps involved in remembering new words.

_____

_____

_____

_____

_____

_____

_____

_____

2. Remembering Words You Need to Know

List a few words that you need to know for one of your courses. Fix those words in your memory using the methods described in this section.

_____

_____

_____

_____

_____

2 Recognizing Word Meanings

2a Sentence Clues

Each time you read books for your courses, you probably discover new words. Sometimes you may take time out to look up an unfamiliar word in a dictionary. But if you had to stop every time you came to a word you weren't sure of, especially when you found many unfamiliar words, reading would become a very tedious process.

You should realize, however, that you can often figure out the meaning of words without using a dictionary. Many times you can discover the meaning of a word by the way it is used in *context*, or you can figure out a word because you know the prefix or suffix attached to the root word.

How to Use Sentence Hints for Word Meanings

Hint	*Example*	*Explanation*
Some sentences give the definition for a difficult word by means of punctuation.	*Origami*—Japanese paper folding—is family fun. The *addax*, a large pale-colored animal much like the antelope, has two spiral horns.	Dashes—, parentheses ( ), brackets [ ] Commas

Hint	Example	Explanation
Sometimes *helping words*, along with punctuation, provide important clues.	Mary felt *perturbed;* that is, she was greatly disturbed by her sister's actions.	Helping words: *that is, meaning, such as, or, is called.*
Some sentences tell the opposite of what a new word means. From its opposite, you can figure out the meaning of the word.	Parents who constantly spank their children can hardly be called *lenient.*	If you are *lenient,* you do not often punish your children. *Merciful* or *gentle* would be a good guess for the meaning of *lenient.*
Sometimes you can use your own experiences to figure out the definition of a word.	The *cacophonous* rattling made Maria cover her ears.	A noise that would make you cover your ears would be unpleasant or *jarring.*
Sentences before or after a sentence containing a difficult word sometimes explain the meaning of the word.	Mozart gave his first public recital at the age of six. By age thirteen he had written symphonies and an operetta. He is justly called a child *prodigy.*	It would certainly take a remarkably talented person to do these things. An extraordinary person, then, would be a *prodigy.*
Some sentences are written just to give the definitions of difficult words— words that readers will need to know in order to understand what they are reading.	One of the remarkable features of the Nile Valley is the *fertility* of its soil. This rich earth that supported plant growth made it possible for Egyptians to thrive in a dry region.	The second sentence, which tells you that the soil was rich and that it supported plant growth, explains *fertility.*
Because some sentences give examples for a new	Select a *periodical* from among the following: *Playboy,*	The sentence doesn't say a *periodical* is a

Hint	Example	Explanation
word, you can build a definition.	*Time, Reader's Digest,* or *Seventeen.*	magazine, but you can figure that out easily from the examples.
Some sentences use a word you do know to help explain a word you do not know.	A *formidable* enemy is one to be feared.	*Formidable*— through the clues in this sentence— means *fearful* or *dreadful.*

Exercise

Using Sentence Clues

The words in italics (slanted type) in each of the following sentences may have a meaning that you do not know. Try to use hints in the sentences in order to make up a definition. After you write the word in the first blank space, write your own definition in the second blank space.

1. After many weeks of work scraping off old paint and varnish that had been applied through the years, we managed to *renovate* the old desk. _____   _____ _____

2. At exam time Carl's hands shook and sweated so much that he could not hold a pen. His heart pounded and his stomach churned, even though he

knew the subject
very well. He re-
ally had a strange
phobia about tak-
ing tests.   _____   _____

3. After several
minutes of coaxing
and encourage-
ment, we managed
to *cajole* grandma
into boarding the
airplane.   _____   _____

4. *Fibrinogen*—a
substance in the
blood needed for
clotting—does not
always work prop-
erly in all human
beings.   _____   _____

5. *Bards*, the
poet–musicians
who followed the
king, were impor-
tant members of
ancient Celtic soci-
ety.   _____   _____

6. Parts of some
sex movies are cut
in order to allow
them to play in
local theatres, but
this film is *unex-
purgated*.   _____   _____

7. *Myopia* (that
is, nearsighted-
ness) not only re-
fers to a physical
disorder but can
also apply to people

who make decisions
without thinking of
the consequences.   _____   _____

8. Many English
teachers discuss
linguistics with
their classes. Lin-
guistics is the
study of speech and
language.   _____   _____

9. If you *in-
sinuate* that he is a
liar, he certainly
won't like that sly
suggestion.   _____   _____

10. The high div-
ing board is
where the swim
team separates the
brave from the
pusillanimous.   _____   _____

2b Word Part Clues

Occasionally, two words may be put together to form a new word
that is not familiar to you. If you look at each new word unit,
though, you can sometimes recognize the new word. Then you can
try to understand the meaning. For example, look at these words:

      bookcase   (book + case)
      offshore   (off + shore)
      backstage   (back + stage)
      upstream   (up + stream)
      hothead   (hot + head)

Words new to you may contain certain groups of letters that
have meanings you can learn. If you don't know what the word

itself means, these groups of letters may help you reach a definition.

When a group of letters with a special meaning appears in front of a word, it is called a *prefix*.

When a group of letters with a special meaning appears at the end of the word, it is called a *suffix*.

The *root* (or *stem*) is the basic part of a word. We add prefixes or suffixes to some roots and create new words. Look at the word *introspective:*

- The root *spect* means "look."

- The prefix *intro* means "within" or "inward."

- The suffix *ive* means "to tend to" or "to lean toward."

If you knew the meanings of those word parts, you might have been able to see that *introspective* means, in a very exact sense, "to tend to look inward." You would not need a dictionary to discover that definition. When we say people are introspective, we mean that they look into and examine their own thoughts and feelings. Maybe you wouldn't be able to figure out all that from the prefix, root, and suffix, but at least you would have some idea of what the word meant.

If you learn some key prefixes, roots, and suffixes, you will gain some idea of the meanings of many words without looking them up in a dictionary.

2b(1) Important Prefixes

These prefixes all mean, in some way, "no" or "not."

Prefix	Meaning	Example
a	not	amoral
in	not	insensitive
im	not	immobile
non	not	nonreturnable
mis	wrongly	misdirected
mal	badly	malformed
anti	against	antisocial
ir } un }	not	{ irresponsible { unattractive

These prefixes all deal with time.

Prefix	Meaning	Example
pre	before	prerequisite
post	after	postpone
ante	before	antedated

These prefixes deal with numbers, one or more than one.

Prefix	Meaning	Example
uni	one	unicycle
mono	one	monologue
auto	self	autograph
bi	two	bifocal
tri	three	tripod
poly	many	polygon

These prefixes all deal with placement.

Prefix	Meaning	Example
ab	away from	abnormal
circum	around	circumscribe
com	with, together	committee
de	down from	deceit
dis	away	discharge
ex	out of	expel
inter	among	intertwine
per	through	perceive
re	again	revoke
sub	under	submarine
super	above	superior
trans	across	transition

2b(2) Important Roots

Root	Meaning	Example
cred	believe	credence
equ	equal	equate
fac, fact	do, make	factory
graph	written	monograph
mis, mit	send	missile
mor, mort	die	mortify

Root	Meaning	Example
nomen	name	nominal
port	carry	portable
pos	place	position
spic, spec	look	spectator
tang	touch	tangible
vid, vis	see	visible
voc	call	evoke

2b(3) Important Suffixes

Suffix	Meaning	Example
able ⎤ ible ⎦	able to be	⎧ manageable ⎨ defensible
al ⎤ ance ⎥ ence ⎥ ic ⎦	relating to	⎧ regal ⎨ resistance ⎪ independence ⎩ heroic
ion ⎤ ism ⎥ hood ⎬ ity ⎥ ment ⎦	state of, quality of	⎧ union ⎪ patriotism ⎨ brotherhood ⎪ legality ⎩ puzzlement
er ⎤ or ⎬ ite ⎦	one who	⎧ writer ⎨ advisor ⎩ Israelite
y ⎤ ful ⎦	full of	⎧ soapy ⎨ wishful

Exercises

1. Word Part Clues

Each word in the following list is made up of smaller parts. In some, two words are put together to make a new word. In others, prefixes, suffixes, and roots help make up the word. Without turning to a dictionary, use your knowledge of word part clues to write your definitions on the blank lines.

1. peacemaker _____

2. misdirected _____

3. postmortem_____

4. constructive _____

5. goalkeeper_____

6. circumspection _____

7. intangible _____

8. henhouse _____

9. revocation _____

10. misnomer_____

2. Word Part Clues

1. Look at the examples in **2b** on p. 11. Write definitions for the words listed there, using your knowledge of the words that make up the new one. Use a separate sheet of paper.

2. Look at the examples of words in the righthand columns next to the prefixes, suffixes, and roots introduced on pages 12–14. Using your understanding of the word parts, write definitions for the words. Don't check a dictionary until you are all finished. (Use a separate sheet of paper.)

3. Word Parts in Words You Know

Make a list of words you already know, including:

1. any three that begin with the prefix *pre* _____

_____

2. any three that begin with *ex* _____

_____

3. two that start with *in* _____

4. two that end with *ible* or *able* _____

5. one that ends with *ism* _____

6. three that end in *ance* or *ence* _____

_____

7. two that end in *er* or *or* _____

8. one that ends in *ful* _____

9. two that begin with *auto* _____

10. two that begin with *uni* _____

4. Combining Word Parts

By combining prefixes, suffixes, and roots, make a word that means:

1. the quality of being carried across _____

2. not able to be believed _____

3. send under _____

4. write alone _____

5. not capable of being placed _____

2c Denotation and Connotation

So far we have looked at the meanings of words in only one way. A bicycle, for instance, means a two-wheeled vehicle. An addax is an animal that is like an antelope and has two spiral horns. What we have been studying up to this point, then, has been the *denotation* of a word—that is, what the word literally means.

But many words have another kind of meaning beyond their surface meaning. The word *black*, for example, denotes "the darkest color" or "the lack of light." Going beyond denotation, we can understand that "black is beautiful" and that having a business "in the black" is also good. On the other hand, you wouldn't want to be known as "the black sheep" of your family or to have people think your heart was black. As you see, even a simple color can have a wide range of possible meanings, depending on how we use it. This is what is meant by *connotation*, the implied (suggested) meaning of a word.

Often words with similar denotations have very different connotations. All the words in the column at the left denote a person opposite in gender to a male. Yet in each case the connotation is different.

> *female*—a member of the sex that produces eggs or bears young
>
> *woman*—an adult female human being
>
> *girl*—a human female who has not matured into womanhood
>
> *lady*—a woman with refined habits and gentle manners
>
> *chick*—a slang word for a young woman

Knowing connotations of words helps you understand language more fully than you might otherwise. You can see from the list above, for example, that *female, girl, chick, woman,* and *lady* should not be used interchangeably, even though the words share similar denotations, and even though many people do ignore the differences among these words. Unless you were commenting on her social behavior, you'd be inaccurate if you referred to a physician who was not a man as a "lady" doctor. (If you *had* to signify the doctor's sex, *woman* would be much more accurate.) And most young women dislike being called *chicks*, although young men talking among themselves would probably not think twice about using the word.

A writer has many options in choosing words to make a point, and you have to be aware that the writer's choice of one word over a similar one can influence you when you read. In fact, writers can make you feel the way *they* want you to feel about ideas and people through connotations. And dictionaries do not usually include in their definitions all the connotations of a word. That's where your own thinking comes in. You need to be able to recognize that writers who use the word *lady* where they could have used the word *woman* may be offending some members of their audience—deliberately or not. (If a writer uses the word *chick*, you are supposed to feel something else altogether!)

The more you get a sense of connotation, the more you will understand how a writer can influence your emotional reactions to words.

Exercises

1. Denotation and Connotation

In the following groups of sentences, the denotations of the words in italics are almost the same. However, because the connotations are different, each sentence says something slightly (or not so slightly) different from the others. Discuss the meaning of each sentence by explaining the connotations and denotations of the words in italics.

   1. The child *lied* about his father's job. _____

_____

     The child *fibbed* about his father's job. _____

_____

     The child *pretended* about his father's job. _____

_____

   2. Martin is a *mediocre* pianist. _____

_____

     Martin is an *average* pianist. _____

_____

     Martin is an *adequate* pianist. _____

_____

3. Mr. Wing lives in a *palace*. _____

_____

Mr. Wing lives in a *mansion*. _____

_____

Mr. Wing lives in a *chateau*. _____

_____

4. Sally seems *pleased* with her new boyfriend. _____

_____

Sally seems *elated* with her new boyfriend. _____

_____

Sally seems *ecstatic* with her new boyfriend. _____

_____

5. Darth Vader is a *villain*. _____

_____

Darth Vader is a *fiend*. _____

_____

Darth Vader is a *miscreant*. _____

_____

2. Denotation and Connotation
   These words all have reasonably clear denotations, but each
has a number of connotations as well. Write the denotation of the
word and at least one connotation.

1. Communist _____

_____

2. welfare _____

_____

3. fascist _____

_____

4. American _____

_____

5. patriot _____

_____

3. Denotation and Connotation

In each of the following groups, the words have similar denotations, but the connotations are often quite different. Discuss the common denotation of the words and then their individual connotations. Use separate paper if you write out your responses.

1. timid, fearful, cowardly
2. broke, bankrupt, penniless, busted
3. slick, clever, devious, sly
4. eccentric, weird, crazy, insane
5. fat, overweight, obese, plump
6. grin, smile, leer, smirk
7. foreigner, alien, outsider, immigrant, wetback
8. argument, quarrel, dispute, debate
9. wife, better half, wifey, "the missus," the little woman, Ms.
10. oldster, elderly, senior citizen, gramps

4. Denotation and Connotation in Poetry

Look at the following poem in two versions; only example A was written by the English poet A. E. Housman (1859–1936). What does the original poem (example A) mean? Why is it better than example B?

Compare the words (in italics) that have the same number above them—for example, compare *rue* with *sorrow*, *laden* with *weighty*, and so on. What do the words in italics denote? What do they connote? Why has Housman chosen the words he has used instead of the words that appear in example B? What *relationships* among the words used in example A fade when the poem is worded as shown in example B? Write your answers on a separate sheet.

(1)   (2)
A. With *rue* my heart is *laden*
(3)
For *golden* friends I had
(4)
For many a *rose-lipt maiden*
(5)
And many a *light-foot lad*
(6)   (7)
By *brooks* too *broad* for leaping

The light-foot boys are laid

The rose-lipt girls are sleeping
(8)   (9) (10)
In *fields* where *roses fade*.

(1)   (2)
B. With *sorrow* my heart is *weighty*
(3)
For *lovely* friends of joy
(4)
For many a *pink-lipt lady*
(5)
And many a *graceful boy*
(6)   (7)
By *lakes* too *large* for leaping

The graceful boys do lie

The pink-lipt girls are sleeping

(8)   (9)   (10)
In *earth* where *flowers die.*

5. Denotation and Connotation for the Proper Meaning

Discuss the connotations and denotations of the words that
have the same numbers above them in the following sentences.
Under what conditions would you use one of the sentences? When
would you use the other? Why? (You might want to look ahead to
Chapter 11.) Which sentence do you find more suitable? Why?
Write your answers on a separate sheet of paper.

          (1)   (2)   (3)   (4)   (5)
1 a. The *youthful chieftain exhorted* his *comrades* to *persevere* until

          (6)   (7)
      they *vanquished* the *foe.*

          (1)   (2)   (3)   (4)   (5)   (6)
   b. The *young leader urged* his *friends* to *stick to it* until they *beat*

          (7)
      the *enemy.*

          (1)   (2)   (3)
2 a. "*Father,* is this the *appropriate hour* for me to *retire?* " my son

      asked.

          (1)   (2)   (3)
   b. "*Dad,* is this the *right time* for me to *go to bed?*" my son asked.

                          (1)   (2)
3 a. At the wedding two *gentlemen escorted* her down the aisle to

                            (3)
      where she stood beside her *groom.*

                        (1)   (2)
   b. At the wedding two *guys lugged* her down the aisle to where

                            (3)
      she stood beside her future *hubby.*

2d   Shades of Meaning

Some words, although they mean nearly the same thing, actually
mean separate, distinct things. *Boat,* for example, refers to a small
craft that is usually open at the top, and *ship* refers to a large
seagoing craft.

The small differences between words help you recognize different types of similar things quickly and clearly. There are, for example, many types of boats and ships, and each type is described by a specific word. Here are a few of them:

barge	a roomy, flat-bottomed boat
battleship	a large, heavily armed warship
destroyer	a small, fast warship
dinghy	a small rowboat
freighter	a ship for carrying freight
schooner	a large sailing ship
scow	a square-ended barge for carrying garbage or gravel

Not only technical words like names of ships have shades of meaning. Even when you are reading about human feelings, you will find out much more if you pay attention to the exact shades of meaning. The following words, for example, all describe some kind of unpleasant feeling, but notice how different each is:

envy	a painful awareness that somebody has something you want
jealousy	hostility toward a rival
suspicion	distrust
resentment	a feeling that someone has wronged you
grudge	a long-lasting resentment
revenge	desire to hurt someone in return for what he or she has done
malice	desire to do harm for evil pleasure

The best place to find the shades of meaning of any word is in a dictionary. The use of a dictionary is discussed in Chapter 3.

Exercises

1. Shades of Meaning in Descriptive Words

Each of the following words describes a kind of leader. Explain the different shades of meaning of each word. In the blank spaces at the bottom, add your own words (and explanations) to the list. Use a dictionary.

1. tyrant _____

2. dictator _____

3. ruler _____

4. president _____

5. chief _____

6. _____

7. _____

8. _____

2. Meanings of New Words: A Review

Using the vocabulary skills explained in Chapter 2, try to determine the meanings of the words in italics in the following sentences.

1. People who say what they mean clearly and simply will never *obfuscate* an issue.

Obfuscate means _____

2. Ben Franklin, who hated to switch back and forth between the glasses he needed for reading and the glasses he needed for seeing things at a distance, solved his problem by inventing *bifocals*.

Bifocals are _____

3. We all compromised a little about what we wanted to do last night except Leroy, who remained *obstinate* and insisted that all he wanted to do was skate.

Obstinate means _____

4. "All elephants are gray. That animal is gray. Therefore that animal is an elephant." That kind of reasoning is an example of a *syllogism*, but clearly the statement is not necessarily true.

A *syllogism* is _____

5. Some chemical compounds show *deliquescence* because they become a liquid by absorbing moisture from the air.

Deliquescence is _____

6. A fragrant perfume or a good aftershave can be a very important, if intangible, asset on a date.

Intangible means _____

7. In early times, farmers *bartered* their goods for animals and supplies.

Bartered means _____

8. "Our hope is that there will be no *reversion* to earlier behavior patterns," the psychiatrist said.

Reversion means _____

9. *Buzz, click, cuckoo, hum, hiss,* and *pop* are examples of a technique in writing called *onomatopoeia,* wherein words imitate the sounds they name.

Onomatopoeia is _____

10. Many people think that excessive television watching has opened the *floodgates* of young minds, admitting a torrent of inane drivel, violent tendencies, and antisocial behavior.

Floodgates are _____

11. It is good that *acrophobia* is not a problem among bridge painters, who can dangle without fear by ropes hundreds of feet off the ground while they work.

Acrophobia means _____

12. The Victorians, who called piano legs "limbs" and regarded pregnant women as being "in a family way" eventually gave rise to a new generation, the Edwardians. Unlike their parents, the Edwardians had no patience with *euphemisms*.

Euphemisms are _____

13. One of the advantages of gold is its *malleability*, which enables jewelers to hammer, bend, and shape gold into almost any shape or design.

Malleability means _____

14. In opera an important singing role is often played by the *contralto*. A *contralto* is the lowest female voice or the voice part between soprano and tenor.

A *contralto* is _____

15. *Scansion* (the analysis of verse for its arrangement of words in pattern) is an important skill in appreciating poetry.

Scansion means _____

3   Using a Dictionary

A dictionary is an important tool to help build your reading skills. Here is what you can find in a dictionary:

- how to spell a word or its special plural form

- whether or not a word is capitalized or abbreviated

- how to break a word into syllables

- how to pronounce a word

- how a word fits into the English system of grammar (what part of speech it is: verb, noun, adjective, and so forth)

- different meanings of a word, along with *synonyms* (words that mean the same) and *antonyms* (words that have the opposite meaning)

- a sentence or an expression that uses a word correctly

- the meaning of important prefixes and suffixes

- the special uses of a word

- the history of a word

- words made from a main word

Some dictionaries also have special sections that tell about these subjects:

- foreign words and phrases

- abbreviations

- addresses of colleges or government offices

- the population of cities and countries

Depending on how complete they are and on what their purposes are, dictionaries vary in length. Unabridged dictionaries—they try to include information on all the words in our language (about half a million!)—take up thousands of pages. Much of your dictionary work in class and at home, however, will involve a *pocket dictionary*, a small book designed to give only those words used most often. The example from the *American Heritage Dictionary* on page 29 and the following discussion will help you improve your dictionary skills.

3a The Guide Words

Two words appear at the top of each dictionary page. Because all the words in a dictionary are arranged in alphabetical order, the guide words tell you what words to expect on any one page. (The lefthand guide word tells you the first word on the page; the right-hand guide word tells you the last word on the page.) If you wanted to look up *salad*, for example, the lefthand guide word *safeguard* is a hint that the word is here, because *sal* comes after *saf*. The righthand guide word is *salient*. *Sala* comes before *sali*, so you know your word must appear between these two guide words.

3b The Main Entry

The word itself first appears in heavy black letters. (This kind of type is called *bold type*.) Periods show where to put a hyphen in case you have to break the word at the end of a line of writing. The main entry, of course, gives the correct spelling.

3c The Pronunciation Key

These groups of letters (coming right after the main entry) tell you how to say the word. (You know from words like *cough*, *bough*, and *through* that spelling is sometimes not helpful in telling you how to pronounce words.) The letters that appear in parentheses, or between slanted lines in some other dictionaries, stand for special sounds. To find out what sound a letter makes in the word you are looking up, check the pronunciation key at the bottom of the page or at the front in a special section. Checking the key at the bottom

Guide words

Main entries

Pronunciation

Part of speech

Special forms and spellings

Meaning

History of the word

Pronunciation key

safeguard / salient   620

assuring unmolested passage, as through enemy lines.

safe·guard (sāf′gärd′) *n.* A precautionary measure or device. —*v.* To insure the safety of; protect.

safe·keep·ing (sāf′kē′pĭng) *n.* Protection; care.

safe·ty (sāf′tē) *n., pl.* **-ties.** 1. Freedom from danger or injury. 2. Any of various protective devices. 3. *Football.* **a.** A play in which the offensive team downs the ball behind its own goal line. **b.** A defensive back closest to his own goal line.

safety match. A match that can be lighted only by being struck against a chemically prepared friction surface.

safety pin. A pin in the form of a clasp, having a sheath to cover and hold the point.

saf·fron (sāf′rən) *n.* 1. The dried orange-yellow stigmas of a kind of crocus, used to color and flavor food and as a dye. 2. Orange-yellow. [< Ar *za'farān.*] —**saf′fron** *adj.*

sag (săg) *v.* **sagged, sagging.** 1. To sink or bend downward, as from pressure or slackness. 2. To droop. [Perh < Scand.] —**sag** *n.*

sa·ga (sä′gə) *n.* 1. An Icelandic prose narrative of the 12th and 13th centuries. 2. A long heroic narrative. [ON, a story, legend.]

sa·ga·cious (sə-gā′shəs) *adj.* Shrewd and wise. [< L *sagāx.*] —**sa·gac′i·ty** (-găs′ə-tē) *n.*

sage¹ (sāj) *n.* A venerable wise man. —*adj.* **sager, sagest.** Judicious; wise. [< L *sapere,* to be sensible, be wise.] —**sage′ly** *adv.*

sage² (sāj) *n.* 1. An aromatic plant with grayish-green leaves used as seasoning. 2. Sagebrush. [< L *salvia,* "the healing plant."]

sage·brush (sāj′brŭsh′) *n.* An aromatic shrub of arid regions of W North America.

sag·it·tal (săj′ə-təl) *adj.* 1. Of or like an arrow or arrowhead. 2. Relating to the suture uniting the two parietal bones of the skull. [< L *sagitta,* arrow.] —**sag′it·tal·ly** *adv.*

Sag·it·ta·ri·us (săj′ə-târ′ē-əs) *n.* 1. A constellation in the S Hemisphere. 2. The 9th sign of the zodiac. [< L *sagittārius,* an archer, Sagittarius.]

sa·go (sā′gō) *n.* A powdery starch obtained from the trunks of an Asian palm. [Malay *sagu.*]

sa·gua·ro (sə-gwär′ō, sə-wär′ō) *n.* Also **sa·hua·ro** (sə-wär′ō). A very large branching cactus of SW North America. [Mex Span.]

Sa·har·a (sə-hâr′ə, -hä′rə). A desert of N Africa.

sa·hib (sä′ĭb) *n.* A title of respect for Europeans in colonial India, equivalent to *master* or *sir.* [Hindi *şāhib,* master, lord.]

said (sĕd). *p.t. & p.p.* of **say.** —*adj.* Aforementioned.

Sai·gon (sī-gŏn′). The capital of South Vietnam. Pop. 1,400,000.

sail (sāl) *n.* 1. A length of shaped fabric that catches the wind and propels or aids in maneuvering a vessel. 2. A sailing ship. 3. A trip in a sailing craft. 4. Something resembling a sail. —*v.* 1. To move across the surface of water by means of a sail. 2. To travel by water

in a vessel. 3. To start out on a voyage. 4. To operate a sailing craft; navigate or manage (a vessel). 5. To glide through the air; soar. [< OE *segl* < Gmc **seglam.*]

sail·boat (sāl′bōt′) *n.* A small boat propelled by a sail or sails.

sail·fish (sāl′fĭsh′) *n.* A large marine fish with a large dorsal fin and a spearlike projection from the upper jaw.

sail·or (sā′lər) *n.* 1. One who serves in a navy or earns his living working on a ship. 2. A straw hat with a flat top and brim.

saint (sānt) *n.* 1. *Theol.* **a.** A person officially entitled to public veneration for extreme holiness. **b.** A human soul inhabiting heaven. 2. A very holy or unselfish person. [< L *sanctus,* sacred.] —**saint′dom** *n.* —**saint′hood′** *n.*

saint·ly (sānt′lē) *adj.* **-lier, -liest.** Of or befitting a saint. —**saint′li·ness** *n.*

Saint-Saëns (săN-säNs′), **Camille.** 1835–1921. French composer.

saith (sĕth, sā′əth). *Archaic.* 3rd person sing. present indicative of **say.**

sake¹ (sāk) *n.* 1. Purpose; motive: *for the sake of argument.* 2. Advantage, benefit, or welfare. [< OE *sacu,* lawsuit. See **sāg-.**]

sa·ke² (sä′kē) *n.* Also **sa·ki.** A Japanese liquor made from fermented rice.

sa·laam (sə-läm′) *n.* An Oriental obeisance performed by bowing low while placing the right palm on the forehead. [Ar *salâm,* "peace."] —**sa·laam′** *v.*

sa·la·cious (sə-lā′shəs) *adj.* Lewd; bawdy. [< L *salāx,* fond of leaping, lustful.] —**sa·la′cious·ly** *adv.* —**sa·la′cious·ness, sa·lac′i·ty** (sə-lăs′ə-tē) *n.*

sal·ad (săl′əd) *n.* A dish usually consisting of raw green vegetables tossed with a dressing. [< VL **salāre,* to salt.]

sal·a·man·der (săl′ə-măn′dər) *n.* 1. A small, lizardlike amphibian. 2. A portable stove used to heat or dry buildings under construction. [< Gk *salamandra.*]

sa·la·mi (sə-lä′mē) *n.* A highly spiced and salted sausage. [< It *salame,* "salted pork."]

sal·a·ried (săl′ə-rēd) *adj.* Earning or yielding a regular salary.

sal·a·ry (săl′ə-rē, săl′rē) *n., pl.* **-ries.** A fixed compensation for services, paid on a regular basis. [< L *salārium,* orig "money given to Roman soldiers to buy salt."]

sale (sāl) *n.* 1. The exchange of property or ownership for money. 2. Demand; ready market. 3. Availability for purchase: *on sale.* 4. An auction. 5. A special disposal of goods at lowered prices. [< OE *sala* < ON.] —**sal′a·ble, sale′a·ble** *adj.*

Sa·lem (sā′ləm). The capital of Oregon. Pop. 68,000.

sales·man (sālz′mən) *n.* A man employed to sell merchandise, insurance, etc. —**sales′man·ship′** *n.* —**sales′wom′an** *fem.n.*

sal·i·cyl·ic acid (săl′ə-sĭl′ĭk). A white crystalline acid, $C_7H_6O_3$, used in making aspirin. [< L *salix,* willow.]

sa·li·ent (sā′lē-ənt) *adj.* 1. Projecting or jutting beyond a line. 2. Striking; conspicuous. [< L *salīre,* to leap, jump.] —**sa′li·ence, sa′li·en·cy** *n.*

of the entry, you see that the *a* in *sake* has the same sound as the *a* in *ate.* You'll notice that the *a* in *sake,* the next entry (meaning a kind of Japanese liquor), is the same *a* as is found in *bar,* giving *sake,* the liquor, a very different pronunciation.

3d   The Parts of Speech

The *parts of speech* tell you how the word is placed in the system of English grammar. The *n.* after the pronouncing letters of *sailor* means "noun." The *adj.* after *saintly* means "adjective." Sometimes a word has different meanings based on what part of speech it is. *Sail* as a noun means "a length of shaped fabric that catches the wind and propels or aids in maneuvering a vessel." As a verb, *sail* means "to move across the surface of water by means of a sail."

3e   Special Forms and Special Spellings

Sagacity is made from *sagacious,* so it is included as part of the entry for *sagacious* instead of as a main entry itself. Notice too that, in addition to singular forms of words, the dictionary often gives you the plural forms. The plural of *salary* is formed by adding *ies* as the final syllable.

3f   The Meanings of the Word

Next, the word is defined. The meanings of words that can be used in more than one sense are separated and numbered in heavy bold print. Usually the most important definitions come first. If you see *syn.,* that is an abbreviation for *synonym.* Words that come after *syn.* have the same meaning as the main word. An example sometimes appears to show how the main word is used.

Some Dictionary Pointers

- Review your skill with alphabetical order. Can you arrange words correctly?
- Use the guide words. They save you time.
- Check all abbreviations and symbols in the special section.

- If you look up a word and it's not where you expect it to be, don't think it's not in the dictionary! Check under several possible spellings. If you couldn't spell the word *crime*, for example, the sound of the word might suggest these spellings:

cryme	krime
kryme	krhyme
criem	crhyme

  If you couldn't spell the word, you might have to check them all before you found *crime!*

- Test the *meaning* you find for the word in the sentence in which you found the word. You may not have picked a definition that works for the word as it is used.

- Try to say the word aloud after you look at the pronunciation key.

3g   The History of the Word

The information that appears in brackets tells the way the word has developed in our language. Many words have origins in foreign languages like Latin (L) or Greek (G). In fact, a good dictionary can be your best first source for *etymology*—the study of the origin and historical development of words. For example, a word like *scrupulous*, which means "having principles," developed from the early use of small, sharp stones in Roman markets. (A stone weighing one twenty-fourth of an ounce was called a *scrupulus* in Latin.) Merchants used those stones for weighing, and merchants who weighed objects honestly were said to be *scrupulous*.

Exercises

1. Order of the Alphabet
   Put the words in this list in correct alphabetical order.

scrimmage   _____

scrub _____

scribble _____

scream _____

scrounge _____

scribe _____

2. Guide Words

The guide words at the top of a certain dictionary page are *intellectual* and *interfere*. Circle the words you would expect to find on that page.

insult	intense	interpol
instruct	intake	interest
intercede	interface	intend
inning	intellect	interstate

3. Guide Words

Under each numbered pair of guide words appear several other words. Circle each word that you would expect to find on a page that shows the guide words.

a. forehand / formula

fortune	Formosa	formulate
forfeit	formalize	formation

b. rabies /radio

racket	raccoon	radiogram
rabid	radius	radical

c. vertex / veto

vex	versus	vessel
vesper	vestige	

d. manward / marcasite

maraud	marcel
mantilla	manx cat

e. foulard / fourpence

fowl	foundry	fountainhead
fraction	fourpenny	

4. One Word, Several Meanings

Each word that follows has several different meanings. Look up each word in a dictionary and write three different definitions. After each definition, write a sentence in which you use the word in that way. Use your own paper.

book

1. *Definition*: a written work for reading
   Sentence: The book I read was *Sissy* by John Williams.

2. *Definition*: a set of tickets bound together
   Sentence: He ripped a ticket from my *book* before I entered the bus.

3. *Definition*: to engage a performer for a show
   Sentence: David Merrick *booked* a Russian dance group for a United States tour.

   turn   sink   part
   fair   block

5. The Right Meaning

The words in italics in the following sentences have many meanings. Use a dictionary to check the definitions, but make sure you select the appropriate definition based on how the word is used in the sentence. Write your meanings in the spaces provided.

1. The carpenter applied a shiny *finish* to the table. _____

_____

2. As they neared the cage of the lioness, they saw her cub

lying near her. _____

_____

3. The sixth issue of the *magazine* was published last week.

_____

4. Are you *content* with the contents of this book? _____

_____

5. Many people considered her face *homely*. _____

_____

6. As the *pivot*, Sargeant Gomez helped turn the battle in his platoon's favor. _____

_____

7. The artist gave the picture a mat *finish*. _____

_____

8. In her talk about bees, she suddenly flew off on a *tangent* and dealt with the poor quality of commercial honey. _____

_____

9. A few years ago, organ transplanting was an *embryo* of an idea; now it is quite common in practice. _____

_____

10. The members enjoyed the home-baked cake at the *collation*. _____

_____

6. Checking Foreign Words

Many words from other languages become part of the English language. Check the numbered words in a dictionary to learn the language they come from, their pronunciation, and their meaning. Fill in this information in the following chart.

Word	Language	Pronunciation	Meaning
1. qua	_____	_____	_____
2. bon homme	_____	_____	_____

Word	Language	Pronun- ciation	Meaning
3. coup d'état	_____	_____	_____
4. bête noire	_____	_____	_____
5. honcho	_____	_____	_____
6. chutzpah	_____	_____	_____
7. yogurt	_____	_____	_____
8. prima facie	_____	_____	_____
9. macho	_____	_____	_____
10. hibachi	_____	_____	_____

7. Pronouncing Words

Use your dictionary to find the correct way to pronounce these words.

1. flaccid
2. epitome
3. quay
4. February
5. mischievous
6. dais
7. brooch
8. carafe
9. library
10. indict

8. Practice in Dictionary Skills

Using the sample from a dictionary on page 29, answer the following questions.

1. What is the plural of _safety_? _____

2. What is the origin of the word _salaam_? _____

3. Which of the words in this sample are written with a capital letter? _____

4. Circle the words that contain the same sound as the long *a* sound in *sale.*

saint, sage, Salem, salient, sahib

5. What is *salicylic* acid used for? _____

_____

6. What part of the world does *sahib* come from? _____

7. What is another spelling for the word *sake*? _____

8. Write the plural of the word *salary.* _____

9. Explain in your own words the meaning of the word *salient* as it is used in the following sentence:

The most *salient* feature of disco music is the heavy beat.

10. The symbol ə is a *schwa* and stands for a vowel sound in a syllable that is not accented. Find three words in which schwas are

used to show pronunciation. _____

_____

9. A Dictionary Review
Using a good dictionary, find the answers to these questions.

1. What is the plural of *hippopotamus*? _____

2. What parts of speech may the word *service* be? _____

3. What language does the word *picnic* come from? _____

What is its origin? _____

_____

4. What do the following words mean?

a. cajole _____

b. rostrum _____

c. ohm _____

d. panacea _____

e. irrational _____

5. Write an antonym and a synonym for each of the following:

	Antonym	*Synonym*
a. placate	_____	_____
b. harsh	_____	_____
c. diligent	_____	_____

Unit Two
Comprehension

4 Reading for the Main Idea

4a **Key Ideas in Sentences**

Although a sentence may give a great deal of information, it usually offers one key idea. Readers must be able to find key ideas in order to understand sentence meanings clearly.

The key idea of a sentence usually tells:

- what a person or an object is

- what a person or an object is doing

A tall girl in a white dress rushed away into the trees just beyond the gate to Stevens Park.

This sentence tells about a girl. We know that the girl rushed away. All the information about her appearance, about where she ran, and about the name of the park adds details. The details are helpful in completing the scene for the reader, and very often we need to rely on details to make the main idea clearer. But the key idea, the main thought, in the sentence is simply *a girl rushed away*.

Here is how to find key ideas in sentences:

- Ask *who* or *what* the sentence is about.

- Ask what the person or object is doing or what is happening to the person or object.

- Learn to separate details from the key idea. Many words in sentences describe things about the subject of the sentence and merely add details around it. If you ask *when, what kind, where,* or *why,* you will find details. As a result it is easier to see the key idea.

(why)   *(what kind)*   *(where)*
Because of new laws, most foreign automobiles in the United

(when)   *(how)*
States now offer safety features at no extra charge.

Who or what is the sentence about? *automobiles*
What do the automobiles do? *offer safety features*
The key idea is *automobiles offer safety features.*

Exercises

1. Key Ideas in Sentences

In each of the following sentences, underline the parts that give the key idea. Here is an example:

<u>Children</u> who live in a ghetto <u>find</u> <u>fun</u> in the street even when they have no toys.

1. Even good schoolyard basketball players have trouble playing fullcourt.

2. A new car can be ruined by a typical Chicago winter.

3. San Juan has nicer apartments than New York and at lower prices.

4. A group of screaming teenagers holding sticks raced along Sutphin Avenue yesterday.

5. In spite of his hate for overnight trips, John camped in the woods of Highland Park because his friends dared him to.

2. Key Ideas in Sentences

Write in the blank lines the key idea in each sentence.

1. A recent issue of *Time* magazine contains an article about attempts by Greenpeace to stop the worldwide slaughter of whales.

_____

_____

2. Was the woman who ran away after the robbery of First National City Bank part of the gang of thieves who stole $400,000 last week at a bank in another part of town?

_____

_____

3. Although television programs sometimes appear to be honest, they may actually be distorting the truth.

_____

_____

4. Do not under any circumstances pick up a hitchhiker on a lonely road at night, no matter how sorry you feel for the person standing there alone.

_____

_____

3. Key Ideas in Quoted Statements
Each of the following sentences was written or spoken by a famous person. On the blank lines, write in your own words the key idea of each statement.

1. "Today men seek the kind of approval that applauds not their actions but their personal attributes." (Christopher Lasch)

_____

_____

_____

2. "A law is unjust if it is inflicted on a minority that, as a result of being denied the right to vote, had no part in enacting or devising the law." (Martin Luther King, Jr.)

---

3. "A culture in its very nature is a set of values, skills, and ways of life that no one member of the society masters." (Jerome Bruner)

---

4. "The person who most considers others is also the one who has the deepest self acceptance." (Erich Fromm)

---

5. "A stubborn and still undecided battle has been raging on the field of my thoughts for the supremacy of one of the two men within me." (Petrarch)

4b Main Ideas in Paragraphs

A *paragraph* is a group of sentences about some related subject. As you read a paragraph, you look for the key idea that each sentence presents. Adding up these key ideas, you see that each sentence helps build the *main idea* of the paragraph, the basic subject that all the sentences are related to. Readers must know what the main idea of the paragraph is in order to understand the information they are reading.

4b(1)   Stated Main Ideas

Often one sentence in the paragraph tells the reader exactly what the rest of the paragraph deals with and therefore gives the main idea. This *main idea sentence* (it is often called a *topic sentence* or *topic statement*) may appear in one of several places.

Main Idea in the Beginning

As the sun went down, the scene from the bridge was beautiful. —**Main idea at beginning** It had been a perfect day. Up and down on either side of New York the bright blue water lay gently rippling, while to the south it merged into the great bay and disappeared toward the sea. The vast cities spread away on both sides. Beyond rolled the hilly country until it was lost in the mists of the sky. All up and down the harbor the shipping, piers, and buildings were still gaily decorated. On the housetops of both Brooklyn and New York were multitudes of people.

—David McCullough

The main idea of this passage is *the view from the bridge was beautiful.* All the sentences in the paragraph illustrate that idea by providing many details.

Main Idea in the Middle

There are 74.5 million television sets in the United States, at least one set for 98 percent of all American homes. Forty-eight percent of all U.S. homes have more than one set, and some families even have a set for every person in the house. *Yet, despite the fact that the number of sets in the United States has* —**Main idea in middle** *virtually reached a saturation point, the amount of time spent watching television has declined steadily since 1976.* Explanations vary from the increasingly poor quality of network shows to the rising popularity of home video equipment, but the fact remains that we are owning more sets but enjoying them less.

The main idea of this paragraph is *despite the fact that the number of television sets in the United States has virtually reached a saturation point, the amount of time spent watching television has declined steadily since 1976.*

Main Idea at the End

Although the buildings are tall, none of them blots out the sky.
People rush about as in New York, but someone always stops
to answer a question about directions. A person will listen
when he or she is asked a question. Often a sudden smile will
flash from the crowds of strangers pushing down State Street.
It is a smile of welcome and of happiness at the same time. And
the traffic: it is tough, noisy, active; but a person never feels as
if he takes his life in his hands when he crosses the street. Of
course, there is always the presence of the lake, the vast,
shimmering lake that shines like an ocean of silver. Something
about that lake each time it spreads out around a turn on ___*Main*
Lakeshore Drive says, "Hello. It's good to see you again."   *idea at*
Chicago is a fine, friendly city.   *end*

The main idea in the paragraph is *Chicago is a fine, friendly
city.* All the sentences in the paragraph support that idea with
details. By stating the main idea at the end, the author summarizes
the point of the paragraph.

Main Idea in More Than One Sentence

Dogs make warm, friendly pets. But they can also be very ___*Main*
troublesome. No one will deny the feeling of friendship when,   *idea*
after a long day's work, a wet pink tongue of greeting licks a
master's hand at the door. And watching television or reading
a book, a man or woman can reach down over the side of the
couch and feel a warm furry patch of life, hear the quiet con-
tented breathing of a good friend. However, try to plan a trip
without your faithful pet and your life is very difficult. Where
will you leave him? Who will feed him? Further, leaving a cozy
house in the midst of winter and facing a howling frozen wind
so the dog may take his walk is no pleasure at all. I often
wonder why people put up with such demands upon their time
and energy.

The main idea in this paragraph appears in two sentences.
Although the first sentence of the selection says that dogs are
warm, friendly pets, only part of the paragraph gives details to
support that idea. Other details in the paragraph show that dogs
are troublesome. An accurate statement of the main idea would
have to include the information in both of the first two sentences:
Dogs make friendly pets, but they can also be troublesome.

Exercise

Stated Main Ideas

    For each of the following paragraphs, put a checkmark next to the sentence that tells the main idea. In the blank space write the main idea in your own words.

1. As soon as the light in the bedroom went out there was a stirring and a fluttering all through the farm buildings. Word had gone round during the day that old Major, the prize Middle White boar, had had a strange dream on the previous night and wished to communicate it to the other animals. It had been agreed that they should all meet in the big barn as soon as Mr. Jones was safely out of the way. Old Major (so he was always called, though the name under which he had been exhibited was Willingdon Beauty) was so highly regarded on the farm that everyone was quite ready to lose an hour's sleep in order to hear what he had to say.

                                                  —George Orwell

_____

_____

2. There is a trick to watching sports on the cable. You check in on all the games, one after another. With a remote channel selector, you can do it without ever leaving the couch. Baseball is the best, because of its leisurely pace. While the Cubs were trying to find a pitcher that day, I could make a tour of tennis, soccer, the HBO movie, and keep up, more or less, with water polo. I have to do a lot of switching around anyhow, because there are no Chicago listings in the Annapolis *TV Guide*. A friend checked this out, and he said not much can be done about it. *TV Guide* is testing a special cable edition in New Mexico, where they have 150,000 cable subscribers and 35 different cable systems. There are only 4,100 cable fans in Annapolis, so it doesn't look good.

                                          —Christian Williams

_____

_____

3. I may be more upsettable than most, but during the years I was involved with carriages and strollers and wagons and tricycles, I was always getting bugged. Why wasn't there, even in the children's section of a department store, a high chair so you could deposit your child and spend your money in some sort of comfort? Why did it have to be a major struggle to get a stroller or a shopping cart across a street; would it cost so much to rake the curbs? And did the entrance to the playground offer the steepest curb of all? Small enough problems, but enough to clue in to the fact that the last people anyone in charge of planning the city are concerned with are mothers and children.

—Joanna Clark

4. Reasoning is a process of thought aimed at reaching or justifying a conclusion. The process involves a consideration of facts and impressions, experiences and principles, objectives and ideals. In planning to embark upon an excursion, one considers the length of time at his disposal, the distances to various destinations, the modes of travel available, the pocketbook, the climates, the accommodations; the mental pictures of places, people, things to see, roads to travel, costs to be incurred, comforts to be enjoyed, discomforts to be endured; places visited in the past, roads already traveled, facilities formerly utilized, costs previously incurred, the advice of friends; the aversion to night travel and crowds, the desire for comfort and service, the dislike of salt water and sand, the scheduling of time and mileage; the aim to visit certain places and people, to attend certain events, to participate in certain activities; the idea of relaxation and refreshment, of self-enlightenment and improvement, of preparation for service and leadership. Not every situation which lends itself to the reasoning process involves so many considerations, but some involve even more. And as to a particular situation, or type of situation, not every person will consider the same things. But the greater the number of things that are considered, the more complex the process becomes. In considering even a relatively simple situation, there is no assurance that reasoning will always lead to the same conclusion, for not all reasoning is logical.

—William Zelermyer

_____

_____

5. Willow Grove, Pa. (UPI)—John Pigford, 7, who acciden-
tally ejected himself 50 feet into the air from the cockpit of a S3
Viking antisubmarine plane on display at a Fourth of July air
show at the Naval Air Base here, died yesterday in a Philadelphia hospital. Pigford, who landed on a concrete runway, suffered severe burns and head injuries. Base spokesman Cmdr.
James Kriebel said that before the accident, thousands of the
125,000 visitors to the annual air show had climbed through
the plane and sat in the cockpit. A complicated procedure was
necessary to activate the ejection system, Kriebel said. "How
he got the right sequence of switches God only knows." Ten
other persons, including John's brother Steve, 8, suffered
minor burns or other injuries in the accident.

—New York Daily News

_____

_____

6. Anyone, really, can bake a good cake. There are many good
mixes for sale at the supermarket, and home cooks report good
results with coffee cakes, streusel, devil's food cakes, and date
nut loaves. Still, it takes a top-notch baker to make a good pie.
There's not a mix around that can offer a moist, flaky crust
that is firm to the teeth and not too soggy. It is a combination
of basic ingredients—flour, shortening, water—and the patient work of a devoted baker that creates the magic of a
well-baked pie.

_____

_____

4b(2) Implied Main Ideas

Sometimes paragraphs do not tell exactly what the basic subject is.
Instead you must decide on the main idea yourself. In order to do
that, you must add up all the details the writer gives and then state
the main idea in your own words.

When a main idea is not stated exactly, but instead the writer *suggests* the idea to you through the information given in the paragraph, the idea is *implied*. An *implied main idea* is one that is suggested. Here is an example:

The first boring task is to prepare breakfast. Johnny, Cathy, and Jed need juice and eggs before a day at school; my husband Bill, coffee and toast before he speeds off to the office. When everyone is finally away, doing something he or she enjoys, I scrape the dishes off into the garbage, then wash them in the sink. I hate it! Afterwards I look forward to making beds, washing the kitchen floor, cleaning the rug in the living room. If I'm lucky the mailman rings the bell so I talk to another human being in the flesh for ten seconds or so. I put up the roast, find some other things to do, all along thinking of the adventures my children meet in the classroom while their housewife-mother watches the house in the suburbs. And Bill, the people he meets, the glamorous lunches, the excitement he sees on the streets everyday: these are things I'll never know from this position. I sweep floors, sew buttons, clink pots and pans—that's my work for the world.

One way to state the main idea of the paragraph is: *My life as a housewife is filled with dull, meaningless tasks.* No one sentence makes that point. Furthermore, the writer never tells us exactly that her life is filled with dull chores. Instead, we add up the details she gives us in order to state the main idea in our own words. She finds making breakfast dull, washing dishes boring, and cleaning the house lonely and tiresome. She envies the excitement her husband finds in his work. Putting all that information together, we conclude that this writer is trying to show us that she leads a dull life as a housewife.

Here is how to state the main idea in your own words:

- Try to figure out what *all* the details in the paragraph are trying to show, not just a few of them.

- Make a complete sentence that (1) names a person or an object and (2) tells what a person or an object is doing.

- Do not look at just a few sentences in the paragraph in order to find out the main idea. Even though the first few sentences express the idea that giving breakfast to the family is dull, it would not be correct to say that *serving breakfast is a dull task* is the main idea of the paragraph. The sentence is true; we know that from statements in the paragraph. But the sentence is not the *main* idea; it is only one narrow idea that helps us build the main idea sentence: *My life as a housewife is filled with dull, meaningless tasks.*

- Do not offer a statement that is *too general* as the main idea. For example, it would be incorrect to say that the main idea of the paragraph is: *The job of the American housewife is dull and meaningless.* The author of the paragraph might agree with this statement. But no details in the paragraph suggest that the writer was talking about the American housewife in general. The author was talking about *herself;* she was showing that *her* job was dull and meaningless, so the main idea should be stated in these terms: *My life as a housewife is filled with dull, meaningless tasks.*

Exercises

1. Implied Main Ideas

Read the following brief passages. Add up all the details in your mind in order to figure out the main idea that is implied. Write a sentence that tells the main idea of the paragraph.

1. For many students drug abuse is the means to a life without drugs. Such students take drugs to support the adaptation they are struggling to make. Once it is established, they are often able to maintain it without drugs. The period of heavy drug abuse often marks the crisis in their lives when they are trying to establish a tolerable relation to the world and themselves. Appealing, tumultuous, sometimes frighteningly empty, the lives of students who turn to drugs are an intense, dramatic revelation of the way students feel today, what they are forced to grapple with not only in the culture, but in themselves.

—Herbert Hendin

_____

_____

2. Naturally, before the true nature of the movements and orientation of the Earth was understood, there could be no confidence that in any one particular year, the sun, as it lowered toward the winter solstice, might not continue to lower indefinitely, disappear, and bring all life to an end. Thus, in the Scandinavian myths, the final end is heralded by the "Fimbul-

winter" when the sun disappears and there is a terrible period of darkness and cold that lasts three years—after which is Ragnarok and the end. Even in sunnier climes where faith in the perpetual beneficence of the sun would naturally be stronger, the time of the winter solstice, when the sun ceased its decline, turned, and began to ascend the heavens once more was the occasion of a vast outpouring of relief.

—Isaac Asimov

_____

_____

2. Implied Main Ideas

In each of the following selections, the main idea is implied. After you read, put a checkmark near the statement that you think best gives the main idea most clearly. Be prepared to explain why the other choices are not correct.

1. Until a person is about nineteen, the brain continues to grow, adding new cells every year. After that, until the end of life, the brain slowly dies, losing several thousand brain cells every day. After the age of twenty-seven, the body becomes brittle. It is harder to recover from injuries, but much easier to get injured. The muscles lose their ability to stretch. But by far, the worst part of getting old is that we become prone to diseases that seem to accompany aging naturally: heart diseases, cancer, arthritis, strokes.

_____a. Old age is a time of much wisdom and experience.

_____b. Staying in shape is important after age thirty.

_____c. Growing older brings on many physical problems.

_____d. Aging is a perfectly natural part of growing.

2. The four feet of space between Gino's and Israel's apartment houses have been long filled with crushed rock and rubbish. Over three years ago, an apartment building in the rear burned down and the city has never finished cleaning away the rubble and the large concrete pieces that once served as a foundation for eight families. "D'you know that a baby died in the fire?" Gino recalled for us on several occasions. Most of the stones have just been ground more deeply into the earth so that the dust adheres to the pants and shoes of the boys who

play in this area every day when the late afternoon light slips
between the houses and throws the shadows of the people
walking by onto the tan wooden fence in the rear.

—Thomas J. Cottle

____a. Buildings burn down and are neglected in cities.

____b. A baby died when a fire destroyed the building near Gino's
house.

____c. Gino and Israel live beside the dirt and rubble of a burned-
down apartment building.

____d. Children enjoy playing with rocks and the earth in the late
afternoon.

3. Main Ideas in Paragraphs: A Review
In the following paragraphs, the main idea is either stated or
implied. (See sections **4b(1)** and **4b(2)**.) Try to determine the main
idea of each selection. Write the main idea in your own words in
the space provided.

1. There is a housing project standing now where the house in
which we grew up once stood, and one of those stunted city
trees is snarling where our doorway used to be. This is on the
rehabilitated side of the avenue. The other side of the
avenue—for progress takes time—has not been rehabilitated
yet and it looks exactly as it looked in the days when we sat
with our noses pressed against the windowpane, longing to be
allowed to go "across the street." The grocery store which
gave us credit is still there, and there can be no doubt that it is
still giving credit. The people in the project certainly need
it—far more, indeed, than they ever needed the project. The
last time I passed by, the Jewish proprietor was still standing
among his shelves, looking sadder and heavier but scarcely
any older. Farther down the block stands the shoe-repair store
in which our shoes were repaired until reparation became impossible and in which, then, we bought all our "new" ones. The
Negro proprietor is still in the window, head down, working at
the leather.

—James Baldwin

_____

_____

2. Each Haida village had a chief, who held that position by virtue of being the highest-ranking member of the lineage, and one or more house chiefs. The village chief (who was also the house chief of his own house) had a special title, the various versions of which translate either as "village master," "village owner," or "village mother." Each village was economically independent, owning its own village site, salmon streams, cod and halibut grounds, berrying and hunting tracts, and of course the camping sites that went with them.

—Phillip Drucker

3. The facts of human population growth are simple. The people of the Earth make up a closed population, one to which there is no immigration and from which there is no emigration. It can be readily shown that the Earth's human population will remain essentially closed—that no substantial movement of people to other planets is likely and that no substantial movement to other solar systems is possible. Now, a closed population will grow if the birth rate exceeds the death rate, and will shrink in size if the death rate is greater than the birth rate. Over the past half-century or so a massive increase in man's understanding and utilization of death control has resulted in a rapid rise in the rate of growth of the human population. So, we have a closed, growing population. And, intriguing as the prospect may be to certain irresponsible politicians, economists, and religious leaders, we will not achieve an infinite population size. Sooner or later the growth of the human population must stop.

—Paul Ehrlich

4. As long as women were brought up and educated very differently from men and as long as their whole mode of life was different, it was safe and suitable to uphold the traditional beliefs as to certain mental sex differences. But as the differentiation in the education of the two sexes lessened so have the actual differences in their abilities and interest. Today the survival of some of these stereotypes is a psychological strait

jacket for both sexes. Witness the fact that some 40 percent of women undergraduates have confessed (the proportion was confirmed in two studies on widely separated college campuses) that they have occasionally "played dumb" on dates; that is, concealed some academic honor, pretended ignorance of a subject, "threw games," played down certain skills in obedience to the unwritten law that the man must be superior in those particular areas. If he *were* superior, the stratagem would not be necessary. "It embarrassed me that my 'steady' in high school," recalled a college junior in an interview, "got worse marks than I. A boy should naturally do better in school. I would never tell him my marks and would often ask him to help me with my homework." Confront the belief "a boy should naturally do better in school" with the fact that the marks of high school girls are generally somewhat superior to those of boys, probably because girls study more conscientiously. Could a surer recipe for trouble be invented?

—Mirra Komarovsky

---

5. Regular charge accounts are those where all purchases made the previous month appear on the next month's statement and payment in full is expected by the due date that month. Some department stores add on interest each month that the account has not been paid; others add no interest charges, although the account is considered to be delinquent. A revolving charge account is one in which the customer can elect to pay a certain portion of the bill each month, and interest charges are added on the unpaid balance. In most department stores, a customer can elect one or the other type of account.

—*Newsday*

---

5 Reading for Information

The first step in reading for specific information is to look for the main idea. In a one-paragraph selection, you add up all the sentences to find the main idea. In a longer work, you add up the main ideas of the various paragraphs in order to figure out the main idea of the whole selection.

But the main idea does not give you all the information you need. Facts and details appear within the paragraphs you read and help develop the main ideas of the paragraphs. These facts and details may paint a more complete picture, may give examples to help you understand the ideas better, may prove a point, or may show how the idea relates to other ideas. To make the best use of these facts and details, you have to be able to

- Find important facts and remember them.

- Separate major facts and details from minor facts and details.

For a particular course, you can have a better sense of how to use a book if you know how your instructor *expects* you to use it. Often your syllabus or course outline tells you just how to approach a book; sometimes your instructor will explain what you are to do with a text.

Do you need to understand ideas or memorize facts from the book? Are you supposed to take the book as absolute truth or as something to think about? Will you be asked to relate the concepts or facts from this book to other material you'll have to read? A course that requires several books may demand different kinds of reading for those several books. Is one book the basic text for the course? Is another book merely a supplement, something added to thorough class instruction? Does a third book repeat the lectures you hear each day? If you ask yourself—and your instructor— some of these questions, you'll know what to do with your text for a given class.

5a **Fact-Finding**

To find and remember important facts, you must be an active, aware reader. Here are nine ways to locate facts:

- Have a definite purpose for reading. Are you reading a page of your biology book to find out how the eye works? Are you reading a chapter of a political science text to learn the meaning of *democracy*? Or do you read only because an instructor made an assignment? Are you reading the newspaper out of general interest or for a specific research project?

- Learn to read for the main idea. If you recognize the main idea easily, the facts to support that idea will stand out.

- Know that all facts and details are not equal in importance. Look only for the facts that relate to the main idea.

- Look for information in groups or units. Facts often appear together in clumps.

- Look for the way the paragraph is put together. How is the information arranged? Has the writer organized the material in terms of a pattern that is easy to see?

- Learn to keep an author's *opinions* apart from the *facts* offered in the writing.

- Question yourself as you read. Stop to think and to let facts sink in before you rush on to other information. Ask yourself, "What does that mean?" or "What does that information tell me?" or "Why is this information here?"

- Use the five *W*'s when you read in order to ask yourself specific questions about the facts.
    1. Ask yourself "Who?" Then look for the name of someone or something.
    2. Ask yourself "When?" Then look for a date (a day, a month, a year) or a time of day or year.
    3. Ask yourself "Where?" Then look for words that show a location or name a place.
    4. Ask yourself "What?" or "What happened?" Then look for some action.
    5. Ask yourself "Why?" Then look for an explanation of some act or event.

- Think about the kinds of questions someone might ask you about the information you have read. Go back after you have finished to reread quickly and review any facts you have learned. Try to summarize the important facts in your mind.

Look at the following selection about an illegal subway ride. The comments in the margin illustrate fact-finding.

Boy, 15, Accused of Driving Subway

New York (AP)—A 15-year-old Queens boy was arrested —*Who?* yesterday on charges of operating an unattended subway train —*What happened?* *Why?*—with passengers aboard on a run from Pennsylvania Station to the World Trade Center. —*Where?*

A unit of information— The train's motorman, who allegedly abandoned the train, was arrested on charges of reckless endangerment, endan- —*Who?* gering the welfare of a minor and endangering property. —*What happened?*

A small but undetermined number of passengers rode the train unaware that the youth allegedly had taken control of it at 34th Street and was running the train as it stopped at seven stations along the route to the end of the line in lower Manhattan. It wasn't clear if a conductor was aboard and if the conductor was aware of the motorman's absence. The train's motorman, Carl Scholak, 46, was arrested at the E line 179th Street station in Queens as he left another train on which he was a passenger.

Who?— Scholak told authorities that he had left his train at the 34th Street station because he was feeling ill, according to MTA officials. But there was no indication that he had closed the doors or stopped the train or notified any other transit —*Less important information* workers before leaving.

Transit officials did not know how the boy could get possession of the hand control and reverser, which a motorman is required to remove and carry upon leaving a cab. Also, the motorman is supposed to lock the cab door and keep the key.

Who?— Metropolitan Transit Authority officials were stunned at the discovery, and the authority's president, John D. Simpson, ordered an immediate investigation. It was not known if the —*Opinion?* welfare of a minor endangerment charges meant that the motorman was being accused of knowingly permitting a 15-year-old to drive the train.

The youth, who was not identified because of his age, was seized by transit police, who were alerted by a towerman who —*Why?* said that a startled passenger reported "a very young person"

at the controls of the E-train on the Independent Subway's
Eighth Avenue line.

Who?— Police said the youth was arrested shortly after midnight —*When?*
as he calmly walked toward the other end of the train at the —*Where?*
World Trade Center with the apparent intention of taking it on
a run back along its route.

He was held on a charge of juvenile delinquency and re- —*What*
leased in the custody of his parents pending disposition of the *hap-*
motorman's case. *pened?*

Authorities said that the parents previously had filed a
petition to have the boy declared a person in need of supervi-
sion.

Scholak, a 15-year veteran with the MTA, was suspended
from duty upon his arrest.

—Newsday

Did you have a purpose in reading? Did you use the words
illegal subway ride in the instructions to help you read for special
information? Did you ask yourself these questions as you read:
What is the main idea? How is the information arranged? Which
facts are most important? What questions might someone ask
about this selection?

Exercises

1. Fact-finding: A Review
Reread the selection beginning on page 56.

1. What is the main idea? _____

_____

2. What are three questions someone might ask about the
selection?

_____

_____

_____

_____

3. Write down three of the most important facts.

_____

_____

_____

_____

4. At what paragraph does the writer start to give you less

important facts about the incident? _____

2. Reading for Facts

Read the following paragraph and answer the questions after
it.

It was the use of the telescope, of course, that opened the
modern age of astronomy and made possible the growth of all
our current theories. Johannes Kepler and Tycho Brahe tried
to answer some questions about the solar system, but it was
Galileo who made the first use of the telescope to observe the
heavens close up. Born in 1564, Galileo added greatly to our
knowledge of the stars before he died in 1642. By means of his
telescope he discovered moons in orbit around Jupiter. Although he saw only four, scientists after him discovered eight
more moons. Galileo also observed that the planet Venus did
not always appear the same size. It was his wise use of the
telescope that helped him understand this important fact: that
the sun and not the earth is the center of the planets.

1. What is the main idea of this paragraph? _____

_____

2. Only one of the following facts is important within the paragraph. Circle it.
   a. Galileo was born in 1564 and died in 1642.
   b. Galileo learned that the earth is not the center of the
      system of stars.
   c. Kepler and Brahe answered questions about the solar
      system.

3. How did Galileo learn about the stars? _____

_____

4. How many moons revolve around Jupiter? _____

5. Galileo's major contribution to our knowledge of the planets was (circle one)
   a. his invention of the telescope.
   b. his study of Brahe and Kepler.
   c. his observations about Jupiter and Venus.
   d. his belief that planets revolved around the sun.

3. Reading with a Purpose
   Read the following excerpt from an article, keeping in mind that you are a student who will eventually be looking for a job. Then answer the questions that follow the article.

Graduate School: A Way to Double Your Money

Despite forecasts of a severe recession and a surge in unemployment, most people who put in their years at graduate school are finding the effort pays—well. Men and women with advanced degrees in business, law and engineering are moving into the work force at salaries of $20,000 and often much more, while those with no more than a bachelor's degree usually start with half as much.

For a couple of years, some employment experts have been predicting that the nation's business schools would soon saturate the market, putting a squeeze on salaries. So far, though, there are few signs of that, at least at the established schools. Demand for new masters of business administration is still outrunning supply, said William Lyhne, assistant director of Executive Compensation Services, a unit of the American Management Association. "There'll never be a glut of M.B.A.'s," he said.

According to Mr. Lyhne, the median national income for 1979 M.B.A.'s with a technical background was $18,500. Many were hired by energy companies. Non-technical students made $18,000.

A few years' work experience also pays. The Amos Tuck School of Business at Dartmouth, for example, says a graduate with no previous work experience will start at $26,000, while one with five years' experience in business typically is offered $30,000.

From school to school, there's a lot of variation in salary offers.

The median for graduates of the business schools at Harvard and Stanford was $27,500 last year. (Harvard isn't yet saying what the figure will be this year, but Stanford's recruiting office predicts a rise of 10 to 12 percent.)

But the University of Michigan's business school reports a median salary of $22,200 last year. At Purdue University's Krannert School of Management the median last year was $23,100. New York University reports that about $25,000 is typical this year.

Placement officers stress that this year's data may be distorted because they reflect the reports of those who have already landed jobs, a group dominated by the top students. As more complete statistics become available, the figures are likely to drop a bit.

Most M.B.A.'s take jobs in finance, manufacturing, accounting and management consulting. N.Y.U. says a quarter of its 1980 class is going into commercial banking and nearly 18 percent into accounting. Another 8.4 percent went into food processing; 6.1 percent, consulting and research, and 4.2 percent, energy. Harvard says its largest group of graduates last year, 41 percent, went into manufacturing, and Michigan says 47 percent took manufacturing jobs and 12 percent entered commercial banking.

Graduates of the leading law schools do even better than M.B.A.'s. At the Harvard Law School, reports Eleanor Appel, the placement director, those of the 550 graduates who join the big New York law firms are signing on at $30,000 to $37,000. Herbert Fried, director of placement at the University of Chicago School of Law, said that big Chicago firms are starting graduates at an average $3,000 more than last year's $25,000.

It's another story for teachers. Graduates of Columbia University's elite Teachers College, with no previous teaching experience, are getting $14,000, says John Buckey, director of placement. A graduate with two years' experience, he says, will start at $16,000. Architects, something of a glut on the market, start relatively low on the scale, too. Graduates of Columbia's architecture school rarely sign on for more than $18,000 or $20,000.

But even that's far better than what job-seekers with mere bachelors degrees can expect. At Barnard College, Kim Healy, associate director of career services, said that English majors who enter the work force directly after graduation generally earn $10,000 to $13,000. "B.A's run the gamut from A to Z," she said, "in publishing you can make as little as $8,000 and in computers you can make as much as $20,000."

—*New York Times*

1. What is the main idea of the article? _____

_____

2. As a student wondering about jobs, you will find some details more important than others. Which of the details are important to you?_____

_____

_____

_____

_____

3. Which questions does this article answer for college students who are thinking about the direction of their future study?

_____

_____

4. In the writer's opinion, are there likely to be too many students with M.B.A.'s in the job market? _____

_____

_____

5. What are some job and salary ranges for students who plan to secure only their bachelor's degree and not to pursue graduate degrees? _____

_____

_____

_____

6. Which details of this article would a school administrator

find most important? _____

_____

_____

_____

7. Which career is most lucrative? Which is least lucrative?
Are you interested in earning as much as you can after you finish
school? What else do you expect of your education? Of your future

job? Use separate paper if you need more space. _____

_____

_____

_____

_____

5b   Major Details, Minor Details

It's obvious that not all facts in a paragraph have the same importance. In the selection on page 56, for example, the subway stop
where the motorman was arrested, the motorman's age, and the
special tools that only the motorman was supposed to have are
among the less important details. Because you do not need those
details to understand the selection, the information they give is
minor. Minor details help round out the paragraph and often hold

our attention to make the material we are reading more interesting. Still, we may ignore minor details if our goal is a clear and quick understanding of what we've read. Details that give major information about the main idea, however, are very important.

Here is how to find major details:

- State the main idea in your own words.

- Look only for information that supports the main idea.

- Read quickly over the words or sentences that give information that is not important to the main idea.

- Look for signal words like *most important, first, finally, the facts are,* and so on.

- Underline the major ideas when you locate them.

Here is how one student separated the major details from the minor details in a passage she was reading for a course in sociology.

Main idea: Sociologists, like anthropologists, get shocked by a culture, but the sociologist looks at his own culture instead of foreign ones.

Anthropologists use the term "culture shock" to describe the impact of a totally new culture upon a newcomer. In an extreme instance such shock will be experienced by the Western explorer who is told, halfway through dinner, that he is eating the nice old lady he had been chatting with the previous day—a shock with predictable physiological if not moral consequences. Most explorers no longer encounter cannibalism in their travels today. However, the first encounters with polygamy or with puberty rites or even with the way some nations drive their automobiles can be quite a shock to an American visitor. With the shock may go not only disapproval or disgust but a sense of excitement that things can *really* be that different from what they are at home. To some extent, at least, this is the excitement of any first travel abroad. The experience of sociological discovery could be described as "culture shock" minus geographical displacement. In other words, the sociologist travels at home—with shocking results. He is unlikely to find that he is eating a nice old lady for dinner. But the discovery, for instance, that his own church has considerable money invested in the missile industry or that a few blocks from his home there are people who engage in cultic orgies may not be drastically different in emotional impact. Yet we would not want to imply that sociological discoveries are always or even usually outrageous to moral sentiment. Not at all. What they have in common with exploration in distant lands, however, is the sudden illumination of new and unsuspected facets of human existence in society.

—Peter Berger

Notice that, by underlining, the student focuses only on details that help explain the main idea directly. Some of these details are the concept of culture shock, the reaction to shocking events, and the kinds of shocking things that a sociologist can find without traveling, in America.

Notice, too, those details the student passes over as not so important. Some unimportant details are the nice old lady being served for dinner, the decrease in cannibalism today, and the experience of the first trip abroad. These minor details make the main idea more vivid, but the main idea can be understood without them.

It's true that you may want to know some information you did not consider of major importance during your first reading. For example, if you read about the subway on page 56, you would not pay attention to the different subway stops involved to help you understand the paragraphs. But if you suddenly realized that you had been on the subway that day and had seen some suspicious things, you might want to go back and check out those details.

Exercises

1. Finding Major Details

Read the following paragraph and answer the questions after it.

In 1915 a professor of geography from Yale studied the relationship between human strength and the climate in which man finds himself. Ellsworth Huntington wrote in *Civilization and Climate* (New Haven: Yale University Press, 1924) that physical vigor is highest on days when temperature moves up and down between 50 degrees and 55 degrees at night and 60 degrees and 70 degrees by day. Mentally man is most fit when the average temperature is a bit over 40 degrees. He understood that human energy is made up of the physical and the mental. Putting this information together he finally decided that the best climate would offer average temperatures of about 40 degrees in the winter and about 60 degrees in the summer. Studying thousands of factory workers and students in different parts of America, he learned that mental and physical activities depend upon conditions of weather. A *change* in temperature, not a stable one, is necessary to keep human energy at its best.

1. Circle the main idea of the paragraph.
   a. Mental and physical activity depend on weather and climate.

   b. Mentally, man is most fit when the average temperature is over 40 degrees.

   c. All animals are affected by the weather.

2. Circle a major detail from the paragraph:
   a. Ellsworth Huntington wrote *Civilization and Climate*.

   b. The best climate is 40 degrees in winter and 60 degrees in summer.

   c. Huntington conducted his study in 1915.

3. Draw a line through the *minor details* that follow (there are two).
   a. Huntington was a professor at Yale.

   b. A change in temperature is best for highest quality in human energy.

   c. The study involved factory workers and students.

   d. Huntington's book, *Civilization and Climate*, was published in New Haven by Yale University Press.

   e. Human energy is measured by mental and physical activity.

2. Separating Major Details from Minor Details
   Read the following paragraph about women in the work force during wartime. Then follow the directions that come after it.

Wars, Women, and Work

In 1890, some 3.7 million American women were working for pay. Two-thirds of them were single, and most of the rest were widowed or divorced. One-third worked as servants. Such patterns did not survive World War II. "To win this war," wrote Susan B. Anthony, II in 1943, "American women *must come out of their homes*." And they did, replacing absent husbands, brothers, and sons in factories and offices around the country. Between 1940 and 1944, Norman Rockwell's "Rosie the Riveter" and 5 million other new women workers swelled the employment rolls. For the first time in U.S. history, wives edged out single women as job-holders; that trend continues. Often overlooked is the role played by World War I in breaking down barriers to women. With 4 million American men under arms, American women became an emergency labor supply—and proved (to the surprise of skeptical managers) that they could do a "man's work." Between 1914 and 1918, the number of women working in the steel industry trebled. The official U.S. government list of occupations in which women replaced men filled some six pages in tiny print. And most working women stayed in the labor force after the war. This fact, the author of a 1920 Labor Department study rightly predicted, "bids fair to encourage a larger share of woman labor in the future."

—*Wilson Quarterly*

1. Circle the main idea of the paragraph.
   a. In 1890, most working women were servants.
   b. Norman Rockwell created "Rosie the Riveter."
   c. Women were called on to fill the gaps created by conscription in time of war throughout history.
   d. Women who entered the job force as a result of wartime needs stayed in the job force even after the wars ended.
   e. Factory managers were skeptical about a woman's ability to earn her keep on the job.

2. Go back to the paragraph and underline the major details that support the main idea.

3. Summarize the major details. _____

_____

_____

_____

3. Finding Major Details
   Read the following selection and answer the questions after it.

Watching What You Eat: Fred Einerman

Fred Einerman's morning often begins with a pre-dawn visit to one of those dreary depots where street food vendors store their pushcarts and pretzels, stew their onions, and skewer their shish kebabs. He's not there from hunger; what he's looking for is dirty cooking implements, insufficient refrigeration, rat droppings, and other hazards to public health.

Einerman, 31, is an inspector for the New York City Health Department. His job takes him in and out of restaurant kitchens all over the city, and, if he still has a healthy appetite at the end of a day, it's no thanks to the sights he generally sees on the job.

"The worst thing I ever saw was a guy mixing a batch of tuna fish with his hands, all the way up to his armpits," he says. "There must have been 100 pounds of tuna fish. It really turned my stomach." What Einerman did about it was condemn the tuna and cite the restaurant for "excessive handling" of the food. Condemning food means discarding it after treating it with motor oil or some equally unappetizing additive to make sure no one can eat it. The citation means Einerman will return in a couple of weeks.

"When I come back, I don't expect to see those violations," says Einerman. He inspects day camps, beauty parlors, and water supplies, as well as restaurants and vendors, and, if the violations haven't been corrected by the time of his second visit, he orders the management to appear at a hearing, where a fine can be levied, and he adds the establishment's name to the restaurant-violations list for publication.

When Einerman finds a serious immediate threat to health—something like rats in the cutlery drawer—he shuts the place down on the spot. If a pushcart food vendor can't produce a license, he has the vendor's cart confiscated by the police.

Einerman, a beefy six-footer, is offered everything from knuckle sandwiches to $20 bribes by people who want to avoid bad publicity, fines, shut-downs, or expensive repair bills. "Sometimes, it can get very hairy. I'm for working in teams, because there are too many things going on that can tarnish a good inspector's name. If you're working alone, it's your word against theirs if they say you asked for a bribe." And a partner also provides an extra pair of eyes. "You might overlook something that someone else will see."

When, off duty, he visits a restaurant and finds its cleanliness wanting, Einerman complains to the management without disclosing that he's an inspector. Sometimes he follows up at work with a suggestion that one of his colleagues pay an official visit to the restaurant. He wishes the public would do likewise. "People should take a second look at what they're eating," he contends, "and if they see something they don't like, they should report it. I've been trying to get people to be aware of what goes on and what their rights are. How many people would ask to see the latest inspection report before they order a meal in a restaurant? That's your right, you know."

Although he and his wife enjoy dining out on weekends, Einerman admits that he's "always wondering what's going on in the kitchen." Even in their lower Manhattan home, he says, he was "extremely paranoid" about cleanliness in the kitchen for the first six months after he took his job.

Einerman, a second-generation New Yorker, earned a degree in education and psychology from Richmond College, intending to become a teacher. But by the time he finished school, teachers were being laid off and there were no permanent jobs to be found.

For a few years, he drifted from job to job, living with his parents and not needing much money. He photographed weddings for a while; he tried selling. One day he heard about an impending civil-service test for the job of "environmental health technician," and he took the test because it "sounded interesting." At the time he was unhappily selling match-book-cover ads. But when he didn't hear about his test results after a few weeks, he forgot about them and continued his quest for satisfying work.

Eventually he went to work in the Consumer Affairs Department. He liked his job, which included office management and purchasing, but he feared he would lose it when the city administration changed. Just after he began worrying, he got a letter about the civil-service test he'd taken four years earlier. He'd passed. A week later, in September of 1978, he became a health inspector.

Einerman says he plans a career in the Health Department, even though he describes his present salary as so low he's ashamed to disclose it. (A department spokesman says the average annual salary for the 100 inspectors is $14,000.)

"There's a big misconception about city employees—that they're lazy, they lay around a lot, they goof off on the job," says Einerman. "That's not me. I like to do the job to the fullest. And I'm doing a job that I know needs to be done."

—Cheryl Morrison

1. State in your own words the main idea of this selection.

_____

_____

2. What are some of the major details that support this main point?

_____

_____

_____

_____

3. In the story, is each of the following details major or minor? Answer by writing *major* or *minor* next to each.

a. Fred Einerman is an inspector for the New York City Health Department. _____

b. Einerman looks for signs of dirty cooking implements.

_____

c. Condemned food is often treated with motor oil to ensure that nobody will want to eat it. _____

d. Einerman inspects beauty parlors. _____

e. For a while Einerman worked photographing weddings.

_____

f. People have a right to see a restaurant's inspection report. _____

g. Einerman is satisfied with his job. _____

h. Restaurants that do not correct violations will have their names published. _____

i. Einerman wishes that more people would complain about restaurants that violate the health code.

_____

j. It took four years for Einerman to find out that he had passed the test for health inspector. _____

k. Einerman plans to spend the rest of his working life in

   the Health Department. _____

5c **Skimming**

Whenever you have to find *specific* facts in a paragraph, look quickly at sentences that offer the needed information. Rapid reading for facts is called *skimming*. When you skim a paragraph or a page, you are searching quickly among sentences for the answer to some question you have.
   Here is how to skim:

- Make sure that you know what information you are looking for. Ask yourself a question.

- Move your eyes quickly from line to line and from sentence to sentence.

- When you think you've found what you are looking for, *stop*.

- Read slowly the part of the line or sentence that tells you what you want to know.

- Think about the question you were trying to answer.

- Does the information you found answer the question?

- Jot down the answer to the question you've asked.

Exercises

1. Skimming

   Skim this paragraph about the Dakota Indians to find out the following information:
   a. What was their other name?
   b. Where did they settle in the seventeenth century?
   c. Who was their leader in the battle of Little Bighorn?
Then write the answers in the answer blanks.

The Dakota Indians lived originally in the Great Lakes region before they were driven out of that region by the Ojibway in the seventeenth century. The Dakotas, better known as the

Sioux, then settled in the North Great Plains and the prairies. But more and more settlers stole away their land and the Sioux, after a bloody battle with Little Crow at their head in 1862, agreed to retire to a reservation. That also was invaded, this time by people looking for gold. In 1874 the Sioux Wars began: a major event there, of course, was the defeat of Custer by Sitting Bull in 1876 at the battle of the Little Bighorn.

1. What was another name for the Dakotas? _____

2. Where did they settle in the seventeenth century? _____

3. Who led them in the battle of Little Bighorn? _____

2. Skimming

Skim this selection about basketball player Nancy Lieberman to find the answers to the questions that follow. Then write the answers in the blanks.

Let the history of basketball, no, the history of civilization, record that last Monday night, with 1:06 left in the first half of a New York Pro Summer League game between the Gailyn Packers and Ka-Har-Lyn at Xavier High School in Manhattan, 6' 4" Al Skinner, late of the Philadelphia 76ers, fouled 5' 10" Nancy Lieberman, formerly of the Old Dominion Lady Monarchs, because she had him beat to the inside. Lieberman went to the line and sank a pair. Two small free throws for woman, two giant free throws for womankind.

Granted the New York Pro Summer League isn't the NBA. But it isn't the 10 a.m. pickup game at the Y either. Notable pros such as Nate Archibald, Ray Williams, Mitch Kupchak, Lloyd Free and Marvin Barnes drop by to mix it up with the likes of old smoothies Harthorne Nathaniel Wingo and Dean Meminger. Some of the players are merely staying in shape, some are trying to set themselves up for one last shot at the big time, and others are auditioning for a spot on an overseas team. Their common denominators are that they each receive the standard salary of two cold sodas after every game and they are all male.

So what's a nice girl like Lieberman doing in a league like this? The original scenario had her becoming America's sweetheart at the end of this month as she led the U.S. women's basketball team to an Olympic gold medal. The boycott ruined that. Plan B began to evolve last month when Paul Williamson, a principal in a Manhattan real estate firm and one of the founders of the fledgling league, suggested to Lieberman's agent, Matt Merola (who numbers among his clients Reggie Jackson and Tom Seaver), that she join the league to improve her skills and to keep in shape during the off-season.

In her first game, Lieberman played about eight minutes for the Bronx Celtics, who are not to be confused with the Boston ones. . . . She was hesitant to shoot in her first game and didn't score, but she did have two assists and four rebounds. She was a little more comfortable in her second outing, scoring seven points with five assists. She even in-your-faced Geoff Huston, who played with the Knicks last year and is now the property of the expansion Dallas Mavericks. "She's a lot better than some of the guys in the NBA," said Huston, being a bit hyperbolic. Still, Archibald says, "She's not a woman out there, she's a player."

Unfortunately, Lieberman wasn't getting much playing time on a team that already had guards Archibald, Free and Earl Monroe on its roster, so after her second game she was traded—given, actually—to the Gailyn Packers, who needed backcourt help. It was in her first appearance with them last week that she showed she really belonged.

—Steve Wulf

1. What league does Nancy Lieberman currently play in?

_____

2. How many points did she score in her second game?_____

3. Where did she go to college? _____

4. Why was Lieberman traded from the Bronx Celtics to the

Gailyn Packers? _____

5d Previewing

Other helpful steps to take in order to read for information come *before* you actually begin reading. You can *preview*—that is, look ahead to the content of a passage—in a number of ways.

Here is how to preview a reading selection:

- *Look at the title.* Does it tell you what you will be reading about? If so, you can then set a purpose for your reading. Furthermore, titles often give the main idea of the selection. The title of the paragraphs on page 56 is "Boy, 15, Accused of Driving Subway." How does that help the reader set a purpose? How does it reflect the main idea?

- *Look for subtitles.* Essays, newspaper articles, and other longer readings sometimes offer help in finding information by printing *subtitles.* Appearing below titles in heavy, dark print or in italics, subtitles suggest the kind of material you will find in a small portion of the reading.

- *Look at the pictures, charts, or drawings.* Often an illustration helps you figure out beforehand what your reading will deal with.

- *Look at the first sentence of each paragraph.* This gives you a quick idea of what the reading involves before you begin to read carefully.

- *Look at the first paragraph carefully.* The first paragraph usually tells just what the reading will be about. Read it, and then stop before going on.

- *Look at the questions that come after the reading.* If you look at the questions *before* you read anything, you then have an idea of what's important. Questions tell you what to expect from a passage. When you read with a knowledge of the questions, you know beforehand what kind of information to look for.

- *Look for key words in different print.* Sometimes heavy bold letters, italics, or even colored ink is used to call the reader's attention to important words or ideas. Titles of books, for example, appear in italics. Noting these in advance can give you important information.

- *Look for a summary.* At the end of a long factual piece, a writer sometimes summarizes the main points. Looking at this summary before you read can help you see more clearly what the selection deals with.

Exercise

Previewing

Before you read the following article, preview it by answering these questions:

1. Read the title. What does the title tell you about the contents of the article? _____

_____

2. Look at the subtitle. What information does the subtitle give you? Can you figure out anything about the article on the basis

of the subtitle? _____

_____

_____

3. Read the first sentence of the article. What does it tell you? Use your own words. What does that first sentence lead you to

expect to find in the article? _____

_____

_____

Welfare Moms Aren't Faring Well These Days

The cost of feeding a family of four went over a hundred dollars a week recently. It is difficult for middle-class families to make ends meet these days, but what must it be like for families on public assistance? Food prices have increased about 27% every year, but food stamp allotments to families on welfare have not been increased since 1974.

Struggling on $199 a month

A typical mother raising her children on public assistance is Sarah Thompson of Brooklyn. "I heard that it costs a family of four $100 a week to eat," she says, "and I've only been getting $199 a month from food stamps to feed my kids and myself. It's really hard for me to hang in there with prices so high."

Sarah clips coupons and buys sale and store brand items. She no longer buys munchies and she limits her children to one treat per shopping trip—each child alternating the choice of a treat.

Lots of Chicken

Sarah knows a dozen ways to cook chicken. "We'll be cackling before long." She laughs when she is asked when was the last time she ate steak. "We eat hamburger." And Sarah has learned the art of reworking leftovers. "We don't throw anything away. We keep everything." Last night's chicken dinner is likely to become tonight's soup and tomorrow's lunch.

5e Previewing Long Material: The Parts of a Book

One of your key tasks at school is to read information from longer works. Your textbooks in biology, math, or business courses offer several hundred pages of material. One professor may require that you read a novel or a play; another may ask you to read an article in a journal; still another may assign a new book that treats the subject of the course in a special way.

Before you read a long book for information, you can use some other effective preview techniques aside from those explained in section **5d.** Here is how to preview a book:

- *Look at the table of contents.* Found in the front of the book, the table of contents is a list of the names of the chapters and the pages on which they begin. If the book is divided into parts, that information also appears in the table of contents. If you study the names of the chapters, you can get an idea of what each section of the book deals with and how the topics relate to each other. Sometimes a table of contents is very detailed: you might find a listing of the topics treated in each chapter.

- *Look at the preface.* Coming before the table of contents, the preface (also called the foreword) is a brief essay in which an author gives reasons for writing the book. The preface is a personal message to the reader. In the preface you get an idea of the kind of reader the author is writing for; of the aims of the book and just what the author expects you to learn as a result of reading it; and of the topics in the book and the best approaches to those topics. Not all books have a preface, as you may know; and sometimes a preface deals with matters that interest the author but may not have much to do with specific ideas in the book. Still, it's good to look the preface over, even if you just skim it, so that you can judge for yourself whether or not to read it carefully.

- *Look briefly at the index.* At the end of a book you may find an alphabetical listing of the topics, subjects, ideas, and names mentioned in the book. A quick look at the index will suggest some of the points the writer deals with and how detailed the book is.

- *Look at one of these special features that sometimes appear in books:*

1. After the chapters in a book a writer sometimes provides a *glossary*, which is a list of difficult words or terms commonly used in the subject the book deals with. The words are listed in alphabetical order; their definitions appear also. The fact that a book has a glossary may indicate that the subject is technical but that the author does try to explain the difficult terms.

2. An *appendix* (plural *appendixes* or *appendices*) at the end of the book presents additional information that is interesting and useful. However, the book is complete without the appendix, and the information we find there is only extra. An appendix may include charts and graphs, special letters or documents, or facts about the lives of the people mentioned in the book. It may just give information to explain something the author felt needed more attention. A look at the appendix, if the book has one, will indicate how a writer deals with special problems.

● *Read the introduction.* Often the first chapter of the book is the introduction. The introduction states the basic problem the author will deal with. It gives background information or discusses the history of the topic. It may summarize what others have said about the subject. It may even explain the method of research the author used. Sometimes—especially in a work of fiction such as a novel, a collection of short stories, or a play—someone other than the author writes the introduction. Such an introduction often explains the book to the readers, pointing out key scenes or ideas worth noting.

● *Look at the bibliography.* At the back of the book, an author sometimes gives a *bibliography*—a list, in alphabetical order, of some or all the books that helped the author to write this book. The bibliography (sometimes called *Works Cited*) indicates the author's range of knowledge and basic interests.

● *Think about what parts the book has and what parts it doesn't have.* A book with a detailed index, a long bibliography, and a number of appendixes may be more appropriate for research than a book with only a short table of contents. Books with glossaries often provide helpful introductions to difficult subjects.

Exercises

1. Using a Table of Contents
     Look at the table of contents that appears on pages 78–79. Then answer the following questions.

1. Explain what you think this book will deal with. _____

_____

_____

_____

2. Which chapter deals with syllabic writings? _____

_____

_____

_____

3. In which chapter would you learn about the Proto-Elamite

system? _____

_____

_____

_____

4. Which of these does the author consider a forerunner of
writing: cuneiform, the Greek alphabet, identifying–mnemonic
devices, monogenesis?

_____

_____

_____

5. Why does the author include a separate chapter on the
terminology of writing?

_____

_____

_____

CONTENTS

CONTENTS

2. Using an Index

Look at the excerpt from an index that appears on page 80. Then answer the following questions.

1. This book has as its main purpose (circle one)
   a. teaching English to college students.
   b. discussing Betty Rizzo and O. J. Simpson.
   c. teaching the rules of punctuation.

2. List the pages on which you would find information about
   a. understanding the use of the semicolon.
   b. the précis.
   c. Tom Seaver.

© 1981 Houghton Mifflin Company.

3. Reading a Preface

Read the foreword that appears below. Then answer the following questions.

 1. A good title for this book would be (circle one)
    a. *A Guide to Mysteries and Double Talk.*
    b. *How to Buy Stocks: A Guide to Making Money in the Market.*
    c. *The Hidden Prejudice: How to Enjoy Growing Old.*

 2. Why has the author written this book? _____

_____

 3. What does the author hope will happen when readers examine the facts in their own minds? _____

_____

Foreword

THIS book is based on a very simple premise: that the stock market is going up.

Tomorrow? Next month? Next year?

Maybe yes, maybe no. Maybe the market will be a lot lower then than it is today.

But over any long period of time—10 years, 20 years, 50 years—this book assumes that the market is bound to go up.

Why?

Because it always has.

Because the market is a measure of the vigor of American business, and unless something drastic happens to America, business is going to go on growing.

Because prices of food and clothing and almost everything else in this country—including stocks—have steadily gone up as the buying power of the dollar has gone down. That's a trend that isn't likely to be reversed.

And so these are the reasons why the author is sold on the value of investing, of buying stocks for the long pull—and not for a quick profit tomorrow.

There's nothing hidden about this prejudice. You'll see it when you read the book. And you will find other prejudices, other opinions, despite an earnest effort to focus this book strictly on facts—the facts about investing that have been obscured all too long by double talk, by financial jargon, and by unnecessary mystery.

Of course it can be said that there are no facts when you

get beyond the simple business of adding one and one. That's true. So let's say that here are the facts as the author sees them—and as plainly as he can state them.

He has only one hope: that they will add up to good common sense in your own mind.

LOUIS ENGEL

4. Using the Table of Contents and Index Together

The table of contents and part of an index on pages 83–86 are from Isaac Asimov's book *The Human Body*. Using them, find on what page or pages there is information about the following subjects.

1. scales and epidermis _____

2. thrombocytes _____

3. apes _____

4. musculature of birds _____

5. bats _____

6. alveolus _____

7. *Annelida* _____

8. baby's first breath _____

9. A-V node _____

10. communication of bees _____

11. blood pressure _____

12. lymph _____

13. bleeding _____

14. sickle-cell anemia _____

15. arm movements _____

16. big toe _____

CONTENTS

INDEX

5. Previewing Long Material: The Parts of a Book

Select a book from the library. Locate the parts of the book in the following list and, in your own words, write what you can find out about the book from each part. If the book does not have one of the parts, discuss what you think that indicates about the book.

1. title and author _____

2. table of contents _____

_____

_____

3. preface _____

_____

_____

4. introduction or first chapter _____

_____

_____

5. glossary _____

_____

_____

6. bibliography _____

_____

_____

7. index _____

_____

_____

6 Recognizing Paragraph Patterns

Paragraphs are important units of thought in the essays and books you have to read. And figuring out the meaning or meanings in a paragraph is your basic challenge as a reader. A helpful clue to meaning often lies in the way a writer arranges information in a paragraph.

Paragraph information often appears in patterns that are easy to recognize. If you know some typical paragraph patterns in which information may appear, you may find it easier to understand what you read. Of course, no writer follows any pattern rigidly. Usually, in any essay or book chapter, many different patterns appear. In a single paragraph, in fact, they often overlap and combine. But being aware of typical patterns in a reading selection can help you follow a writer's thoughts and ideas.

6a Ordering of Ideas

6a(1) Time Order (Chronology)

Some paragraph ideas are put together so that we see them in the time order in which they happened. You must keep in mind the *sequence*: one idea follows another and relates to an event or idea that comes before. This order is often used to tell a story or to explain how to do or make something.

In the southwestern desert in the late 1840s, the U.S. Cavalry needed an animal capable of covering vast distances with little need for food or water. Major Henry Constantine Ways, a cavalry officer, decided that the perfect solution was a camel.

He proceeded to read everything he could on the subject of camels, what breeds there were, their habits and history. He also compared the climates of the American southwest and the Middle East, finding that they were very similar. His studies finished, Major Wayne then wrote a formal proposal to the War Department in Washington. Eventually his plan was read by Senator Jefferson Davis who, as a student of history, was well acquainted with the role camels had played in the life of the Middle East. It took Davis and Wayne nearly five years to get Congress to see the wisdom of using camels in the west, and by the time they did, despite the fact that camels proved to be every bit as useful as Wayne said they would be, the transcontinental railway soon made camels obsolete.

—Gerald Carson

6a(2)   Place Order

Some paragraph details are put together so that we see them in terms of their place in a room, a building, or some outdoor scene. These details follow a direction that traces movement from one part of a scene to another. A writer, especially when describing something, may give details from left to right, from near to far, from east to west, or in some other clear place order.

As I look around this room in this third-rate boarding house, my eyes are greeted first by the entrance to its gloomy interior. The door is painted a dirty cream color. There is a crack in one panel. The ceiling is the same dingy color with pieces of adhesive tape holding some of the plaster in place. The walls are streaked and cracked here and there. Also on the walls are pieces of Scotch tape that once held, I presume, some sexy girls, pictures of *Esquire Magazine* origin. Across the room runs a line; upon it hang a shirt, a grimy towel, and washed stump socks belonging to my roommate, Jack Nager. By the door near the top sash juts a piece of wood on which is hung—it looks like an old spread. It is calico, dirty, and a sickly green color. Behind that is a space which serves as our closet; next to that is the radiator, painted the same ghastly color. The landlady must have got the paint for nothing. On top is Jack's black suitcase, his green soap dish, and a brightly colored box containing his hair tonic. Over by the cracked window are a poorly made table and chair. On top of the table, a pencil, shaving talcum, a glass, a nail file; one of my socks hangs over the side. Above the table is our window, the curtains of cheese cloth held back by a string. There is also a

black, fairly whole paper shade to dim such little sunlight as
might enter.

—John J. Regan

6a(3)   Order of Importance

Some paragraph details are put together so that we know which
ideas the writer thinks are more important. In this kind of paragraph the least important idea comes first, and the writer tells the
other details in order of growing importance. Of course, the most
important idea comes last.

Robert Hooke's work in science was varied and important
through the 1700s in England. In the first place he served as
the head of the Royal Society, a group of the day's leading men
of science; there he urged new tests and experiments to advance knowledge. He helped provide a means by which men
could discuss their ideas with others who shared their con-
cerns. Hooke was also a well-known architect whose advice
about the design of buildings was welcome. He designed a
large beautiful house in London where the British Museum
now stands. Unfortunately Hooke's building burned down; the
six long years of work he did on it were wiped out by a careless
servant. Of all Hooke's gifts to mankind, however, the most
important was his own research in science. He studied the
movement of planets and improved tools for looking at the
heavens. He invented the spiral watch spring. And, of course,
it was Hooke who first described the cell as a basic part of
plant tissue.

Once you know the way the writer orders details, you can
follow the sequence more easily. In time order, events come one
after the other. In place order, objects appear in relation to other
objects. In order of importance, you learn the writer's opinion
about which ideas are more crucial than others.

How to See Paragraph Arrangement

- Certain words in paragraphs give you hints about how the
  ideas are arranged.

- For *time order* look for words that tell time, such as *when,
  then, first, second, next, last, after, before, later.*

- For *place order* look for words that locate, such as *there, beside, near, above, below, next to, under, over, alongside, beneath, by, behind, on.*

- For *order of importance* look for words that help us judge importance, such as *first, next, last, most important, major, greatest, in the first place.*

Exercises

1. Ordering of Ideas

1. In the example of *time order* (pages 88–89), circle the words that help you see that paragraph details are arranged in time order.

2. In the example of *place order* (pages 89–90), circle the words that help you see that paragraph details are arranged in place order.

3. In the example of *order of importance* on page 90, circle the words that help you see that paragraph details are arranged in order of importance.

2. Understanding Sequence

Look at the following details from the example of time order (pages 88–89). The details are not arranged in the correct time order. Put a *1* in front of the first thing that happened, a *2* in front of the second, and so on.

_____a. Jefferson Davis became interested in the plan.

_____b. Major Wayne studied all he could about camels.

_____c. In 1855 Congress approved funds for the experiment.

_____d. The Southwest had a need for a durable animal.

_____e. The railroads soon made camels unnecessary.

_____f. Camels proved to be valuable in the west.

3. Understanding Sequence

1. Reread the example of place order (pages 89–90). Put a *1* next to the item described first in the paragraph, a *2* next to the item described second, and so on.

_____a. things hung on the wall

_____b. the ceiling

_____c. the window

_____d. the entrance

_____e. the closet

_____f. the walls

_____g. the table

_____h. things on top of the radiator

_____i. the radiator

_____j. things on top of the table

_____2. In what order are the details arranged?
a. top to bottom
b. left to right
c. around the room
d. from big things like walls to small, personal items

_____3. What kind of picture does the writer give of the room?
a. hopeful and cheery
b. run-down and gloomy
c. poor but proud

4. Understanding Sequence

The following details all come from the example on page 90. Put a checkmark next to the statement that is most important in the paragraph. Then put a circle next to the statement that comes last in the paragraph.

_____a. Robert Hooke was a scientist.

_____b. Hooke's own research in science included the investigation of a watch spring and the discovery of the cell.

_____c. He was a well-known architect.

_____d. A building he designed was burned by a careless servant.

_____e. Hooke served as chief of the Royal Society.

5. Understanding Sequence

Read this paragraph. Then answer the questions that follow.

My older brother Steve, in the absence of my father who died when I was six, gave me important lessons in values that helped me grow into an adult. For instance, Steve taught me to face the results of my behavior. Once when I returned in tears from a Saturday baseball game, it was Steve who took the time to ask me what happened. When I explained that my softball had soared through Mrs. Holt's basement window, breaking the glass with a crash, Steve encouraged me to confess to her. After all, I should have been playing in the park down Fifth Street and not in the alleyway. Although my knees knocked as I explained to Mrs. Holt, I offered to pay for the window from my allowance if she would return my ball. I also learned from Steve that personal property is a sacred thing. After I found a shiny silver pen in the wardrobe of my fifth-grade classroom, I wanted to keep it, but Steve explained that it might be important to someone else in spite of the fact that it had little value. He reminded me of how much I'd hate to lose to someone else the small dog my father carved from a piece of cheap pine. I returned the pen to my teacher, Mrs. Davids, and still remember the smell of her perfume as she patted me on the shoulder. Yet of all the instructions Steve gave me, his respect for life is the most vivid in my mind. When I was twelve I killed an old brown sparrow in the yard with a BB gun. Thrilled with my marksmanship, I screamed to Steve to come from the house to take a look. I shall never forget the way he stood for a long moment and stared at the bird on the ground. Then in a sad, quiet voice, he asked, "Did it hurt you first, Mark?" I didn't know what to answer. He continued with his eyes firm, "The only time you should even think of hurting a living thing is if it hurts you first. And then you think a long, long time." I really felt rotten then, but that moment stands out as the most important lesson my brother taught me.

1. How many lessons did Steve teach his brother? _____
2. List the lessons in your own words.

_____

_____

_____

_____

_____3. In the story about the pen, Steve taught his brother which
of the following lessons?
a. respect for life
b. respect for personal property
c. responsibility for his actions
d. the value of honesty
e. sympathy for people with problems

_____4. According to the writer, which was the most important
lesson Steve taught?
a. respect for older people
b. the value of honesty
c. respect for personal property
d. responsibility for one's actions
e. respect for life

6. Understanding Sequence
Read this paragraph. Then answer the questions that follow.

A coin-operated vending machine was invented by the Greeks
2,000 years ago. It stood in a temple, and when a worshiper
put a coin in the slot, it automatically produced a measured
amount of holy water. The coin fell onto a small pan hung from
one end of a delicately balanced beam. Its weight caused the
beam to dip; the beam's opposite end rose, opening a stopper
valve and allowing the holy water to flow out. When the pan
carrying the coin had been tilted enough, the coin slid off. Free
of its weight, the down end of the beam bobbed upward again
and the up end swung down, closing the valve and cutting off
the holy water. Surprisingly, the device closely parallels one
used in today's flush toilets.

—Murray Rubenstein

_____1. What action starts the machine in motion?
a. the balance beam moving
b. the valve closing
c. the pan tilting too much
d. the coin dropping in the hole

_____2. What causes the valve to open to let out water?
a. the coin dropping in the slot
b. the end of the beam with the pan going up

   c. the end of the beam without the pan going up
   d. the coin sliding off the pan

_____3. What causes the coin to slip off the pan?
   a. the end of the beam with the pan dipping too low
   b. the water pushing the coin off the pan
   c. the water ceasing to flow
   d. the machine shaking

_____4. What closes the stopper valve and turns the machine off?
   a. the coin weighing down the pan
   b. the beam swinging back to its original position
   c. the pan tilting too much
   d. the coin falling off the pan

_____5. The balance beam moves like what playground device?
   a. a merry-go-round
   b. a seesaw
   c. a swing
   d. a jungle gym

7. Understanding Sequence

Read this paragraph. Then answer the questions that follow.

I am back in Alabama now after a quarter of a century, and I am trying to sort out my impressions of this state which, along with Mississippi, is probably all that is truly left of the Old South. After driving around the state for several days in pouring rain, I awakened in Mobile to a cleansed and miraculous world. Stepping out on the balcony of the Malaga Inn, I was startled by the strength of the sun because it was not yet ten o'clock in the morning, and it was still early spring. The Spanish Plaza, in front of me, was half in the sun and half in shade, and at this hour it was a quiet and deserted place. A man with a paper was whistling loudly on the porch of a house across the street, and it struck me that I had never before seen a person read a newspaper and whistle at the same time. Somewhere behind the house a carpet was being beaten, and in the parking lot of the inn someone was trying to start a car with points that had been damaged by the rain. A bakery truck braked quickly at the corner, its tires squealing loudly enough to cause the whistler to lower his newspaper. These sounds came singly, measuring off the silence of a morning that was just beginning.

                                             —Randolph Wolfe

    1. What state and town was the writer describing? _____

_____

____2. The writer was standing
      a. in a parking lot.
      b. on a house porch.
      c. on the balcony of an inn.
      d. on the sidewalk.

    3. What was right in front of the writer? _____

_____

____4. The house with the porch was
      a. across the street.
      b. behind the writer.
      c. on the corner.
      d. on the writer's left.

____5. What was going on behind the house?
      a. A man was reading a paper.
      b. A bakery truck braked quickly.
      c. A car was starting.
      d. A carpet was being beaten.

8. Ordering of Ideas

    1. Of the three sample paragraphs on pages 93–95, which

paragraph places details in space order? _____

    2. Which paragraph places details in order of importance?__

    3. Which paragraph places details in time order? _____

9. The Ordering of Ideas Through Several Methods

    The following selections show the arrangement of details in a variety of ways. On the blank lines after each selection, explain the order that the writer has selected.

1. Once in a long while, four times so far for me, my mother brings out the metal tube that holds her medical diploma. On the tube are gold circles crossed with seven red lines each—

"joy" ideographs in abstract. There are also little flowers that look like gears for a gold machine. According to the scraps of labels with Chinese and American addresses, stamps, and postmarks, the family airmailed the can from Hong Kong in 1950. It got crushed in the middle, and whoever tried to peel the labels off stopped because the red and gold paint came off too, leaving silver scratches that rust. Somebody tried to pry the end off before discovering that the tube pulls apart. When I open it, the smell of China flies out, a thousand-year-old bat flying heavy-headed out of the Chinese caverns where bats are as white as dust, a smell that comes from long ago, far back in the brain. Crates from Canton, Hong Kong, Singapore, and Taiwan have that smell too, only stronger because they are more recently come from the Chinese.

Inside the can are three scrolls, one inside another. The largest says that in the twenty-third year of the National Republic, the To Keung School of Midwifery, where she has had two years of instruction and Hospital Practice, awards its Diploma to my mother, who has shown through oral and written examination her Proficiency in Midwifery, Pediatrics, Gynecology, "Medecine," "Surgary," Therapeutics, Ophthalmology, Bacteriology, Dermatology, Nursing, and Bandage.

—Maxine Hong Kingston

_____

_____

_____

2. There are three essential qualities for vulture country: a rich supply of unburied corpses, high mountains, a strong sun. Spain has the first of these, for in this sparsely populated and stony land it is not customary, or necessary, to bury dead animals. Where there are vultures in action such burial would be a self-evident waste of labor, with inferior sanitary results. Spain has mountains, too, in no part far to seek; and the summer sun is hot throughout the country. But it is hottest in Andalusia, and that is the decisive factor. The sun, to the vulture, is not just something which makes life easier and pleasanter, a mere matter of preference. His mode of life is impossible without it. Here in Andalusia the summer sun dries up every pond and lake and almost every river. It drives the desperate frogs deep into the mud cracks and forces the storks to feed on locusts. It kills the food plants and wilts the fig trees

over the heads of the panting flocks. Andalusia becomes like
that part of ancient Greece, "a land where men fight for the
shade of an ass."

—John D. Stewart

_____

_____

_____

6b Listing of Details

Information in a paragraph sometimes appears just as a series of
facts or details. Though all statements relate to the main idea, each
fact is not expanded. The paragraph presents a listing of information.

In the following paragraph, notice how the writer lists a series
of details to support the topic.

In 1935 the depression in America was five years old and
deepening. America had over 19,000,000 people on relief, one
in every six or seven of the population. As FERA administrator, Harry Hopkins had spent $323,890,560 on relief in the
first ten months of 1934, almost a third more than in 1933. In
1935 Congress appropriated $4,880,000,000 for the Work Re-
lief Bill. *Time* estimated uncomfortably that of the 19,000,000
on relief, 20 percent were unemployables, or "chronic de-
pendents." Over the country the debate ran, "Most people out
of work couldn't hold jobs if they had them." For the first time
since 1911, marriages had fallen in 1932 below the one-million
mark, though the population had risen from 93,000,000 in 1911
to 125,000,000 in 1932. In 1935, according to the President's
inaugural statement of 1937, one-third of American families
were "ill-fed, ill-clothed, and ill-housed." The mean income of
13,000,000 families was $471 annually, including income from
gardens and part-time labor. For these families the average
expenditure for food was $206 annually. The middle third of
American families received a mean income of $1,076; the upper
third received an average of $2,100.

—Don M. Wolfe

Exercises

1. Listing of Details
Read the foregoing paragraph and answer these questions.

1. What is the main idea? _____

2. List five details the writer gives to support the main idea.

_____

_____

_____

_____

_____

2. Listing of Details
Read the following paragraph and answer the questions after it.

The boys you worshiped when you first came down into the street remain with you all your life. They are the only real heroes. Napoleon, Lenin, Capone—all fiction. Napoleon is nothing to me in comparison with Eddie Carney, who gave me my first black eye. No man I have ever met seems as princely, as regal, as noble, as Lester Reardon who, by the mere act of walking down the street, inspired fear and admiration. Jules Verne never led me to the places that Stanley Borowski had up his sleeve when it came dark. Robinson Crusoe lacked imagination in comparison with Johnny Paul. All these boys of the Fourteenth Ward have a flavor about them still. They were not invented or imagined: they were real. Their names ring out like gold coins—Tom Fowler, Jim Buckley, Matt Owen, Rob Ramsay, Harry Martin, Johnny Dunne, to say nothing of Eddie Carney or the great Lester Reardon. Why, even now when I say Johnny Paul the names of the saints leave a bad taste in my mouth. Johnny Paul was the living Odyssey of the Fourteenth Ward; that he later became a truck driver is an irrelevant fact.

—Henry Miller

1. For the writer, are the real heroes those in books or the ones he knew personally?_____

2. What are the names of some of the real heroes? _____

_____

_____

_____

3. What were some of the things these heroes did? _____

_____

_____

_____

_____

4. How do you think the writer feels about the street he grew up on? _____

_____

3. Listing of Details

Read the following paragraph and answer the questions after it.

I know how a prize watermelon looks when it is sunning . . . among pumpkin vines and "simblins"; I know how to tell when it is ripe without "plugging" it; I know how inviting it looks when it is cooling itself in a tub of water under the bed, wait-ing; I know how it looks when it lies on the table in the shel-tered great floor space between house and kitchen, and the children gathered for the sacrifice and their mouths watering; I know the crackling sound it makes when the carving knife enters its end, and I can see the split fly along in front of the blade as the knife cleaves its way to the other end; I can see its halves fall apart and display the rich red meat and the black seeds, and the heart standing up, a luxury fit for the elect; I know how a boy looks behind a yard-long slice of that melon, and I know how he feels; for I have been there. I know the taste of the watermelon which has been honestly come by, and I know the taste of the watermelon which has been acquired by art.

—Mark Twain

1. What experience is the writer trying to capture by listing all the details? _____

2. List the main details that capture this experience.

_____

_____

_____

_____

3. The details in lines 4 through 11 are arranged in a kind of time order. Explain what happens in those lines to show the time sequence.

_____

_____

4. Listing of Details
Read the following paragraph and answer the questions after it.

There are many kinds of doors. Revolving doors for hotels, shops, and public buildings. These are typical of the brisk, bustling ways of modern life. Can you imagine John Milton or William Penn skipping through a revolving door? Then there are the curious little slatted doors that still swing outside de-natured bar-rooms and extend only from shoulder to knee. There are trapdoors, sliding doors, double doors, stage doors, prison doors, glass doors. But the symbol and mystery of a

door resides in its quality of concealment. A glass door is not a
door at all, but a window. The meaning of a door is to hide
what lies inside; to keep the heart in suspense.

—Christopher Morley

1. How many types of doors are mentioned? _____

2. List the different types of doors. _____

_____

_____

_____

_____

3. What do all doors have in common? _____

_____

_____

4. What does the last sentence do for the paragraph? _____

_____

_____

_____

6c Comparison and Contrast

In order to describe an unfamiliar object or idea, an author will
often relate the unfamiliar object to a familiar one. Not many of
you, for instance, know what a *bowler* in the game of cricket does.
If you learned that a bowler is much like a pitcher in baseball,
however, you could understand the bowler's job. Then, by also
considering how a bowler is *not* like a pitcher, you could get an
even better idea of what a cricket bowler does.

The technique of relating one object to another by showing
how they are alike and how they are different is called *comparison*

and contrast. Throughout the following paragraph, the author shows how life in a hotel is different from life in a normal home by comparing and contrasting the advantages and disadvantages.

For a child in a big hotel, there were distinct advantages. In addition to having so many recreational facilities available, I never had to do many of the things kids hate to do—like make my bed, wash the dishes, take out the garbage, or even clean my room. There was always someone on the staff who was paid to take care of such chores. On the other hand, there were disadvantages. Never was I able to eat breakfast in my pajamas. I had to dress for every meal. Nor could I ever raid the icebox. And privacy was something very hard to come by. Growing up in a hotel is like growing up in a goldfish bowl. Everybody always seemed to know what everybody else was doing at every given moment. Gossip was the name of the game.

— *These details explain advantages.*

— *These details explain disadvantages.*

—Tania Grossinger

Another type of comparison and contrast allows the writer to state one point and discuss *both* objects in regard to that idea; then to state another point and discuss both objects in regard to *that* idea; and so on.

The New York *Times* and the New York Daily *News* are really quite different. The two newspapers do not even look alike. Each page of the *Times* is twice the size of each page of the *News.* And as a tabloid—a smaller newspaper—the *News* uses many more pictures as a way to report events. They are also different in regard to types of stories each presents. The *News* is concerned with human interest stories, many about sensational people or events. The *Times*, although it does not neglect human interest, offers more news of worldwide importance. Furthermore, the styles of writing are not alike. The *News* stresses brief, simple reporting in everyday language. The *Times*, on the other hand, is much more formal and detailed; its articles take up several columns and are filled with background material and events that may have bearing on the present story.

— *One point: how they look*

— *Another point: the stories*

— *Another point: the style of writing*

Here are some tips for understanding comparison and contrast:

- Look for key words that help relate the two objects or ideas. These
  words point to like ideas:

similarly	in addition	in the same way
also	further	likewise

  These words point to ideas that differ:

but	on the other hand	still
although	in contrast	in spite of
however	yet	even so
nevertheless	conversely	nonetheless

- Look for a sentence or two that tells just what is being compared to
  what.

- As you read, keep in mind the two ideas that the writer is comparing
  or contrasting. Ask yourself, "What things are being compared?
  Why are they being compared? How are the things alike or different?

Exercises

1. Comparison and Contrast
Read example 1 on page 103 and answer the following questions.

1. Underline the two sentences (they are not together) that
tell what is being contrasted.

2. What are some advantages of living as a child in a large

resort hotel? _____

_____

3. What are some disadvantages of being a child in a big

hotel?_____

_____

2. Comparison and Contrast
Read example 2 on page 103 and answer the following questions.

1. What is the main idea of the selection? _____

_____

2. How do the newspapers compare in appearance? _____

_____

3. How are the stories in the *Times* different from the stories

in the *News*? _____

_____

4. What kind of writing does the *Times* offer? How is it differ-

ent from the writing that appears in the *News*? _____

_____

3. Comparison and Contrast in Long Selections
Read this selection and answer the questions that follow it.

The early feminists fought for the right to be equal with men.
Then women found themselves with the freedom to study and
think, but it was too often at the price of sacrificing a personal
life. So they went back into the home. In the present generation, women who have devoted themselves to homemaking
have rediscovered its hardships and limitations and are de-
manding the right to leave the home. But this time they do not
want to give up anything homemaking entails. They would
have the period of child rearing considered a special episode.
In their view, the woman with a job is to be more admired as a
mother and is more stimulating as a wife. It would be well to
ask: is this an expression of anything more than another swing
of the pendulum?
    The problems facing articulate, educated women remain
as vivid today as they have been throughout European history. The continuous care given to small children, a husband,
and a household usually is incompatible with the single-minded
pursuit of a career. The life style of the good wife and mother
contrasts sharply with that of the good scientist, artist, or
executive.

    —Margaret Mead and Frances Balgley Kaplan

   1. In the first paragraph what two groups of women are be-

      ing compared? _____

____2. The early feminists
      a. were willing to give up their personal lives to gain the
         freedom to study and think.
      b. wanted to have the freedom to study and to think at the
         same time as they enjoyed homemaking.
      c. wanted to spend their whole lives devoted to their
         families.
      d. wanted freedom but were not willing to pay the price of
         giving up their personal lives.
      e. were willing to pay any price for equality.

____3. The modern feminists
      a. are willing to give up their personal lives to gain the
         freedom to study and think.
      b. want to have the freedom to study and to think at the
         same time as they enjoy homemaking.
      c. want to spend their whole lives devoted to their
         families.
      d. want freedom but are not willing to pay the price of
         giving up their personal lives.
      e. are willing to pay any price for equality.

   4. What two life styles are compared in the second para-

      graph? _____

____5. The writer feels that
      a. the problems women face have changed through his-
         tory.
      b. having a family is better than having a career.
      c. having a career is better than having a family.
      d. the two life styles can fit together.
      e. the two life styles cannot fit together.

4. Comparison and Contrast in Long Selections
   Read this selection and answer the questions that follow it.
(*Wasichus* is an Indian word for "white men.")

I came to live here where I am now between Wounded Knee
Creek and Grass Creek. Others came too, and we made these

little gray houses of logs that you see, and they are square. It is a bad way to live, for there can be no power in a square.

You have noticed that everything an Indian does is in a circle, and that is because the Power of the World always works in circles, and everything tries to be round. In the old days when we were a strong and happy people, all our power came to us from the sacred hoop of the nation, and so long as the hoop was unbroken, the people flourished. The flowering tree was the living center of the hoop, and the circle of the four quarters nourished it. The east gave peace and light, the south gave warmth, the west gave rain, and the north with its cold and mighty wind gave strength and endurance. This knowledge came to us from the outer world with our religion. Everything the Power of the World does is done in a circle. The sky is round, and I have heard that the earth is round like a ball, and so are all the stars. The wind, in its greatest power, whirls. Birds make their nests in circles, for theirs is the same religion as ours. The sun comes forth and goes down again in a circle. The moon does the same, and both are round. Even the seasons form a great circle in their changing, and always come back again to where they were. The life of a man is a circle from childhood to childhood, and so it is in everything where power moves. Our tepees were round like the nests of birds, and these were always set in a circle, the nation's hoop, a nest of many nests, where the Great Spirit meant for us to hatch our children.

But the Wasichus have put us in these square boxes. Our power is gone and we are dying, for the power is not in us any more. You can look at our boys and see how it is with us. When we were living by the power of the circle in the way we should, boys were men at twelve or thirteen years of age. But now it takes them very much longer to mature.

—John G. Neihardt

1. The two things being compared are _____

   and _____.

2. List the ways in which Indian life depends on the circle.

_____

_____

_____

_____

_____

___3. The Indians
   a. always lived in square houses.
   b. lived in round tepees but then decided to move into
      square houses.
   c. lived in round tepees but then were forced to live in
      square houses.
   d. will never move from round tepees.
   e. like the wild country.

___4. This selection was spoken by Black Elk to John Neihardt
      almost fifty years ago. What happened to Black Elk's tribe
      once they moved into square houses?
   a. Everyone fell ill and died.
   b. Boys took longer to grow into men.
   c. The tribe stayed mighty.
   d. They had to move to other houses.
   e. They forgot the old way of life.

   5. Put a circle around all the words in the selection that
      suggest roundness (*ball*, for example) and a square around
      all words that suggest squareness.

___6. Black Elk feels that
   a. circles and squares both have strong magic.
   b. squares give much power, but circles make the tribe
      weak.
   c. circles give much power, but squares make the tribe
      weak.
   d. it is good for children to spend more years learning how
      to grow up.
   e. it is time to give up the old ways of life.

6d Cause and Effect

In this kind of paragraph, you learn either *why* something happened or what happened *as a result* of something. The writer may
explain conditions or events that *cause* a certain situation or may
discuss conditions or events that *result* from a situation. The fol-

lowing selection tells about a common effect in humans, and then it explains the causes that scientists have found.

Have you ever had the experience of putting money into a soda machine or a pay phone and, instead of getting soda or a dial tone, you get nothing? Even though you know it's just a machine, how many of you find yourselves kicking the machine or giving it a frustrated shake? It may interest you to know that scientists have studied this behavior, which is called the *pain-attack mechanism*. Pigeons were trained to peck at a disk mounted on a wall and to expect the reward of some grain every time they did so. Scientists found that, when they didn't reward the pigeon as it expected, the bird became very agitated, attacking the wall disk and even other pigeons in the same box. In similar experiments, monkeys, rats, and pigeons also reacted violently when they were given an electric shock for no reason. From these results, scientists decided that animals, and in a sense this includes us, will respond to a painful event by fighting back. The event can be physical pain, such as an electric shock, or emotional pain, such as expecting a reward and not getting it. But it also seems that getting yelled at or being fired, like losing a lover or losing money in a soda machine, will trigger anger or aggression in humans.

Cause and effect are important in much of the scientific and technical material you will read in college. As those of you who study science already know, many scientific discoveries were made because a scientist studied cause and effect in natural events. In the passage you just read, you saw how behavioral psychologists studied an *effect*, aggression, to see if they could discover some possible *causes* for it. The pain-attack mechanism provides an explanation for an important cause-and-effect relationship.

- If the writer tells why something happened, what happened because of something, or what might happen because of something, you can expect reasons to explain causes or effects.

- Look for word clues: *because, since, as a result, therefore, consequently, so.*

- Remember that many causes can contribute to a single situation and that many effects can grow from a single cause.

In our everyday life we frequently consider causes. For instance, we avoid eating food that smells bad or touching something that is glowing hot, because we know what effect tainted food or redhot objects will have on us. So also, when we read a passage, we can look for reasons (causes) behind events described (effects).

Exercises

1. Cause and Effect
Reread the paragraph on page 109 and answer these questions.

1. What situation will the writer try to explain by giving causes?

_____

2. What cause did scientists find for the type of angry, violent behavior described in the article?

_____

_____

3. In what situations and in what way does the pain-attack mechanism apply to pigeons and other animals?

_____

_____

_____

4. How does the pain-attack mechanism apply to humans?

_____

_____

_____

5. Describe any personal experiences you have had that might relate to the pain-attack mechanism. Do your experiences support or contradict the cause-and-effect pattern described in the article?

_____

_____

_____

_____

2. Cause and Effect
Read this paragraph and answer the questions that follow it.

Why is Broadway rehashing so many older plays and musicals instead of presenting new works that relate directly to the 1980s? In the last few years, theatergoers have been offered _West Side Story, Camelot, The King and I, The Music Man, Oklahoma, Dracula_ and _Look Back in Anger,_ good plays all, but ones that enjoyed runs anywhere from seventeen to fifty years ago. Even many new works, like _Annie_ and _A Day in Hollywood / A Night in the Ukraine_ are simply adapting established characters from other media. Part of the reason may be the tremendous cost of mounting a production in New York these days. A producer asked to invest a few hundred thousand dollars in a production may be expected to prefer a play of proven merit and past success to a new, untried work. Another explanation might be that during the 1960s New York theater went into a decline and very few young playwrights were given a chance to establish themselves, creating a void between the writers of the fifties and today. Whatever the cause, Broadway is running a great risk, for if no new plays or musicals are given a chance today, what will Broadway have to revive tomorrow?

1. What effect is the writer trying to explain? _____

_____

2. What examples does the writer give to show that theater

productions do not relate to today? _____

_____

_____

3. What causes does the writer give? _____

_____

_____

_____

4. Would you call these causes psychological, economic, sociological, political, artistic, or scientific? Why?

_____

5. What does the author say is the danger of relying so heavily on revivals? What will be the ultimate effect of all the causes he mentions?

_____

_____

_____

_____

3. Cause and Effect
     Read this paragraph and answer the questions that follow it.

Why does a person turn to a life of crime? There is no simple answer, but psychologists believe that some clues lie in the early life of the criminal. A child raised in an unhappy home, or by a strict parent or parent substitute, or a child raised in poverty runs the risk more than others of turning against the law. Some investigators believe that there is something in the basic personality which forces someone into crime. Several people suggest that it is a feature of the genes—something within the human cell tissue—that determines criminal action. And, of course, there is solid evidence to suggest that pressures of present-day society give rise to crime. Even an unlikely type for crime might turn to it because he or she is unable to face the hectic pace and style of life our present age demands.

1. For what effect is the writer trying to find the cause?

_____

2. Put a checkmark next to the causes that were suggested in the paragraph. Cross out the causes that were not mentioned.

____a. bad schooling

____b. genes

____c. poverty

____d. bad upbringing and childhood

____e. bad friends

____f. an evil heart

____g. pressure of modern society

____h. a desire to get rich quick

____i. personality

____j. insanity

____3. The writer
   a. does not say one cause is more important than the others.
   b. says that genes are the most important cause of people becoming criminals.
   c. says that poor upbringing is the main cause of people becoming criminals.
   d. says that the pressure of modern society is the main cause of people becoming criminals.
   e. says that people become criminals for no reason at all.

Unit Three
Interpretation and
Evaluation

7 Making Inferences

Inference is a process by which readers use hints to gather information. In making inferences, you go beyond surface details and "read between the lines" to reach information logically. When you read, certainly, you develop ideas from the exact information you have before you. Factual details in what you read provide the basis of your knowledge. But not every bit of information is easily apparent or clearly stated. Hints or suggestions may appear that you have to build upon with your own knowledge and experience in order to understand something fully. Because information is not always stated in exact terms, we must supply our own information from details or ideas that are only suggested by the writer. We can't always be certain that what we supply is absolutely right. But if we follow hunches that are based on evidence, we can be fairly sure about some things, even if they are only hinted at.

Of course, a page of writing does not offer the only opportunity you have to learn more about something by means of hints or suggestions. In understanding human behavior, you've been using your inference skills for most of your childhood and adult lives.

How? Let's take an example. Your supervisor comes to work one Monday morning at 9:30. (She's usually there waiting for you as you punch in at 9:00 sharp.) She mumbles to herself under her breath and shakes her head from side to side, biting her lip. She doesn't say "Hello" as she usually does, but instead, staring straight ahead of her, she storms past your desk and the desks of your co-workers. At her office she turns the doorknob roughly, throws open the door forcefully, and then slams it loudly behind her.

What do you *infer* from her behavior? Clearly, she's angry about something. You conclude that she's angry by adding up all that you see and by relying on what you know about her usual behavior. No one had to tell you that she was angry. From her appearance, her actions, her "body language," and her behavior, it was safe for you to infer that she was irritated about something.

In making inferences, you have to be careful not to go too far beyond the information at hand. Otherwise, your inferences might not be correct. For example, could you assume that the supervisor we have described was angry because she had had a fight with her son? Not at all. Nothing in what you saw or observed suggested that. On the other hand, you might have heard her mumble an angry remark to herself about her son as she passed by you. Or you might know for a fact that she fought with him often and that, when she did, her behavior resembled the behavior she displayed that morning. Then you might safely say to yourself, "Well, I guess she's been at it with Pepé again!" The point, of course, is that inferences must be based on valid, available information, not simply on vague suspicions or wild guesses.

Look at the picture on page 116. In a sentence describe the main idea of the picture—that is, what the picture is about.

You probably wrote something like *A man is sitting on a park bench holding an umbrella.* That states pretty much the subject of the picture. Now look back at it to answer these questions.

_____1. The person in the picture is
     a. about twenty years old.
     b. about forty years old.
     c. about eighty years old.

_____2. The picture was taken
     a. on a hot summer day.
     b. on a snowy winter evening.
     c. on a rainy spring day.

_____3. The scene takes place
     a. on a crowded city street.
     b. in a quiet city park.
     c. near a country farm.

If you picked answer *b* for question 1, how did you know that the person was about forty? If you picked answer *c* for question 2, how did you know that the scene probably took place on a rainy spring day? If you picked answer *b* for question 3, how did you know that the picture was taken in a quiet city park? None of the answers you picked is stated by the main idea of the picture: *A man sits on a park bench holding an umbrella.*

To answer the first question, you looked at the man's face and saw that, although his features were not young and smooth like those of a man of twenty, they weren't aged enough to belong to a man of eighty either. The hints from the picture enabled you to reject the extremes and to infer that the man was about forty.

For the second question you had to look at what the man was wearing. You knew that, in a sweater and suit coat, he was dressed too warmly for a hot summer day but not warmly enough for a snowy winter one. You inferred that it was spring by the leaves in the background, and you inferred that it was raining by the presence of the man's open umbrella.

For the third question you eliminated answer *a* easily, because no crowds are to be seen. The presence of concrete and long benches allowed you to infer that the scene was not a farm but a park. And the length of the bench, long enough for many people to sit on, tells you that the park was located where many people need a place to sit, probably in a city.

In reading, too, inference is an important skill, because it helps us fill in information a writer only suggests. Look at the following paragraph and answer the questions after it.

After lunch Diane took her bike and sneaked quietly into the yard. She moved carefully to the plot of soil under the oak in back of the house as she checked to see that nobody watched her. She leaned her bicycle against the tree and bent down. All around dark clouds rumbled noisily in the sky; a streak of yellow zig-zagged far away, and she trembled. Digging swiftly in the hot earth, she made a small hole and quickly took a crushed ten-dollar bill from her pocket. After she slipped the money into the ground and covered it, she breathed deeply and smiled. She was glad *that* was over! Now no one would find it or know how she got it. Certainly it would be there later when she wanted it.

_____1. Diane is probably
     a. a teen-ager.
     b. a young mother.
     c. a child of three or four.

_____2. About the money, Diane probably
     a. got it as a gift for her father.
     b. earned it.
     c. got it in a suspicious way.

_____3. This event probably took place
     a. on a snowy winter afternoon.
     b. before a summer rainstorm.
     c. one night during Easter.

_____4. After she hides the money, Diane feels
     a. very guilty and sorry.
     b. relieved.
     c. worried that someone saw her.

To answer all these questions, you needed to use inference skills. The sentences about Diane give only hints about the questions asked. Not one answer is stated exactly in the paragraph.

You know Diane was a teen-ager from her actions and thoughts, which were too advanced for her to be three or four.

Further, a young mother would not *generally* bury money in the ground. Answer *a* is correct for question 1.

Because she sneaked into the yard and because she looked to see if anybody watched her, you infer that Diane has done something wrong. When she thinks that no one will know how she got the money, you guess that she received it in a suspicious way. Answer *c* is correct for question 2.

The noisy clouds and the streak of yellow—thunder and lightning, surely—suggest that a storm is coming. *Hot earth* suggests the summer. Besides, Diane goes out after lunch, so the scene is not a nighttime one. Answer *b* is correct for question 3.

You can infer from Diane's deep breath and from the statement "She was glad *that* was over" that she is relieved after she hides the money. Answer *b* is correct for question 4.

Building Inference Skills

- Try to read beyond the words. Fill in details and information based on the writer's suggestions.

- Question yourself as you read. "Why is Diane hiding the money?" you might have asked as you read. "Why are there clouds and lightning in the sky?" Supply the answers on the basis of the writer's hints and your own experience.

- If a writer describes a person, try to understand the person from how she moves, what she says, what she looks like. You can infer things about a person's character from the way she behaves. Try to build a picture of the person in your mind; base your picture on the writer's description of action and appearance.

- If a textbook or a teacher asks a question you cannot answer easily from what you have read, remember to use inference. Return to the part of the reading where you expect the answer. Then see if the writer suggests something that you yourself have to supply in clearer terms.

Exercises

1. Inferring Details from a Cartoon

Look at the following cartoon. Then try to use your inference skills to answer these questions.

"What do you say? Shall we get down to some serious bowling?"

———1. The man who is speaking probably
    a. is tired from a long day's work.
    b. is a championship bowler.
    c. cannot enjoy himself by just sitting around and joking with his friends.
    d. is angry because the bowling lanes are crowded.

———2. There are no women among the five men—probably because the men
    a. are divorced.
    b. do not like women.
    c. are spending a "stag" night out.
    d. are meeting their wives after bowling.

———3. The four men to whom the man in the center is speaking are at the bowling alley essentially to
    a. socialize for an hour or two.
    b. practice bowling for the league game.
    c. take lessons from the man who is speaking.
    d. discuss important business deals.

———4. The humor in the cartoon is based on the idea that
    a. people at bowling alleys should not have to be convinced to bowl.

b. few of the people have any real interest in bowling.
c. the man who speaks does not realize that having fun at a bowling alley does not have to include bowling.
d. all of these.

2. Making Inferences

Read the following selection, in which a former migrant worker describes the treatment he received. As you read, try to use inference skills such as those offered in this chapter. Then answer the questions after the selection.

I began to see how everything was so wrong. When growers can have an intricate watering system to irrigate their crops but they can't have running water inside the houses of workers. Veterinarians tend to the needs of domestic animals but they can't have medical care for the workers. They can have land subsidies for the growers but they can't have adequate unemployment compensation for the workers. They treat him like a farm implement. In fact, they treat their implements better and their domestic animals better. They have heat and insulated barns for the animals but the workers live in beat-up shacks with no heat at all.

—Roberto Acuna

1. Write in your own words the main idea of this selection (see section **4b**).

_____

_____

____2. We may infer that the author believes that
   a. migrant workers should stop complaining and get back to work.
   b. farm owners are mistreating workers.
   c. veterinarians are better than medical doctors.
   d. workers should be treated like farm tools.
   e. growers are unable to figure out how to supply migrant workers with running water.

____3. The attitude of farm owners toward migrant workers is one of
   a. neglect.
   b. fairness.

    c. hostility.

    d. favoritism.

____4. What inferences can we draw from the passage about what motivates the farm owners?

    a. Workers can be replaced easily at no cost to owners.

    b. Farm owners are cruel people who like to make others suffer.

    c. The government causes farm owners to mistreat their help by paying them money to do so.

    d. Farm owners can't distinguish between humans and animals.

3. Making Inferences

Read the following selection and answer the questions after it.

The impact of the American periodical press also has been technological and social. The large, mass-circulation magazines have influenced the smaller magazines, which in many instances seek to imitate their appearance and to emulate the high quality of their printing, layout, and make-up. They also have influenced magazines around the world. Europe, for example, is given to publishing magazines resembling *Life* and *Look*, and almost no heavily industrialized country is without its imitator of *Time* (*The Link* in India, *Elseviers* in the Netherlands, *Tiempo* in Mexico, *Der Spiegel* in Germany, and *L'Express* in France, for example). The social effect has to do with the discharge or failure to discharge its social responsibilities. These responsibilities the magazine press shares with all communications media, printed or electronic. They include the obligation, in a political democracy such as is the U.S.A., to provide the people with a fair presentation of facts, with honestly held opinions, and with truthful advertising. All but the subsidized periodicals hold—or seek to hold—to these goals within a certain framework: that of the business order, the private initiative, profit-making system.

—Roland E. Wolseley

1. In your own words write the main idea of this selection (see

section **4b**). _____

_____2. We may infer about magazines like *Life, Look,* and *Time* that
   a. they are resented in European countries.
   b. they sell very well throughout the world.
   c. they are respected as models for foreign magazines.
   d. they do not discharge social responsibilities.
   e. their production costs are extremely high.

_____3. The writer believes that magazines
   a. must make a profit at any costs.
   b. should not compete with television for advertising.
   c. should be subsidized.
   d. should imitate European models.
   e. should not accept untruthful advertising.

_____4. We may infer about the author's knowledge of the subject that
   a. he knows very little about Asian or African periodicals.
   b. he knows a great deal about European and American magazines.
   c. he knows a great deal about European magazines but not much about American magazines.
   d. he has worked as a magazine layout editor.
   e. none of these.

4. Making Inferences
   Read the following selection and answer the questions after it.

Greek mythology is largely made up of stories about gods and goddesses, but it must not be read as a kind of Greek Bible, an account of the Greek religion. According to the most modern idea, a real myth has nothing to do with religion. It is an explanation of something in nature; how, for instance, any and everything in the universe came into existence: men, animals, this or that tree or flower, the sun, the moon, the stars, storms, eruptions, earthquakes, all that is and all that happens. Thunder and lightning are caused when Zeus hurls his thunderbolt. A volcano erupts because a terrible creature is imprisoned in the mountain and every now and then struggles to get free. The Dipper, the constellation called also the Great Bear, does not set below the horizon because a goddess once was angry at it and decreed that it should never sink into the sea. Myths are early science, the result of men's first trying to explain what they saw around them. But there are many so-called myths which explain nothing at all. These tales are pure entertainment, the sort of thing people would tell each other on a long winter's evening. The story of Pygmalion and Galatea is an example; it has no conceivable connection with any event in nature. Neither has the Quest of the Golden Fleece, nor Orpheus and Eurydice, nor many another. This fact is now generally accepted; and we do not have to try to find in every mythological heroine the moon or the dawn and in every hero's life a sun myth. The stories are early literature as well as early science. But religion is there, too. In the background, to be sure, but nevertheless plain to see. From Homer through the tragedians and even later, there is a deepening realization of what human beings need and what they must have in their gods.

—Edith Hamilton

_____1. The author believes that mythology
    a. has nothing to do with religion.
    b. was discovered by means of Pygmalion and Galatea.
    c. is a very modern idea.
    d. is pure entertainment.
    e. has to do with science, religion, and literature.

_____2. Which of the following statements is true?
    a. Every myth exhibits a connection with some natural event.
    b. Not all myths attempt to explain an event in nature.
    c. Angry gods and goddesses appear in all myths.
    d. All myths refer to long winter evenings.
    e. Evidence of Greek bible stories appears in all myths.

_____3. In regard to modern ideas on myth, the author
    a. is impressed by and agrees with them.
    b. refuses to accept any of them.
    c. adds to them her own point of view.
    d. has no comments to make.
    e. none of these.

5. More Practice with Inference
    After you read the following selection, use inference skills to answer the questions.

The morning of New Year's Day was cold and overcast: flat light coming from a yellow sky; empty streets. Christmas wreaths hung in dark windows of McFeely's bar, on West Twenty-third Street. A solitary man crossed an asphalt playground on Horatio Street, trailing a plume of cigarette smoke. There were four padlocks on the front of Ponce Sporting Goods Sales, on Madison Street, and Joe's Spanish-American Record Shop ("Candies—Reg. Nylons—Panty Hose—Latest Hits") was also locked, as were the Misión Pentecostal and Jehovah's Witnesses buildings down the block. An elderly Chinese man wearing a blue ski jacket with a fur collar moved slowly across Mott Street at Grand. A long subway train came rattling and rumbling down the ramp of the Manhattan Bridge into Manhattan. Six teen-agers with two footballs began throwing passes in the small plaza between St. Andrew's Church and the Municipal Building, behind the United States Courthouse on Foley Square. At the Ng Yung grocery, on lower Broadway, a man was putting boxes of red apples on the sidewalk; a pile of ice left to melt in the gutter remained solid. Seagulls were flapping around the Department of Sanitation dock on the Hudson near Twelfth Street. No boats were moving on the river, and parts of it were frozen and white.

—*The New Yorker*
January 19, 1981

_____ 1. The main idea of this paragraph is
   a. to show the effects of cold weather on New York City.
   b. to describe an area of Manhattan on January 1.
   c. to demonstrate the ethnic variety of people who live in New York.
   d. to show how hard people work in the city during early morning hours.
   e. to argue against laws that keep businesses closed on holidays.

_____ 2. We may infer that most of the stores and other establishments are closed because
   a. the weather is much too cold.
   b. there are no customers available.
   c. it is too late at night.
   d. the noise of the subway train disturbs people in the shopping area.
   e. it is a holiday.

_____3. The sporting goods store probably has four padlocks on it
because
   a. the owner does not want to encourage people from the
      Misión Pentecostal to come by.
   b. the store has been robbed many times before.
   c. the police require four locks for safe protection of
      neighborhood establishments.
   d. there is valuable merchandise inside that requires pro-
      tection from robbery.
   e. all of these.

8 Understanding Figurative Language

To make language clearer, more interesting, and more vivid, we all use expressions that are not literally true. We make comparisons in speaking and writing. *Figurative language*—language that compares—paints a picture.

People frequently use figurative expressions when they speak:

1. "I worked *like a dog* last night!"

2. "Either spend that fifty dollars or put it in the bank. You can't *have your cake and eat it too.*"

3. "I told him to stop *bugging me.*"

None of these expressions is literal—that is, not one means *exactly* what it says. The speakers are not really talking about dogs, cake, or bugs.

In example 1, the speaker tries to show how hard she worked, and she compares herself to a dog to achieve the effect she wants.

In example 2, the person is saying that you cannot both use something up and keep it to use later. He states a familiar figurative expression. With it he compares the person he's talking to with someone who wants to eat a piece of cake and, at the same time, to save it for later—an impossible thing to do.

In example 3, the speaker compares someone to an insect, even though she is really talking about a person. The expression "bugging me" suggests in this sentence that the person is behaving like an annoying bug—a mosquito, perhaps, or an ant.

With informal and familiar figurative expressions like these, you rarely see a picture in your mind as a result of the comparisons being made. But writers who use *original* figurative language expect you to picture the comparisons they have made so that you can see something more easily. Look at these two statements:

1. A yellow light was slanting over the high walls into the jail yard.

2. A sickly light, like yellow tinfoil, was slanting over the high walls into the jail yard. (George Orwell)

In example 1, the writer certainly has painted a picture for the reader. You can see the jail yard, the high walls, and the yellow light slanting over it. There are no figurative expressions here; the description is literal. But in example 2, because of *figurative language*, the picture is much more vivid. You know that light cannot be ill or of bad health (only living things like people or animals can get sick.) Yet by calling the light *sickly* and thereby comparing it to some living thing, Orwell makes us see unhealthfulness in the scene. Then he makes the picture even clearer by comparing the light to yellow tinfoil. Of course, there is no tinfoil here: you would not expect there to be any on the walls outside a prison. But by means of the comparison, the writer is trying to paint an original picture in your mind. If you have ever seen (or can imagine) yellow tinfoil, you can picture the kind of light Orwell wants you to see as it slants over the jail yard walls.

Writers have many different ways of using figurative language to create vivid pictures. Sometimes nonhuman things are given human features. (This kind of comparison is called *personification*.)

1. The sun *yawned* through the trees. (The sun is being compared to a person yawning.)

2. An idea *spoke* within him, *racing through* his mind. (The idea has the quality of a living thing: it speaks and races.)

Sometimes we make comparisons using the word *like* or the word *as*. (This kind of figurative expression is called a *simile*.)

3. The tree bent in the wind *like an old man praying*. (A tree is compared to an old man at prayer.)

4. The moon looked *as white as a skull*. (The moon's color is being compared to the color of a skull.)

Some comparisons are only suggested. One of two objects being compared is said to *be* the other object, but the things compared are usually quite different from each other. (Implied comparisons like those that follow are called *metaphors*.)

5. His *blackberry* eyes darted nervously. (The eyes are being compared to blackberries so that you can see the eyes as small and black.)

6. A brown, withered *leaf of a hand* fluttered gently on her lap and then lifted up to wipe a tear away. (The hand is being compared to a leaf to suggest frailty and the approaching end of life.)

For special effects, we exaggerate some comparisons. (A figurative expression that exaggerates is called *hyperbole*.)

7. He roared with the force *of a thousand lions*. (The force of his roar is exaggerated by being compared with the roars of lions.)

In newspapers, magazines, and textbooks, you can expect to find figurative language to make a point clearer or more lively, and often both. In poetry and other forms of creative writing, writers often use figurative language in subtle and complex ways. As a reader, you must recognize figurative expressions so that you can understand a writer's point fully.

Understanding Figurative Language

- Make sure that you are aware that the writer is making a comparison. In example 6, the writer is talking about a woman's hand. By introducing the idea of a leaf, the writer has not changed the topic suddenly to a discussion of leaves! The writer is merely making this description more vivid by comparing the hand to something else.

- Keep clearly in your mind just what is being compared to what. Don't lose the basic point by getting confused about the comparison and forgetting what the writer is explaining in the first place. In example 3, you are supposed to see the tree better because it looks like an old man at prayer; you should not, however, expect to hear anything further about religion or praying. (There are, however, *extended metaphors* that carry the implied comparisons further. Especially in poetry, you should watch for additional words that continue and extend a simple comparative theme.)

- Look for such words as *like* and *as*, which often introduce comparisons.

- Try to figure out why the writer has made the comparison. Why, in example 1, has the sun been compared to a yawning man? Why, in example 4, is the moon compared to a skull?

Exercises

1. Understanding Figurative Language

Each of the following sentences from a professional writer makes a comparison. Explain in your own words what the comparison means. Tell also why you think the writer makes such a comparison. Use a separate sheet of paper to record your answers.

1. An aged man is but a paltry thing,
   a tattered coat upon a stick, . . .
   —William Butler Yeats

2. Blow, blow thou winter wind
   Thou art not so unkind
   As man's ingratitude . . .
   —William Shakespeare

3. When Duty whispers low, *Thou must,*
   The youth replies, *I can.*
   —Ralph Waldo Emerson

4. A wicked whisper came and made my heart as dry as dust.
   —Samuel Taylor Coleridge

5. My father's body was a globe of fear
   His body was a town we never knew . . .
   —Michael Ondaatje

2. Common Figurative Expressions

The figurative language in the following sentences appears often in our own talk and conversation. On a separate sheet of paper, explain the meaning of the figurative expressions that appear in italics.

1. I've really been *climbing the walls* since I quit smoking.

2. Zoe *flipped* when she heard the news.

3. When I told my father I wrecked his car, he *hit the roof.*

4. "Day of the Dead" was so scary I almost *jumped out of my skin.*

5. My brother Kevin *eats like a horse* and *sleeps like a log.*

3. Figurative Language in Poetry

Explain the meaning of each figurative expression printed in italics in the following lines of poetry. Write your answers on a separate sheet of paper.

1. *As a white candle*
   In a holy place
   So is the beauty
   Of an aged face

   —Joseph Campbell

2. The buzz saw *snarled* and rattled in the yard.
   —Robert Frost

3. *Love walked alone*
   The rocks cut her tender feet
   And the brambles tore her fair limbs.
   —Stephen Crane

4. Look *like the innocent flower*
   But *be the serpent under it!*
   —William Shakespeare

5. Because I could not stop for Death—
   He kindly stopped for me—
   The Carriage held but just ourselves—
   And Immortality.
   —Emily Dickinson

4. Understanding Figurative Language in Poetry

In this selection, "Dream Deferred" by Langston Hughes, you will find that the poet uses a variety of figurative images to show what happens to a dream that is deferred—put off, in other words. Read the poem with an eye toward understanding how each figurative expression helps you to understand what Hughes is talking about. Then answer the questions.

Dream Deferred ("Harlem")

What happens to a dream deferred?

Does it dry up
like a raisin in the sun?

Or fester like a sore—
And then run?
Does it stink like rotten meat?
Or crust and sugar over—
like a syrupy sweet?

Maybe it just sags
like a heavy load.

Or does it explode?

—Langston Hughes

1. What things are being compared in the first, second, and third lines?

_____

_____

2. Explain the image of something drying up "like a raisin in the sun."

_____

_____

3. In line 4, Hughes says that something deferred can "fester like a sore." What does *fester* mean? How can a dream be like a festering sore?

_____

_____

4. Why does Hughes think it is necessary to give the reader so many different pictures of a deferred dream? Why isn't one enough?

_____

_____

9 Drawing Conclusions and Predicting Outcomes

Careful readers *interpret* what they read; that is, they try to explain and to understand ideas brought out by their reading. One way to build your skill at interpreting is to try to draw conclusions from what the writer tells you.

A reading selection gives you information about a topic. Good readers are able to use that information on their own in order to know what to expect next. Paragraphs or larger readings present information to support a topic, but they do not always state all the possible results of the events the writer discusses. In fact, if you must answer questions after you read, those questions often involve conclusions you must draw on your own.

You have to put together facts and details logically in your own mind in order to draw correct conclusions. You have to think ahead to events or ideas that might come from information the writer gives, information that forces you to *predict* how things come out. Even though you might not know for sure, you have to use evidence you find in your reading to forecast what will happen.

Read the following selection and answer the questions after it, which involve drawing conclusions.

Ever since our departure, the seagulls have been following our ship, apparently without effort, almost without moving their wings. Their fine, straight navigation scarcely leans upon the breeze. Suddenly, a loud plop at the level of the kitchens stirs up a greedy alarm among the birds, throwing their fine flight

into confusion and sending up a fire of white wings. The seagulls whirl madly in every direction and then with no loss of
speed drop from the flight one by one and dive toward the sea.
A few seconds later they are together again on the water, a
quarrelsome farmyard that we leave behind, nesting in the
hollow of the wave, slowly picking through the manna of the
scraps.

—Albert Camus

_____1. The seagulls are following the ship because
     a. the men are playing with them.
     b. they are angry at the noises from the ship.
     c. they are hungry.
     d. they are confused.

_____2. The "loud plop at the level of the kitchens" is probably
     a. the sound of a dead bird falling from the sky.
     b. the drop of the engine or anchor to slow the ship down.
     c. a man falling overboard.
     d. the sound of leftover food hitting the waves.

_____3. The men probably throw scraps overboard because
     a. they have to get rid of unwanted garbage and leftovers.
     b. they like the seagulls.
     c. the seagulls are hungry.
     d. the seagulls annoy them.

_____4. The men will probably
     a. try to shoot one of the birds.
     b. travel on, leaving the gulls to their meal.
     c. feed the birds whenever the birds are hungry.
     d. shout and make noises to keep the annoying birds away.

We can tell from the way the birds behave at the end that they
were probably hungry and are following the ship for food; therefore answer *c* is correct for question 1.

From the plopping sound near the kitchen, we conclude that
someone has thrown food overboard and pick answer *d* for question 2.

In question 3, we can reach a conclusion from the way the men
behave. Nothing in the paragraph suggests how they feel about
the gulls: we don't know if the men like the birds or are annoyed by
them. We also do not know whether the men know if the seagulls
are hungry or even whether the men *care* that the birds may be
hungry! The only safe conclusion is that the men want to dispose of
their garbage: answer *a* is correct for question 3.

In like manner, the only thing we can predict about a future event is that the men will leave the birds behind as the ship moves forward.

How to Form Conclusions and Predict Outcomes

- Be sure you know the main idea of the selection.

- Be sure you understand all the facts or details that the writer gives to support the idea.

- Check on difficult vocabulary. Did you use sentence *clues* (section **2a**) to figure out that *manna* had something to do with food? (Any food supplied as if by a miracle—like the food that came to the Jews in the wilderness—is called *manna*.)

- Look out for the logic of action. Did you follow the sequence (section **8a**)? Did you put events together in the right order of time or place to help you predict what would happen?

- Look at the way characters are described. Can you tell from their personalities—from the way they think and feel—just how they might act?

- Ask yourself after you read: what will happen as a result of these actions or events?

- Be careful to build your conclusion on evidence you find in what you read and not on your own opinions, likes, and dislikes. Of course you need to use your own experience to help figure out how things may happen. But most of your conclusions must be based on what you read in the selection.

Exercises

1. Drawing Conclusions and Predicting Outcomes

Read the following passage and then answer the questions, most of which are based on your ability to draw conclusions or predict outcomes.

Few people passed. The man out of the last house passed on his way home; she heard his footsteps clacking along the concrete pavement and afterwards crunching on the cinder path before the new red houses. One time there used to be a field there in which they used to play every evening with other people's children. Then a man from Belfast bought the field and built houses in it—not like their little brown houses but bright brick houses with shining roofs. The children of the avenue used to play together in that field—the Devines, the Waters, the Dunns, little Keogh the cripple, she and her brothers and sisters. Ernest, however, never played: he was too grown up. Her father used often to hunt them in out of the field with his blackthorn stick; but usually little Keogh used to keep *nix* and call out when he saw her father coming. Still they seemed to have been rather happy then. Her father was not so bad then; and besides, her mother was alive. That was a long time ago; she and her brothers and sisters were all grown up, her mother was dead. Tizzie Dunn was dead, too, and the Waters had gone back to England. Everything changes. Now she was going to go away like the others, to leave her home.

—James Joyce

_____1. The title that would best express the main idea of this selection is
   a. A Quiet Street.
   b. How Tizzie Dunn Died.
   c. Dreams.
   d. Everything Changes.
   e. Buildings Old and New.

_____2. About her past life the woman has
   a. no thoughts at all.
   b. generally pleasant thoughts.
   c. thoughts filled with pain.
   d. regrets.
   e. anger.

_____3. If her father had found the woman playing in the field when she was younger, he would probably have
   a. sent her home.
   b. chased the other children away.
   c. yelled at her for playing with Keogh the cripple.
   d. told her mother.
   e. beaten her.

_____4. We may conclude that the woman's home is probably in
   a. England.
   b. Ireland.
   c. New York.
   d. Chicago.
   e. none of these.

_____5. About the idea of leaving home the woman is
   a. deeply worried.
   b. somewhat concerned.
   c. greatly relieved and happy.
   d. frightened because of her father.
   e. sorry because of her mother.

_____6. One conclusion we *cannot* safely draw on the basis of this selection is that
   a. the Waters family returned to England because they were unhappy where they lived.
   b. the woman's father grew worse as the years went on.
   c. the houses built by the man from Belfast changed the way the neighborhood looked.
   d. the woman lives on a quiet street.
   e. Ernest did not join in the games of the young children.

2. Drawing Conclusions and Predicting Outcomes
Read the following selection and answer the questions after it.

The American companies are altering plants and equipment and are introducing dramatically redesigned automobiles in a two-level fight. First, they plan to produce smaller, fuel-efficient cars to compete with the imports. Second, they intend to use highly sophisticated equipment and manufacturing systems that will increase the industry's lagging productivity and provide cars that are less expensive to produce and can be manufactured with fewer workers.

New plants are being constructed; old ones, abandoned or remodeled. Traditions that have existed for decades—emphasis on styling, size, power—are being left behind. It was not long ago that American automobile men denigrated the Volkswagen and other foreign automobiles. Funny-looking cars, they would say. Bathtubs upside down. Wind-up toys. Terrible styling. Then things began to change.

The encroachment of foreign cars on American shores now has auto makers testing cars like the Volkswagen Rabbit and the Toyota Celica—imitating them, trying to understand what makes them tick. They are investigating competitors' cars and making major alterations in their own. It is a desperate struggle to match competition, particularly that of foreign automobiles. But it is also a struggle to survive.

_____1. We may conclude that the automobile industry in the past had
   a. big cars that did not use gas well.
   b. highly sophisticated equipment.
   c. highly productive plants.
   d. inexpensive cars.
   e. many new plants.

_____2. What outcome can we predict if the automobile industry does not win its fight to become competitive with foreign auto manufacturers?
   a. Americans will abandon the automobile.
   b. American auto companies will try a new approach.
   c. American auto companies will go out of business.
   d. American auto companies will return to their old methods.
   e. All the foreign companies will back off from American markets.

_____3. Why are American companies investigating how foreign cars work and why they appeal to the American public?
   a. They want to prove that foreign cars are unattractive.
   b. They want to prove that foreign cars are unsafe.
   c. Americans have forgotten how to make cars.
   d. Foreign cars are using illegal devices.
   e. Americans want to copy the methods of foreign auto makers.

3. Drawing Conclusions and Predicting Outcomes
Read the following selection and answer the questions after it.

The Manus baby is accustomed to water from the first years of his life. Lying on the slatted floor he watches the sunlight gleam on the surface of the lagoon as the changing tide passes and repasses beneath the house. When he is nine or ten months old his mother or father will often sit in the cool of the evening on the little verandah, and his eyes grow used to the sight of the passing canoes and the village set in the sea. When he is about a year old, he has learned to grasp his mother firmly about the throat, so that he can ride in safety, poised on the back of her neck. She has carried him up and down the long house, dodged under low-hanging shelves, and climbed up and down the rickety ladders which lead from house floor down to the landing verandah. The decisive, angry gesture with which he was reseated on his mother's neck whenever his grip tended to slacken has taught him to be alert and sure-handed. At last it is safe for his mother to take him out in a canoe, to punt or paddle the canoe herself while the baby clings to her neck. If a sudden wind roughens the lagoon or her punt catches in a rock, the canoe may swerve and precipitate mother and baby into the sea. The water is cold and dark, acrid in taste and blindingly salt; the descent into its depths is sudden, but the training within the house holds good. The baby does not loosen his grip while his mother rights the canoe and climbs out of the water.

—Margaret Mead

1. Without using a dictionary, try to determine the definitions of the following words. Refer to the line in which the word appears for hints to its meaning.

   a. lagoon (line 3) _____

   b. verandah (line 6) _____

   c. rickety (line 12) _____

   d. slacken (line 15) _____

   e. punt (line 17) _____

   f. precipitate (line 19) _____

   g. acrid (line 21) _____

____2. The main idea of this paragraph is
   a. to show how Manus babies learn about water.
   b. to show how the mothers raise their children.
   c. to show how to survive the dangers of the sea.
   d. to illustrate the way in which Manus families pass their time.
   e. all of these.

____3. The Manus houses are built
   a. in the mountains.
   b. in bush country.
   c. on slats above the lagoon.
   d. with shells from the sea.
   e. by the villagers at a festival.

_____4. We can conclude that a Manus child who falls by accident
into the sea with the mother
   a. will probably drown.
   b. will probably be all right.
   c. will probably be attacked by sharks.
   d. will be rescued by the father.
   e. will swim to safety.

_____5. Manus mothers probably take their children onto the water
after they reach the age of
   a. five weeks.
   b. eleven weeks.
   c. nine months.
   d. ten months.
   e. a year.

_____6. When traveling as a baby with its mother, the Manus child
   a. rides in a backpack.
   b. sits in a straw carriage.
   c. hangs from the mother's neck.
   d. paddles a canoe.
   e. all of these.

_____7. As rowers along the lagoon, Manus mothers are
   a. not so good as the fathers.
   b. quite inexperienced.
   c. quite capable.
   d. usually involved in accidents.
   e. unable to dodge low-hanging shelves.

10   Generalizing

Another way to help you interpret what you read and to get deeper meanings from it is to develop skills in generalizing.

When you generalize, you extend meanings beyond the specific ideas you read about. Generalizing allows you to apply information you've learned in a broader, less specific sense. You add up facts and details and draw from that particular information some general ideas or principles.

In Chapter 9 you learned about drawing conclusions and predicting outcomes. These skills are closely related to generalizing. *Generalizing* carries you a step beyond a conclusion you can draw about a specific set of details. It's almost as if *you* develop a concept or a rule based on material you've read.

Read the following selection and the questions and discussion after it.

One rainy morning in 1955, Harry Van Sinderen left his home in Washington, Connecticut, to drive to his office in New York, about a hundred miles away. The rain turned into a downpour—the heaviest he could remember. Switching on the car radio, he learned that he was in the midst of a tropical storm that had swung inland from the coast, and that streams were flooding all through northern Connecticut. A few minutes later he got worse news: a dam on the Shepaug River above Washington had broken, and the resulting flood had wiped out the center of the town, with considerable loss of life and property.

Harry drove on to New York, walked into his office, and wrote out his resignation as chairman of the board of the export–import company he had managed for many years. He then drove back to Washington, through the still-pouring rain, and appointed himself Chief Rebuilder of the town. He was sixty-six years old at the time.

—John Fischer

——1. Harry Van Sinderen was probably
   a. interested in urban planning.
   b. interested in tropical storms.
   c. slightly insane.
   d. not making enough money on his job.

——2. Mr. Van Sinderen's actions suggest
   a. that people should not go outdoors in tropical rain-storms.
   b. that a manager's job is often dull.
   c. that driving a car to and from work each day is a great drain on one's energy.
   d. that people late in life can change careers to find more meaningful work.

——3. Harry Van Sinderen would agree
   a. that personal success in business and finance is a person's key aim.
   b. that service to the community in a time of crisis is more important than personal goals.
   c. that people should carry heavy insurance in case of disasters like flooding.
   d. that unexpected storms in Connecticut are violent.

Based on Van Sinderen's concern for damage to the city from the rainstorm, and based on the statement that he made himself Chief Rebuilder of the town, the idea that he has an interest in urban planning is clear. Even though he may have acted strangely in giving up his job with his company, and even though people often leave jobs for work that pays more, we have no evidence to make us believe that he is either slightly insane or underpaid for the work he does now. And just because he found himself in the midst of a heavy downpour, we cannot conclude that he had a special interest in tropical storms. Only answer *a* is a fair conclusion for question 1.

In question 2, however, we must be able to go beyond the conclusions we have drawn from the paragraph. Van Sinderen, a man of sixty-six years, suddenly resigned one job to take on another that he thought was important. We can generalize from his actions and say that they suggest that age does not have to stop a person from making major changes in his or her life's work. Based on Harry Van Sinderen's action, we've developed a general rule: people late in life can change their careers to find more meaningful work. This is not a general statement that everyone would agree

with, but information in the paragraph supports the generalization. For question 2, only answer *d* is correct.

All the other statements in question 2 are generalizations too,
but there is no reason to believe that they are true, based on information given in the selection. It's a general rule that people should
not go out in tropical storms. But Mr. Van Sinderen really
benefited from his ride in the heavy rains—they helped him make
an important decision. And although it's often generally true that
driving each day drains energy, nothing in the paragraph supports
that idea. Further, even though Mr. Van Sinderen quit his job, and
even though we suspect, in general, that a manager's job often has
moments of dullness, we cannot support that idea from information
in this paragraph. For question 2, then, we would have to reject
choices *a*, *b*, and *c*.

Question 3 also requires us to make some rule based on information we have in the paragraph. Though we know generally that
financial and business success is a key aim for many people, we do
not know that Mr. Van Sinderen would agree. (In fact, his quitting
a high-level job suggests that those forms of success are not essential to him.) Choice *a*, then, is not correct. Choice *c* is also a
generalization, and a very reasonable one at that. Many people
would agree that heavy insurance can help in times of disaster. But
there's nothing in the passage to show that Mr. Van Sinderen
agrees with that idea. We have to rule out choice *c*, therefore.
Choice *d* is not correct either. It is much too broad. It suggests
that any unexpected storm in Connecticut is violent. How can we
make that generalization from this paragraph, which talks about
only one storm?

For question 3, then, only answer *b* is correct. Mr. Van Sinderen did make a personal sacrifice by giving up his secure job as
chairman of the board; he made that sacrifice in order to help in
rebuilding his town after a very serious storm. His actions suggest
that he would agree that, in times of crisis, people should give up
their own personal goals to serve their communities. That is a fair
generalization from this paragraph.

How to Generalize with Care

- Make sure you understand the main idea and key details from
  the reading.

- Make sure you can draw conclusions or predict outcomes based
  upon information you have read.

- Think about how you might apply the writer's ideas in different situations.

- Don't go *too* far beyond the information the writer gives when you try to generalize. Otherwise you face the problem of making statements that are too broad in their scope. Statements that are too general often do not admit any exceptions.

Exercises

1. Generalizing

Read the following passage, in which an older person discusses his concern about the younger generation's unwillingness to accept leadership. When you finish, examine the statements after the selection. Put a checkmark next to the statement that, on the basis of the passage, is a correct generalization.

Are we so sure, after all, that older people are wiser than the young? The fashion of today is to call youth into counsel and ask the advice of those whose careers have scarcely begun. Heaven forbid that we should be thought surly and despotic! We must also remind each other that the technological trend goes against the claims of seniority. Significant changes of method used to occur about once in thirty years. Each generation could learn from the last, make its own contribution and look forward to another ten years of superior knowledge and valued experience. Changes have now become more frequent, taking place within the decade, and the value of experience comes, therefore, to be called in question. Seniority may signify no more than being out of date and out of touch. It is the younger men who have been on the computer course and the present directors may not even know the language. It is doubtful, moreover, whether the present-day technologists will respond to any sort of leadership. They are absorbed in their own electronic world and unable to communicate with those who have not attended the same sort of polytechnic. There was a time for leadership, many believe, but that time has gone. There is no place for kingship, they claim, in the world of today.

—C. Northcote Parkinson

_____1. Technical changes come from the young.

_____2. Older people are out of touch with recent scientific advances, because things today change so quickly.

_____3. Older people should be consulted more often for technological advice, because they have had so many more years of experience.

_____4. The new technology causes people to reject leadership.

_____5. There is a feeling of uncertainty today, because we are no longer sure who can make the wisest decisions.

_____6. Young people feel that older people who offer advice are just being surly and despotic.

_____7. Seniority has less place in today's technology than in the past.

2. Generalizing

Read the following selection and then answer the questions, most of which are based on your ability to generalize.

In adapting the principle of democratic government to the family we run into some obvious difficulties. The child does not elect his parents and he is not a responsible and functioning citizen in the society of his family. His father cannot be guided by the popular will of an electorate or a governing body to whom he is responsible. He cannot be guided by the popular will of his children either, unless he is prepared to lose his sanity and his life's savings. If he is an earnest, democratic father, he may go in for family councils and such things, but this is likely to become a hoax in the name of democracy which any five year old can spot in a minute.

We need to rescue the American father from the unreasonable and false situation into which we have put him in the name of democracy. We will have no tyrants either, for authority does not mean tyranny. And authority of the kind I speak does not require physical force or the exercise of power for the sake of power. It is a reasonable and just authority (as authority must be in a democratic society) exercised confidently as the prerogative of a father, deriving its strength from the ties of love that bind a parent and child.

—Selma H. Fraiberg

——1. The author believes that fathers
    a. should not have any authority in the family.
    b. should set up family councils to act as authorities in the family.
    c. should base authority on physical force.
    d. must be a figure of authority in the family.
    e. none of these.

——2. The author probably feels that democracy
    a. is a failure.
    b. cannot be applied to all aspects of society.
    c. is not a concern of fathers.
    d. is not preferred to tyranny.
    e. is an unfortunate expression of popular will.

——3. We may assume that the author believes that young children
    a. need strict parents.
    b. should have nothing to say about the governing of a family.
    c. can easily sense a situation of fraud within the family.
    d. should be able to elect their own parents.
    e. all of these.

  4. Put a checkmark next to statements with which the author probably would agree.

    ——a. Authority does not depend on physical strength.

    ——b. The ties of love do not allow the use of authority.

    ——c. Only responsible, functioning citizens should have the rights of democracy.

    ——d. Obeying the children's will always forces parents to become insane.

    ——e. Problems in adapting principles of democratic government to families may be easily overcome.

11 Evaluating Ideas

The skills described in Chapters 1 through 10 help you understand and interpret what you read. But effective reading is more than just understanding. You must be able to read in a *critical* way— which means that you have to *evaluate* a writer's ideas once you understand them. When you evaluate, you judge the worth of what you read.

Here are some important questions to ask yourself in evaluating what you read:

- Does the author carefully separate objective fact from his or her own opinion?

- Does the passage present the facts completely, specifically, and accurately?

- Does the author seem reliable? Can you see what strengths or experiences make the author qualified to write about a topic?

- Does the author make any claims that seem outrageous or unsupportable?

- Does the author make his or her intent or point of view clear?

- Does the author take into account other points of view on the topic?

- Does the author try to appeal more to your emotions or to your reason and common sense?

- Do your emotions get in the way of your ability to judge an author's statements fairly?

- Does it seem that the author is slanting information in such a way as to prejudice your ideas? Is he or she using propaganda?

The following sections will help you sharpen your critical reading.

11a Fact and Opinion

Most reading samples contain ideas based on fact *and* opinion. Of course it's not always easy to keep the two apart. Further, a writer often combines the two in such a way that you do not always notice where fact ends and opinion begins. In a philosophy course you may spend much time discussing just what is a fact or an opinion, but here we only want you to be able to distinguish between two types of statements as you read.

Facts are statements that tell what really happened or really is the case. A fact is based on direct evidence. It is something known by actual experience or observation.

Opinions are statements of belief, judgment, or feeling. They show what someone thinks about a subject. Solid opinions, of course, are based on facts. However, opinions are still somebody's view of something and are not facts themselves.

Look at the following statements, which come from Dee Brown's *Bury My Heart at Wounded Knee: An Indian History of the American West.*

1. In 1848 gold was discovered in California.
2. In 1860 there were probably 300,000 Indians in the United States and Territories, most of them living west of the Mississippi.
3. Now, in an age without heroes, the Indian leaders are perhaps the most heroic of all Americans.

In sentence 1 we see a statement of fact. We have evidence of the discovery of gold in California in 1848. If we checked sources, we would see that the statement is true.

The use of numbers, dates, and geography in sentence 2 creates a sense of fact. But the word *probably* suggests some doubt, and we cannot accept the statement as completely factual. That doesn't make it wrong or untrue. It just makes it partly an opinion. Because Dee Brown is a scholar in American Indian history, most people would accept his statement as fact. But it is still his educated judgment that 300,000 Indians lived in the United States in 1860. The writer's education and background tell us to rely on his statement, and we accept it as true without much thought. It is possible, though, that some people have other views on this subject.

Keeping Fact and Opinion Apart

- Look for words that *interpret*. In the first of the following sentences, we have details that describe facts—without any evaluation of these facts. In the second sentence, the writer interprets the details for us.

  The man leaning against the fence had brown eyes and black hair touching his shoulders.
  A handsome man leaned against the fence.

  It's somebody's opinion that such a man is handsome. Other words that interpret—there are countless examples—are *pretty, ugly, safe, dangerous, evil, attractive, well-dressed, good*, and so on.

- Look for words that serve as clues to statements of some kind of opinion. Some words like *probably, perhaps, usually, often, sometimes, on occasion* are used to limit a statement of fact and to indicate the possibility of other opinions. Other words say clearly that an opinion will follow; these are words like *I believe, I think, in my opinion, I feel, I suggest*.

- Before you accept a statement of fact and before you agree with a statement of opinion, question the skill of the author. Is he or she reliable? Why should you take his or her word?

- Test the writer's opinion by asking whether a different opinion is possible. You do not have to agree with the different opinion (or with the author's, for that matter). You just have to be able to see if there is another view.

- Some authors give us statements from other writers or authorities in order to illustrate their own ideas. Make sure you can tell the source of any statement that appears in what you read.

In sentence 3 we have a clearer example of the author's opinion. Here, too, the statement is not wrong. It is just clearly not a statement of fact. In the first place, the word *perhaps* tells us that the author himself believes other ideas are possible. It is true that many people would agree that Indian leaders are the most heroic. Others might say, however, that leaders during World War II or leaders of countries in times of crisis were the most heroic. Others would say that leaders on Vietnam battlefields were the most heroic. None of these statements is incorrect. All, however, are opinions.

To judge a writer's work you have to be able to tell opinion from fact. Often writers mix fact and opinion even within the same sentence, with some words representing facts and others representing opinions. Think about the following sentence:

The double-digit inflation rate that we have had for the last three years looks as though it will continue despite the economic proposals made by the new Reagan administration.

When this sentence was written early in the Reagan administration, double-digit inflation had lasted for three years and was a historical fact. It was also a fact that Ronald Reagan was the new president of the United States and that his administration had made some strong economic proposals.

However, the prediction that double-digit inflation will continue is only the writer's opinion. Another opinion is this writer's idea that inflation will continue despite Reagan's proposals. In fact, some other writer might have predicted the opposite—that inflation would decrease as a result of Reagan's proposals. Still another writer might have agreed that inflation would continue but might have blamed the new economic proposals for continuing the problem.

When you have a mixture of fact and opinion in a single statement, you must decide whether the main point of the sentence is essentially fact or opinion. In the last example, the main point of the sentence was to make a prediction, so the sentence basically offers an opinion, even though it contains many facts. Consider another example:

The suave and handsome William Darius paid fifteen thousand dollars cash for his extravagant, solid gold watch. He said, "It was worth every penny."

Even though the words *suave, handsome,* and *extravagant* state opinions, the first sentence states many facts—the man's name is William Darius; he paid cash; he spent fifteen thousand dollars; and the watch is made of solid gold. Even more important, the main point of the sentence is to report the fact that a particular man bought a particular watch for a particular amount. Thus the sentence is basically factual.

Similarly, the point of the second sentence is to report what Mr. Darius said. What he said was an opinion, but it was a fact that he said it. So the second sentence is also basically factual.

Exercises

1. Fact and Opinion
In the following sentences underline each word that presents a fact, and circle each word that presents an opinion. After each sentence write whether the sentence basically represents *fact* or *opinion.*

1. Many people believe that the Yankees are the greatest sports franchise in American history, and there is some evidence to

support this. _____

2. The Yankees have won more championships than any other

team in any sport. _____

3. No other team can boast such great athletes as Babe Ruth,

Lou Gehrig, Joe DiMaggio, and Reggie Jackson. _____

4. It is this combination of outstanding athletes and natural superiority that enables the Yankees to beat the Red Sox all the

time. _____

5. It will be many years before another team wins enough

championships to challenge the Yankees' record. _____

2. Fact and Opinion
Read the following selection and answer the questions, which are based on your being able to tell fact from opinion. The author has taught English in an intermediate school in Brooklyn.

Education's No Lark

It's time to turn back the clock in our schools. Getting an education is not *fun* and was never meant to be. Education is hard work and much of that work is very boring. But after 12 years of phonics and arithmetic, literature and geometry, history and languages, taught in the traditional way, students emerge as educated persons.

Students so educated need no special tutoring to pass specific courses or to take college entrance exams. They'll take the tests cold, will do well, average or below and will either go or not go to college. Not everyone is college material.

There is no "special program" of education that will produce results that are as good as those produced by textbooks, classroom lessons, homework and tests. You can pour billions of dollars into flashy learning projects, individualized instruction and teacher-aide salaries but none of these can replace good old fashioned discipline—in learning and classroom behavior.

I have to laugh when I hear parents refer to their children as "gifted." Only a small percentage of any given population is above average in intelligence. The average person possesses an average brain and needs average, everyday instruction. Even those children who are truly gifted are generally so in only one area, e.g., math, languages or science, and do not require an entire curriculum based on that label.

When I was in school, the few gifted children enriched their own courses of study by doing extra credit assignments and/or special projects on their own time. They sat in the classroom with the rest of us and learned the basic subjects— only *they* learned them better.

No additional monies were needed to educate these children. Those who were genuinely gifted proved it when the time had come for us to take our college entrance tests. Their superiority became apparent. They earned scores of 1200 and above and we average students ended up in the 900-1100 range. They got into Columbia and Princeton. We went to the state colleges. Those who scored below 900 didn't go to college.

Today, some of us read *The National Enquirer;* some read *Harper's*. Some of us watch Channel 7; some watch 13.

Most people are not born with super brains. The standards for American education and the methods by which it is possible to attain them have been set for centuries. With a few minor changes, they can still work for us and for generations to come. We must adhere to these standards, using teachers and textbooks, homework and tests. A few of our children will be members of the intellectual elite. Most will not.

—Camille Belolan

1. Which of the following statements are accurate statements of the author's beliefs?

   _____a. Children who are gifted should get special programs.
   _____b. Beating children is just as good as fancy programs.
   _____c. The traditional approach to education is better.
   _____d. Nobody today is as smart as the previous generation.
   _____e. Communism is the cause of today's ills.

2. The writer defends her assertion that no major changes in American education are needed by saying that:

   _____a. students today are little different from those in the past.
   _____b. so few gifted students really exist that it doesn't matter what we do to them.
   _____c. students used to go to Princeton, but today no one is smart enough to go there.
   _____d. some people watch Channel 7.
   _____e. none of these.

3. Which of the following statements represent the author's opinion?

   _____a. Prepared students do not need special tutoring.
   _____b. A student who is beaten will learn more thoroughly.
   _____c. Most kids today are nitwits.
   _____d. Students who are not prepared for college shouldn't go to college.
   _____e. Assigning homework and giving tests are valid means of educating students.
   _____f. Parents who say their children are gifted are only ashamed to admit the truth.
   _____g. White students are smarter than black students.
   _____h. Most people are not born with super brains.

3. Clues to Fact and Opinion

   Write *fact* before each statement of fact; write *opin.* before each statement of opinion. Then circle any clue words that help tell you whether the statement expresses fact or opinion.

——1. A final peace treaty should be good for both Israel and Egypt.

——2. The two countries have been battling each other for thirty years.

——3. Until there is a final treaty, the Palestinian problem will not be solved.

——4. Many people feel that the treaty will bring permanent peace to the area.

——5. The situation will probably remain tense and dangerous for some time.

——6. In the long run, however, I think that the rewards of peace will be so great that neither country will want war.

4. Judging the Truth of Statements

Read each of the following statements and choose the phrase that best completes each sentence.

——1. "The cashier at the local supermarket says that it is a fact that wheat prices will be going down soon." This statement gives
   a. a reliable fact about wheat prices.
   b. the writer's own opinion.
   c. the opinion of someone who should know.
   d. the opinion of someone who is not an expert on the subject.
   e. the only opinion anyone oculd possibly have on the subject.

——2. "I believe that this government cannot endure permanently half slave and half free." (Abraham Lincoln) This statement expresses
   a. a fact.
   b. a guess.
   c. the opinion of someone who should know.
   d. the opinion of someone who is not an expert on the subject.
   e. the opinion of someone other than Abraham Lincoln.

——3. "Hurting other people is wrong." This statement expresses
   a. a fact.
   b. the opinion of someone who should know.

c. an opinion that should not be believed without further evidence.

d. the opinion of someone who is not an expert on the subject.

e. an opinion that most people would agree with.

11b **Evidence**

Sometimes, when writers state their opinions, they just assert an opinion without providing any support. In such cases you have no particular reason to believe their opinions unless you trust them as authorities or experts. Any writer—even an "expert"—who states opinions without giving any supporting evidence probably should not convince you.

More often, writers will try to convince you to share their opinions by presenting various facts or evidence, just as a lawyer presents evidence in a court case to support the opinion that the accused is innocent or guilty of a crime. Just as a jury must evaluate the evidence carefully to decide whether to accept a lawyer's opinion about the accused, so must you evaluate the evidence presented in what you read to decide whether to accept the writer's opinion. The following questions will help you to evaluate the evidence offered in support of any opinion you find expressed in your reading.

• Can the facts be trusted?

• Are the facts given in an objective way?

• Do the facts really support the opinion being expressed?

• Are the facts not really relevant to the point being made?

• Have unfavorable or negative points been left out?

• Do the facts prove the opinion, or do they only suggest that the opinion is reasonable?

If two writers give opposite opinions, you should judge which one gives the better evidence. Whose facts are more reliable, are more complete, are expressed more objectively, and support the opinion more fully?

Many times, writers will try to convince you to share their opinions. They may use all their persuasive skill to try to make you believe that tall people make better presidents, or that Sandy

Koufax is the only great baseball pitcher, or even that people who use marijuana should be shot. Only a careful reader can avoid falling for an emotional or poorly reasoned argument.

Exercises

1. Evidence Backing Up Statements

For each of the following statements, write *E* if the statement is backed up properly by evidence, write *N* if there is no supporting evidence, and write *I* if there is evidence but it is improperly used.

____a. Rosa must be crazy to buy a new Cadillac.
____b. There is no way Rosa can afford a new Cadillac on her salary, because she works only part-time at a minimum-wage job.
____c. Rosa must be involved in some kind of criminal activity to make a lot of money, because she is driving a new Cadillac.
____d. Rosa can afford a new car; she told me a rich uncle left her a lot of money.
____e. Rosa's old jalopy turned out to be a classic car. I read in the paper that a museum offered her a new Cadillac in exchange. She must have accepted because I saw her car at the automobile museum.

2. Evidence in Longer Passages

Read the following passages and answer the questions after each.

There is a considerable body of anecdotal information suggesting chimpanzee intelligence. The first serious study of the behavior of simians—including their behavior in the wild—was made in Indonesia by Alfred Russel Wallace, the co-discoverer of evolution by natural selection. Wallace concluded that a baby orangutan he studied behaved "exactly like a human child in similar circumstances." In fact, "orangutan" is a Malay phrase meaning not ape but "man of the woods." Teuber recounted many stories told by his parents, pioneer German ethologists who founded and operated the first research station devoted to chimpanzee behavior on Tenerife in the Canary Islands early in the second decade of this century. It was here that Wolfgang Kohler performed his famous studies of Sultan, a chimpanzee "genius" who was able to connect two rods in order to reach an otherwise inaccessible banana. On Tenerife, also, two chimpanzees were observed maltreating a chicken: One would extend some food to the fowl, encouraging it to approach; whereupon the other would thrust at it with a piece of wire it had concealed behind its back. The chicken would retreat but soon allow itself to approach once again—and be beaten once again. Here is a fine combination of behavior sometimes thought to be uniquely human: cooperation, planning a future course of action, deception and cruelty. It also reveals that chickens have a very low capacity for avoidance learning.

—Carl Sagan

1. What is the main opinion being expressed?

_____

_____

2. What are the chief pieces of evidence used to back up this opinion? _____

_____

_____

_____

3. How well do you think each piece of evidence supports the main opinion?

_____

_____

_____

_____

Man has been communicating by pictures longer than he has been using words. With the development of photography in this century we are using pictures as a means of communication to such an extent that in some areas they overshadow

verbal language. The science of semantics has studied the con-
veyance of meaning by language in considerable detail. Yet
very little is known as to how pictures convey meaning and
what their place is in the life of man.

—Paul R. Wendt

1. What is the main opinion expressed in this passage?

_____

_____

2. What evidence is given to support this opinion?

_____

_____

3. State one other opinion expressed in this passage.

_____

_____

4. What evidence is given to support this other opinion?

_____

_____

_____

5. How well are the opinions in this passage supported by
evidence?

_____

_____

6. What kinds of evidence might make the opinions more con-
vincing?

_____

11c **Your Opinion**

Whether you accept any writer's opinions depends also on your own opinions—both your opinions about the subject and your opinions about the piece of writing. Before you read any particular selection, you may have such strong beliefs on the subject of the selection that any author will have a very hard time trying to change your mind. On the other hand, you may be so unfamiliar with the subject that you are ready to believe whatever the writer says. As you read the piece of writing, you may be so bored or so amused that your attitude toward the ideas presented may change. In order to evaluate fairly the ideas expressed in a piece of writing, you need to become aware of your own opinions and reactions.

As you read, you will usually respond with some reactions and ideas of your own. Some of the thoughts that pop into your head may be good—that is, they can be developed further and supported convincingly. At other times, your thoughts may turn out to be unsupportable—perhaps the result of a prejudgment or bias or perhaps the result of not thinking carefully enough. Until you stop to write these thoughts down and think them through with care, you won't know which are worth keeping. Much of your opinion, whether positive or negative, will depend on these moment-to-moment thoughts, and you'll need to sort them out.

One way to sort out your thinking is by keeping a reading journal, a kind of diary of your thoughts about your reading. Every time you finish reading a selection, you write out your thoughts and reactions to it. You should not summarize or simply repeat what the reading stated. Instead you should say whether you liked or agreed with the passage and why. If there were any ideas you objected to, you might give the reasons for your objections. If the reading reminds you of something you have experienced, describe that experience and how it is related to the reading. If other things you know support the writer's opinions, discuss those things. If you dislike the writer's attitude or whole way of looking at the subject, explain exactly what is wrong with the writer's approach.

It does not matter exactly what you say about the reading in the journal as long as you put down your ideas and develop them.

Do not be satisfied with expressing an opinion in a single sentence
or two. Go on to explain your ideas further, to give examples, to
discuss why you feel as you do, or to think your thought through in
any other way that strikes you. After writing your ideas down and
discussing them for a while, you may end up changing your
mind—or you may find yourself even more firmly committed to
your original position.

Look at this sample from a reading journal. It offers a reaction
to the selection on pages 88–89 in Chapter 6.

It's really amazing to think how America could be different if
camels had become a part of the old West. Imagine the Lone
Ranger riding on a camel? It really makes you think that the
people who lived back then really were building a new world,
one that didn't necessarily have to be the way we see it on
television. My uncle once told me that the Army tried using
zebras for a while, but they were too wild to be useful. I didn't
believe him, but maybe he was right. I should ask my teacher
or look it up.

Do you see how the author of this reading journal entry wasn't
summarizing the material he read but was commenting on it?
Notice, too, that he adds some of his own information.

Next, read this reading journal entry about the paragraph on
page 105 in Chapter 6. Can you spot the difference?

I disagree with that Margaret Mead and Frances Balgley
Kaplan paragraph I read. I don't think there are as many
women who have a choice between home and a career as they
think. Lots of the women I know have babies before they're
old enough to know any better and then they're stuck, like my
sister. Now she wishes she'd waited. True, the paragraph does
say that today women are given the choice, sometimes a very
difficult choice, between home and career. I guess they're
writing about the difference between my sister and me. I'm
waiting until I finish school before I even think about having
kids. I'd like to have children, but there's no way I'm going to
throw away all the work I've done. I guess that's what Mead
and Kaplan mean. Maybe I don't disagree after all.

Notice here that the woman who wrote this entry began by
disagreeing with the selection. But after working out her thoughts
on paper, she found that she actually agreed. It's better to come to
conclusions like this in the privacy of a journal than on a test or
while talking in class.

Exercises

1. Set aside a notebook to be used as a reading journal for the rest of the semester. Every time you have a reading assignment, write down and develop your thoughts in response to your reading by making an entry in the journal. At the end of the semester, read through your entire journal and write down as a final entry your observations on how the journal helped you, on how your thinking developed through the journal, or how your use of the journal changed throughout the semester.

2. Read the following passage, and then write down your thoughts in the journal. You may wish to develop your ideas about how the author John Holt's views about learning apply to you. Do you know when you do not know something? How do you know you know something? Can you think of any ways to decide better whether or not you know something?

How can we tell whether children understand something or not? When I was a student, I generally knew when I understood and when I didn't. This had nothing to do with marks; in the last math course I took in college I got a respectable grade, but by the end of the year I realized I didn't have the faintest idea of what the course was about. In Colorado, I assumed for a long time that my students knew when they did, or did not, understand something. I was always urging them to tell me when they did not understand, so that with one of my clever "explanations" I could clear up everything. But they never would tell me. I came to know by painful experience that not a child in a hundred knows whether or not he understands something, much less, if he does not, why he does not. The child who knows, we don't have to worry about; he will be an A student. How do we find out when, and what, the others don't understand?

—John Holt

11d   The Writer's Technique

An important way to develop critical skills is to be aware of the writer's technique in any selection you read. Once you know what the writer is doing with his or her material—once you know what effect he or she is trying to create—you can judge what is said more fairly and clearly. The writer's technique often involves the features discussed in sections **11d(1)** through **11d(5)**.

11d(1)   Style

In general, style is the way a writer picks words and puts them together. The style usually tells you who the writer expects to read the work. If the sentences are long and the words are difficult, the writer expects an educated reader. If the language is rich in slang expressions and current phrases, the writer is talking to a more general group. If the words are very technical, the writer is aiming for a special audience who knows the language of what's being discussed. Some writers pick words with deep emotional appeal in order to urge their readers to act. Other writers choose a more impartial style.

A writer who wants to convince you of how urgent her or his problem is might use short sentences so that, as you read along, you become wrapped up in the fast tone. During World War II, Winston Churchill said, "We shall fight them on the beaches. We shall fight them street by street. We shall never give up." Here he used repetition and short sentences effectively to show how committed England was to keep fighting. If he had said, "We shall fight them on the beaches and in the streets and never give up," the basic message would have been the same, but the style would not have added anything to the listener's appreciation.

11d(2)   Tone

Tone is the attitude the writer takes toward a subject. Authors may write about something they respect or about something they hate. A writer may be angry. A writer may be impatient. A writer may take a humorous view of a subject. Or a writer may be ironic—saying one thing but really meaning the opposite.

Oscar Wilde was asked by a judge during his trial, "Are you trying to show contempt for this court?" and Wilde replied, "On the contrary, I'm trying to conceal it." The tone of his response was much more effective than if he had said, "Yes I am." The irony made his contempt appear much stronger, so strong that Wilde appeared not to be able to restrain it.

11d(3)   Mood

Mood is a state of mind or feeling at a particular time. Often writers create a mood so that they can make you respond in a certain way.

Edgar Allan Poe said that sibilants (words that contain the *s* sound, like *snake*, *sinister*, and *shadow*) help create a mysterious mood, and he used sibilants often: "And then did we, the *s*even, *s*tart from our *s*eats in horror, and *s*tand trembling, and *sh*uddering and agha*s*t."

11d(4)   Purpose

Writers write for a reason. Some wish to give information. Some want to persuade you to believe something. Others try to push you into taking some action related to a subject of deep meaning to them. Some writers write to amuse or entertain.

Advertising is a good example of writing with a purpose—that is, writing to make you buy a certain product. Another example is editorials in newspapers. Editorials aim at gaining public support for a political position.

11d(5)   Point of View

A writer's own beliefs and ideas often determine how he or she looks at a given subject. In this sense, *point of view* means "opinions" or "attitudes," though there are a number of other meanings that make it a rather complex term to use. Our concern here is for the way a writer's own interests and beliefs influence the writing we must read. A communist, for example, would look at Cuban government in a very different way from a man or woman who believes in democracy. A Catholic would not look at ideas on abortion in the same way as a Protestant or a Jew. A black woman might have much stronger views on the treatment of sickle-cell anemia than a white woman might. Sometimes an author's point of view forces him or her to *slant* the writing. Slanted writing leans toward one way of looking at a problem and leaves out ideas that might disagree.

Of course, these techniques often blend together in any sample of writing. Style and tone are not often possible to separate, and they both clearly relate to purpose and point of view. Also, the writer's style often creates a mood.

Furthermore, an author's technique often yields many results. Writing may be both humorous and ironic. An author may wish to give information in order to persuade you to do something, and in so doing he or she may write in a style that is very emotional.

Mark Twain once said that "Man is the only animal that blushes, or needs to." This is a much more effective way to communicate his point of view than if he had said, "People, unlike animals, do things that they are ashamed of." As Twain and other humorists discovered, people will listen to any argument if it is put in a humorous or entertaining way.

The point in seeing the writer's technique is to help you notice that what the author says relates to *how* the author says it. What we discuss here is just a beginning of the study of writing technique. In literature courses you may go much further into the subject.

Exercises

1. The Writer's Technique

Read the following statements. In each blank space, write the letter of the remark that answers that question. You may use the same letter more than once. You may use more than one letter for each answer.

a. Magazine editors frequently complain to us about the unsuitability of many manuscripts submitted to them. Not only are the manuscripts unsuitable, but no postage is sent for their return. In their own interests, writers and others are advised *to enclose postage for the return of unsuitable material.*

b. A mother bird sat on her egg. The egg jumped. "Oh, oh!" said the mother bird. "My baby will be here! He will want to eat. I must get something for my baby to eat!" she said. "I will be back!" So away she went.

c. Try a little *peripate*—a little strolling—with a friend in Greece this spring. Beaches are warm; villages scenic at Greek Easter; temples and tavernas open to the air. You can swim, sail in warm crystal-blue waters, even island-hop.

d. The diseases brought about by pollution can be conquered. The waters of our lakes and rivers can be clean again, our land fertile, and our air fragrant. All this lies within our grasp.

e. The black community and black women especially must begin raising questions about the kind of society we wish to see established.

f. Shall we sit by and watch the cancer of poverty destroy our young? Shall we watch babies starving, young children with swollen bellies full of air, families by the thousands burying their newborn in unnamed graves? Is this America the beautiful?

g. My brother is a wonderfully wise person; he knows exactly how you should run your life. He is also truly generous: he will give you all the hot air you ask for.

h. More women than men own stock; 51 percent of all shareholders are women.

_____ 1. Which statement is written in a highly emotional style?

_____ 2. Which statement is written in a humorous tone?

_____ 3. Which statement presents an ironic tone?

_____ 4. Which statement is designed to persuade you to believe something?

_____ 5. Which statement is written from the point of view of a speaker for women's liberation?

_____ 6. Which statement is written in a style suited for people who are authors?

_____ 7. Which statement tries to force you to take some action?

_____ 8. Which statement sets a mood of rest and pleasure?

_____ 9. Which statement is designed to give information?

_____10. Which statement is written in a style suited for children under six?

2. The Writer's Technique
Read the following opening sentences of short stories. Then complete with the best answer the statement that follows each.

_____1. "The thousand injuries of Fortunato I had borne as I best could, but when he ventured upon insult I vowed revenge." (Edgar Allan Poe) The tone of the person speaking is
   a. matter-of-fact.
   b. ironic.

    c. angry.

    d. humorous and silly.

    e. sad.

——2. "One view called me to another; one hill top to its fellow, half across the county, and since I could answer at no more trouble than the snapping forward of a lever, I let the country flow under my wheels." (Rudyard Kipling) This opening sentence sets a mood of

    a. quiet peacefulness.

    b. hurried discovery.

    c. uncertain fear.

    d. friendliness.

    e. disappointment.

——3. "In the Bureau of . . . but it might be better not to mention the Bureau by its precise name. There is nothing more touchy than all these bureaus, regiments, and government offices, and in fact any sort of official body." (Nikolai Gogol) The point of view of the teller of this story is that of a person who

    a. is afraid of getting officials upset.

    b. is an outspoken enemy of the government.

    c. is an army officer.

    d. knows no fear.

    e. is a criminal.

——4. "If I was setting in the High Court in Washington," said Simple, "where they do not give out no sentences for crimes, but where they give out promulgations, I would promulgate. Up them long white steps behind them tall white pillars in the great big marble hall with the eagle of the U.S.A., where at I would bang my gavel and promulgate." (Langston Hughes) Simple speaks in the style of someone who

    a. knows a great deal.

    b. is very powerful.

    c. speaks a foreign language.

    d. is impressed by power and big words.

    e. is very old.

3. Style

    Read the following sentences about shoes and doors. Then answer the questions after them.

a. One, two, button my shoe;
   Three, four, shut the door.
b. After tying my shoelaces, I went out the door and locked it firmly.
c. In the early years the child still has difficulties with basic tasks like opening and shutting doors; the child cannot even begin to do such delicate tasks as putting on shoes and tying them.
d. I heard a noise. I was startled. I jumped out of bed, nearly tripping on the shoes I had left in the middle of the floor. I went downstairs to check the front door. It was swinging wide open. I slammed it shut and wondered what to do next.
e. It was an old pair of shoes, the high buttoned kind, the kind my grandmother used to wear. She was a proud woman who always chose her clothes carefully. And she kept many secrets, too. Often in the middle of the day I would see her closing the door to her sewing room and staying there for hours.

_____1. Which version sounds as if it comes from a mystery story?

_____2. Which version is from a children's nursery rhyme?

_____3. Which version sounds as if it is spoken by a person who is determined?

_____4. Which version sounds as if it is the beginning of a personal memory?

_____5. Which version sounds as if it comes from an article on child development?

11e   Techniques That Twist the Truth

As a critical reader, you have to be able to judge unfair writing. Sometimes a piece of writing will not use truthful methods if its purpose is to force you to have a certain opinion about a subject. *Propaganda* (particular ideas forced on the public by organizations with special interests) is often developed by the use of unfair writing and logic. Any information that leaves out or alters facts in order to press a special point of view is called *biased*, *prejudiced*, or *slanted*.

Be on your guard for propaganda.

- Look out for words used for emotional effect: *commie, liberal, pinko, John Bircher, queer, activist, hippie.*

- Look out for words that have special connotations (see pages 16–18).

- Try to recognize the following methods of propaganda.

1. The writer tries to combine a famous person's name with an idea so that people, liking the person, will like the idea too.

Reggie Jackson plays the field in Murjani jeans.

2. The writer quotes a famous person who approves of or agrees with an idea so that the reader will approve of it too.

Jacques Martin, the famous French chef, says, "Margarine is just as good as butter." Why are *you* still using butter?

3. The writer says that everyone is doing something (or thinking in some way) so you should do it, too.

Every farmer, every hard-working city man knows the dangers of the welfare system.

4. The writer uses very positive words in regard to an idea so that only general statements appear.

Every driver loves this stunning, efficient, and completely safe automobile. Add a bit of sunshine to your life—take a ride in a glamorous, high-fashion car!

5. "Stacking the cards" is a technique whereby the writer presents only facts that tend to make you agree with her or him.

There's nothing wrong with drinking before driving. Not one person at our party was hurt on the way home—and believe me not too many people there were sober!

6. The writer uses bad names about a person or product.

Only a nitwit like Lorna would buy a Japanese car. Those things look like wind-up toys.

We can see the effect of slanted writing by studying the following set of statements.

There is no point in working. The money just goes to the no-good government and the cheating landlord. You just break your back to make the boss rich.

Look, you do the best you can. Taxes are high and rent is impossible. But if you do not work, you give up your pride and the few comforts you have. Of course, the boss has to make a fair profit from your work; otherwise, he would not hire you. You just have to live on what is left over.

Every American should be proud to work and support the system. Your taxes go to making this country great. And by helping the landowners and the factory owners make money, you are strengthening the backbone of the nation. Hard work makes good Americans.

The first version is slanted against work by telling only part of the story and by name-calling—making it appear that everybody is out to take advantage of the poor worker. The third version slants the case in the opposite direction by "stacking the deck" in favor of those benefiting from the worker's labor, by using only positive language, and by pressuring the reader to follow a group. Only the second version gives a balanced view, expressed truthfully.

Exercises

1. Slanted Writing
    Read the following sentences. Write *truthful* after those sentences that use only truthful methods. Write *slanted* after those sentences that use unfair writing techniques.

   1. Crazy Eddie has prices so low he's practically giving mer-

chandise away. _____
   2. Our records indicate that she was late with her rent once,

but all other times she was prompt with her payments. _____
   3. He's a no-good, low-down, side-winding skunk. And that's

the truth. _____
   4. This is the down-home way for everyday people to have

fun, so you all come to Uncle Bill's Hamburger House. _____
   5. Poor people should be the first ones to suffer in these times of economic crisis. It's not the fault of hard-working, honest people that the poor are poor, so why should we have to pay for the fact

that they don't have enough to eat? _____

6. We all know these people aren't our kind, so I don't see why we should allow them to move in. _____

2. Techniques That Twist the Truth

Comment briefly on how each of these statements slants the truth.

1. Anybody who voted for that candidate is just a bigot who would probably be glad if a nuclear war started.

_____

_____

_____

_____

2. Our own senator enjoys the coastline and visits it weekly for rest and relaxation. How could anyone urge the construction of a solid mile of high-rise apartment houses right at the beach?

_____

_____

_____

3. I don't earn very much and we don't have too much money in the bank, but simple folk like us must support the local clubhouse with all the cash we can.

_____

_____

_____

_____

4. Since 50 percent of all deaths involving college students are violent, we know that college students are reckless maniacs with no regard for their own safety.

_____

_____

_____

5. Mickey Juanez of the Chicago Hawks says, "I drink *Bebida* beer after all my rough games." Everyone is drinking *Bebida* beer. Isn't it time you tried it?

_____

_____

_____

Unit Four

The Basic Study Skills

12   Taking Notes

There are several ways to gather information for your courses. You'll have to listen to your instructor's lectures and *take notes* on what he or she says. You might want to *underline* key ideas in a text you own and must read. You might also want to write a *summary* of a paragraph, a page, or a chapter in a book, or you might prefer to make an *outline* (see Chapter 13).

Any time you gather information you must

- Be brief.

- Be clear.

- Be logical.

An essential method of gathering information is to listen to your teacher's lectures and to copy down what you hear. There are many ways to take notes effectively.

Obviously, those who take shorthand will have a much easier time taking down most of what a teacher says than those whose handwriting is slower. But even if you can't write as quickly as the teacher speaks, it is still possible to keep up.

You have to listen for key ideas. Don't try to copy every word the instructor speaks. You might miss statements that are important if you struggle to be too complete. You don't have to write down all the examples given to make a point as long as you list the key ideas.

Don't worry if you cannot spell a word correctly. Just try to get it down as best you can so that *you* understand it. You can always check the spelling later on (you might have to write the word on an exam and you should know how to spell it correctly). Also, check any vocabulary words you do not know.

If the instructor assigns pages to read before the lecture, *read them*! Reading prepares you for the content of the day's session. If you were not able to do the reading before the class began, look the pages over right after class. You can eradicate confusion in your mind that way.

Usually, the lecture begins with a statement that explains what the day's work will be. Try to write down carefully the instructor's opening remarks.

Use abbreviations, symbols, even pictures to help you write quickly. You can also write little notes to yourself as reminders. Number the ideas or underline them, and indent to set things off.

Whenever the instructor writes on the chalkboard, copy down the information you see there. If there's a diagram or chart, copy it slowly and carefully into your notes so you will understand it later on. Chalkboard information tells you what the instructor thinks is important in the day's work.

Put a date on each lecture so that you follow a clear sequence when you study for exams later on.

Make sure you come to class on time so that you don't miss the early part of the session. Aside from giving the aim of the lecture in the first few minutes, the instructor may also give exam dates, assignments, and general announcements early in the class.

Now that you have read some ideas on note taking, assume that you were sitting in class and that your teacher gave as a lecture the information you just read. Here are one student's notes on that lecture. Compare the student's notes with the "lecture" itself.

How to take notes from lecture:

1. listen for key ideas
   a. don't copy every word
   b. "   write every example

2. forget spelling and vocab! check words later on

3. *read assignment <u>before</u> class, also after lecture to evatakate (check sp. & meaning!) confusion*

4. *tchrs opening statement expl. day's work — copy carefully.*

5. *use abbrev., symbols, pictures, etc. write notes to myself number, underline, indent*

6. *ideas on board import. copy what tchr. writes be careful with diagr. & charts*

7. *put date on each lect.*

8. *come to class on time (ugh!)*
   a. *get aim of lessen*
   b. *get announc. of tests, etc.*

Exercises

1. Taking Notes: A Review

Look at the handwritten notes on pages 174–175. Answer these questions.

   1. Write down five abbreviations the student used. _____

2. What two symbols appear? _____

3. What comments does the student make to himself or herself in the note? _____

_____

_____

_____

_____

4. What misspelled words do you find? (See items 3 and 8a in the notes.) _____

_____

5. Copy down one statement made in the lecture that does not appear in the student's notes.

_____

_____

_____

2. Taking Notes

1. Imagine that you heard the information on figurative language in Chapter 8 given as a lecture. On a separate sheet of paper, take notes on that information.

2. Watch the evening news on television. On a sheet of paper, take notes on one of the important news stories. Then get a member of your family or a friend to listen as you tell about the news story. See how close your version is to the actual story, as a means of determining how well you've taken notes.

3. Read a newspaper article, taking notes about it as you go. Wait a while and then, from your notes, write the story yourself in your own words. Afterwards check to see how accurate your version is.

4. Make a list of symbols for the following words, which appear often in the classroom:

homework	test
exam	page(s)
quiz	read

13 Underlining, Summarizing, and Outlining

13a Underlining

One way many students use to gather information is to underline. Underlining helps you call attention to main points. When you study later on, you need to examine only the ideas you've underlined. Of course you need to be able to spot main ideas and major details. (See sections **4b** and **5b**.)

Here is how to underline:

- Underline only main ideas and major details. That way you can quickly recall the most important parts of a reading selection, and you will not get bogged down.

- Write notes or comments in the margin. The margins are a good place to put your observations or any ideas that occur to you as you read. Notes in the margin can also remind you to refer to other sources or to something that the teacher said. You can even write the main idea of the paragraph in your own words here. Circle words or ideas that interest you. Use brackets [], asterisks (*), or other symbols to catch your eye when you go back over the paragraph. Most bookstores sell markers or highlight pens that will allow you to write directly on the page and still read through your markings.

Be sure you own any book in which you plan to use underlining as a study technique. People who read a book after you read it aren't going to have the same purpose in reading it that you have, and marking up a book that doesn't belong to you can actually make it more difficult for another person to read.

Look at this paragraph by Vine DeLoria, Jr., to see how one student used underlining to gather information.

Why didn't the gov't do this?
why is it better to have a park there?
check definition
this sounds like a good idea

I wish the <u>Government</u> would <u>give</u> <u>Alcatraz</u> to the <u>Indians</u> now occupying it. They want to create <u>five centers on the island</u>. One center would be for a① <u>North American studies</u> program; another would be a② spiritual and medical center where Indian <u>religions</u> and <u>medicines</u> would be used and studied. A third center would concentrate on③ <u>ecological</u> studies based on an Indian view of nature—that man should live *with* the land and not simply *on* it. A④ <u>job-training center</u> and a⑤ <u>museum</u> would also be founded on the island. Certain of these programs would obviously require Federal assistance.

five centers on Alcatraz

Some <u>people</u> may <u>object</u> to this approach, yet <u>Health, Education and Welfare</u> gave out <u>ten million dollars</u> last year to *incredible!* ✱ (non-Indians) to study Indians. [Not <u>one single dollar</u> went to an Indian scholar or researcher to present the point of view of Indian people.] And the studies done by non-Indians added nothing to what was already known about Indians.

Exercises

1. Underlining
Read the article on page 90. Use underlining to show important information.

2. Underlining
Review Chapter 5 of this book, "Reading for Information" (pp. 54–87), by underlining important ideas.

3. Underlining
Read a chapter in a textbook assigned for another one of your courses. Underline and make other marks to highlight important information.

4. Underlining
Read the following pages from a textbook on marketing. Underline and make other marks to highlight important information from page 180 to page 182, top:

A *marketing strategy*, then, encompasses selecting and analyzing a target market (the group of people whom the organization wants to reach) and creating and maintaining an appropriate marketing mix (product, price, distribution, and promotion) that will satisfy those people. Let's see what is involved.

Selecting and Analyzing Target Markets

A *target market* is a group of persons for whom a firm creates and maintains a marketing mix that specifically fits the needs and preferences of that group. When choosing a target market, marketing managers try to evaluate possible markets to determine how entry into them would affect the firm's sales, costs, and profits. Marketers also consider whether the organization has the resources to produce a marketing mix that meets the needs of a particular target market and whether satisfying those needs is consistent with the firm's overall objectives. They also analyze the size and number of competitors who already are selling in the possible target markets. For example, the marketing manager for a swimwear company might consider the following factors in selecting a target market or markets:

Racing swimwear is designed for function (plain and lightweight) and is inexpensive to produce. Recreational swimwear, however, is designed for appearance and can be expensive to manufacture.

The product line for racing swimwear can be small, requiring only one or two styles. For recreational swimwear a company must have a large product line for all ages, sizes, and tastes.

The distribution of athletic swimwear would be limited to sports stores; for recreational swimwear it would include almost all clothing stores.

The advertising for racing swimwear would be limited mainly to sports magazines, while advertising for recreational swimwear would probably have to appear in several types of media.

The prices of athletic swimwear possibly would be higher than those of recreational swimwear because there are fewer competitors.

Even though there are three swimwear producers that make all athletic swimwear, there is only one that would be a strong competitor.

Marketing managers may define a target market to include a relatively small number of people, or they may define it to encompass a vast number of people. For example, a women's swimwear manufacturer may select as its target market young women athletes in high school and college and in professional competition. Or this firm may try to reach women of all ages who swim for recreation, a much larger target market. Although a firm may focus its marketing efforts on one target market through a single marketing mix, a business often focuses on several target markets by developing and employing several marketing mixes. Compare Bic's strategy with Ronson's, for example. Bic produces one type of disposable cigarette lighter and directs it at one target market. The maker of Ronson lighters, however, aims at several market groups by manufacturing several types of lighters, promoting them in a variety of ways, selling them at various prices, and distributing them through numerous types of outlets.

The proper selection of a target market is not a simple task. It requires that marketing managers consider many factors and make a number of decisions. In Chapters 3 through 5 we discuss a variety of concepts, activities, and decisions related to selecting and analyzing target markets.

Creating and Maintaining a Satisfying
Marketing Mix

Marketing managers must develop a marketing mix that precisely matches the needs of the people in the target market. Before doing this, they collect in-depth, up-to-date information about those needs. The information might include data regarding the age, income, race, sex, and education level of people in the target market; their preferences for product designs, features, colors, and textures; their attitudes toward competitors' products, services, advertisements, and prices; and the frequency and intensity with which they use the product. With these and other data marketing managers are better able to develop a product, price, distribution, and promotion system that satisfies the people in the target market.

Consider Kawasaki's marketing strategy. Kawasaki views its target market as consisting mainly of males in the 18–34 age group who use a motorcycle for commuting and for weekend entertainment. Although marketers at Kawasaki recognize that some people buy motorcycles for other purposes, they believe the heart of the market to be defined by these characteristics. Kawasaki motorcycles have been designed specifically for the American market. The company produces twenty-two models that range in price from $400 to $2,500. To communicate with the target market, Kawasaki advertises through television, radio, newspapers, and magazines such as *Newsweek, Sports Illustrated, Popular Mechanics, Playboy, Oui,* and *Penthouse.*[5]

Marketing plans—both objectives and strategies—provide purpose and direction to marketing activities. To execute and achieve marketing plans, however, managers must develop an organizational structure for the marketing unit that facilitates the effective performance of marketing activities.

13b **Summarizing**

A *summary* is a brief statement about something you have read. In a summary you use your own words to pinpoint the main ideas the writer makes, but in a shorter way.

Here is how to prepare a summary:

- Decide what is the main idea the author is communicating (see section **4b**). Make that main point the most important statement in your summary.

- Keep the most important supporting ideas and major details (see section **5b**). The main supporting ideas and major details will give your reader an overview of all the points that the author was making.

- Rewrite the sentence in your own words to leave out unimportant words and to emphasize the most important ideas. Check in a dictionary any difficult words used by the writer before you use them.

- Use transition words like *first, second, third, on the other hand, because,* and *although* to show how different statements fit together. Make lists that add together many different examples, reasons, or other major points.

Remember that your summary is designed to save you time when you go over the material again, so make sure your summary is about a third as long as the original material.

The following summary is based on the paragraphs about Alcatraz on page 179. Note that the summary has about 50 words but that the selection itself contains more than 150 words.

Indians holding Alcatraz should keep it to create five centers: one for North American Studies, one for studying Indian medicine and religion, one for ecological studies, one for job training, and one for a museum. This approach is not wrong considering HEW gave ten million to non-Indians—not Indian scholars—to study Indians.

As with note taking and underlining, here you are perfecting a skill that is meant to save you time when you study for a test or when you review material for any reason. Notice how the main points about Alcatraz Island's use by native Americans has been maintained. The paragraph has been condensed and, like condensed soup, it's a lot dryer than the original! What's missing is the author's style. Subjective—that is, personal—phrases like "I wish" and "some people may object" have been omitted. But you'll notice that each major point the author raises is still present in the summary.

This summary, combined with your own recollection of reading the paragraph, is probably all you'll need to jog your memory when you have to recall what you've read next week or next month or next semester.

Exercises

1. Summarizing

Summarize the selection about Robert Hooke that appears on page 90. Use the following space for your summary.

_____

_____

_____

_____

_____

_____

2. Summarizing

Read and summarize a headline story in today's newspaper. Use the following space for your summary.

_____

_____

_____

_____

_____

_____

_____

_____

3. Summarizing

Summarize the following passage from a textbook on writing.

FITTING THE PERSUASION TO THE AUDIENCE

The more you understand your readers, the better chance you have of persuading them. Readers of course vary. But even though you may not know them all individually, you can know where they, as a group, are likely to stand on the question you are dealing with. You can estimate what they already know about the subject, what opinions and attitudes about it they now have, what issues they are most concerned with, and what kind of evidence will be most influential with them. Out of this knowledge you decide what kinds of appeals will best help you to persuade them. Making this decision is a major part of your prewriting. The following advice will help:

1.   *Have specific readers in mind.* Whom are you trying to persuade—your parents, your instructor, your classmates, the readers of your college newspaper, or others? An essay written for one of these will not necessarily be persuasive to the others. A paper addressed to the world in general is not aimed at anybody in particular. You will write more purposefully if you begin prewriting by defining the particular set of readers for whom you are writing.

2.   *Identify with your readers.* Once you have identified your readers, you can begin to identify *with* them. In this sense, *identify* means putting yourself imaginatively in their place and seeing the problem from their point of view. If persuasion is

necessary, your readers do not at present share your beliefs. Your purpose is to lead them toward these beliefs. In order to lead them, you must start where they are. Only by understanding their present attitudes can you hope to change them. This kind of initial identification with the reader is not a trick; you are not pretending to be something you are not. You are simply trying to establish an area of agreement that you intend to broaden.

You have already seen a good example of how a writer leads an audience to a new point of view in the stop-and-frisk essay, "Three Points of View," on page 20. There the student author began by identifying with the attitude he assumed his classmates would take, that of an innocent citizen subjected to the indignities of the stop-and-search procedure. Then he asked them to look at the situation through the eyes of the officer making the search, and in so doing he led them to modify their original attitude. Finally he combined both views in a larger one that would be acceptable not only to the citizen and the officer but to all fair-minded people. In all this there was no trick and no dishonesty. The student was simply following a strategy designed to lead his audience to the conviction that, when conducted by a capable officer, the stop-and-search procedure protects everybody's legitimate interests.

3. *Be careful about the tone of your writing.* As you saw in Chapter 8, the tone reveals an attitude toward the readers. Your tone should help strengthen your identification with your readers; it should certainly avoid anything that will increase the distance between you and them. You can be angry or indignant about the situation you are trying to change or about those who allow that situation to exist. But you cannot be angry or indignant with your readers, not if you want their agreement. Nor can you talk down to them. You are trying to establish a partnership with them. Such a partnership requires mutual respect, and anything in your tone that lessens that respect will work against your purpose.

4. *Provide the evidence your readers need to accept your beliefs.* If you respect your readers, you will not ask them to accept your unsupported opinions, any more than a businessman would expect his partner to take his word for it that a proposed investment will be profitable. Normally both partners would go over the evidence in detail until both were satisfied. As a writer you have an obligation to spell out in detail why you think a reader should accept your conclusions. It is not enough that the writer believes the argument is sound. It is the reader who must be persuaded.

5. *Make your paper easy to read.* When you are asking your readers to agree with you, make their job as easy as possible. Highly complex arguments, confused structure, technical terminology, abstract diction, complex statistics—all these make communication difficult. Since the writer leads the reader, you should do everything you can to make it easy for the reader to follow your writing.

13c **Outlining**

The outline provides a more formal summary of a writer's ideas. Instead of in a paragraph, however, information you gather appears in a special manner. Main ideas are numbered with Roman numbers. Supporting ideas have letters or Arabic numbers and appear under the main headings. This kind of arrangement lets you see at a glance how the key ideas relate to each other and how the writer has backed up important points.

The form of an outline looks like this:

Title

I.   First main idea
    A.   Supporting idea
        1.   Detail
        2.   Detail
        3.   Detail
            a.   Minor detail
            b.   Minor detail
    B.   Supporting idea
        1.   Detail
        2.   Detail
    C.   Supporting idea

II. Second main idea

The following pointers should help you make good outlines.

- Make sure only main ideas form main headings.

- Make sure all the subheadings relate to the main headings you place them under.

- Make sure all the headings in a series are of the same type.

- Make sure all the headings are clearly different so that they don't overlap. (If there is too much overlapping, you must reorganize the information.)

- Make sure that, whenever you break down a heading, you have at least two subheadings.

- Make sure to include everything important that appears in the selection you are outlining.

- Make sure all the items are indented correctly.

- Make sure you put a period after each letter or number.

The most effective kind of outline is the sentence outline. Each item on the outline is expressed as a complete sentence. You may make a less complete outline by using only short groups of words. Decide how complete an outline you need for your purpose.

The following sentence outline is based on the selection about Alcatraz on page 179.

I. The Government should give Alcatraz to the Indians now occupying it.
    A. Indians will create five centers.
        1. One would serve for a North American studies program.
        2. Another would be a spiritual and medical center.
        3. A third would study ecology.
        4. Two other centers would be founded.
            a. One would be for job training.
            b. One would be a museum.
    B. Indian programs will require Federal assistance.
II. People may object to allowing Indians to run their own programs.
    A. But HEW gave $10 million for Indian study last year.
        1. All money went to non-Indians.
        2. No Indian scholar got money to give the view of the Indians.
    B. Studies by non-Indians added nothing to knowledge.

Take a look at the summary of this same paragraph on page 182. The advantage of a short paragraph summary is that it can be done quickly, and for most material you need as a study aid, a summary will do. But when you need to see each idea in relation to every other, when you need to see how each major and minor point fits into the overall structure, making an outline is a better way to do it. All the ideas contained in the paragraph about Alcatraz from page 179 are laid out in a clear and easy-to-read fashion in this sentence outline, with each main idea set off by a Roman numeral, each major point set off by a capital letter, each minor point set off by an Arabic number, and any subdivisions of minor points set off by small letters.

Doing a full-sentence outline well takes time, so be sure the material you're outlining is important enough to deserve the work!

Exercises

1. Outlining
Outline the paragraph about Broadway plays that appears on page 111. Use a separate sheet of paper.

2. Outlining
Outline the article about Indians that appears on pages 106–107. Use a separate sheet of paper.

3. Outlining
On a separate sheet of paper, outline the selection about newspapers that appears on page 103.

4. Outlining
On a separate sheet of paper, outline the following pages from a communication textbook.

DELIVERING THE SPEECH

One advantage, just mentioned, of a presentation that is oral as compared with one that is written is the opportunity for the speaker to convey his or her meanings more vividly through effective use of body and voice.

Body Communication

Body communication refers to what listeners see in the speaker's delivery as opposed to what they hear. Four of the most important aspects in body communication are posture, facial expression, eye directness, and gestures.

Posture   A common tendency of inexperienced speakers is to slouch. They stand with their weight mainly on one leg, sometimes shifting back and forth in a slow uneasy teeter. Or, instead of slouching, they stand with their feet wide apart as if straddling a ditch, or with feet close together like a prim schoolgirl. Either way, the effect is one of self-conscious awkwardness. With such a posture, the speaker conveys little sense of feeling at ease or of showing any real desire to communicate with his or her listeners.
A speaker's posture should be alive and erect (yet not rigid like a fence post), with the weight distributed about equally on both feet and leaning forward just a bit instead of away, as if subconsciously wanting to escape.

Facial Expression The face is the mirror of our emotions. A speaker who is unsure of him- or herself or the message and indifferent or apprehensive concerning the audience will reveal these moods unmistakably on his or her countenance. Such a speaker will be unlikely to arouse much feeling of rapport or interest or confidence in him or her on the part of the audience.

The speaker's face should instead reveal a lively interest in the message and genuine warmth and rapport with the listeners. If you can forget your anxiety by becoming really absorbed with your ideas and audience, your facial expression will reinforce rather than detract from the message.

Eye Directness Inexperienced speakers seem to want to look everywhere except toward the audience: at their notes, at the floor, at the ceiling—even out the window. Yet such indirectness destroys any sense of communicating with the listeners. Moreover, it robs the speaker of the benefits of reading the feedback in his or her listeners' eyes and faces.

A speaker should look the listeners in the eye. One should see them as individuals who, one hopes, will respond with interest, understanding, and belief. In so doing, one should avoid focusing too long on any one person, but include instead the entire audience, as if in a lively conversation with them all.

Gestures One of the most frequently asked questions by beginning speakers is, "What should I do with my hands?" An answer that many have found helpful is to think of speaking as something that involves the whole body, including hands and arms—then let your hands respond accordingly. (This happens in informal conversation, anyway.)

Gestures may be used for various purposes: to *describe* (as the spiral staircase gesture), to *emphasize* (raising the index finger with "Now, just a minute . . ."), to *enumerate* ("There are three good reasons . . ."), or to *point* (pointing to a location on a graph or diagram—usually with a pointer).

One's gesturing will be more effective if the following principles are kept in mind:

1. Gestures should involve the whole body—not just the hands. For example, in pointing to a diagram, turn the whole body instead of pointing with one hand as if the arm were attached loosely at the shoulder.

2. Gestures should be varied. The speaker should avoid relying on a single gesture, such as a right-hand chop repeated over and over. With two hands and the variety of gestures just described, such distracting monotony can be easily avoided.

3. Gestures should be definite and complete. It helps to think of a gesture as consisting of three stages: approach, stroke, and return. Too often a gesture fails to rise above a timid approach. To be effective, it should include an uninhibited motion (above waist level), with the stroke (climax

of the motion) coordinated with the stressed syllable of the word it reinforces: "The *sec*ond objection . . ."; ". . . shaped like *this* . . . ." The return follows naturally from the stroke.

4. Gestures should be spontaneous. Gestures that are specifically rehearsed appear stilted, besides contributing to a sense of self-consciousness. The speaker should be so absorbed with the message and the audience that gesturing occurs spontaneously as a natural response to the occasion—just as in an animated conversation.

It is not necessary, of course, to gesture constantly. Between gestures, the hands may be clasped loosely in front (often at waist level) or behind, or simply left to hang freely at the sides. Not recommended is the belligerent-looking hands-on-the-hip stance, or the hands-stuffed-in-the-pockets posture, although one hand slid casually into a pocket may be acceptable in an informal situation, if not left there indefinitely. In fact, the speaker should avoid "freezing" in any position, for the longer he or she remains frozen, the more uncomfortable he or she will feel—and the audience as well.

Body communication is an important aspect of an oral presentation. If ineffective, it can detract from the message. If effective, it can reinforce it—by as much as 20 percent, according to one authority.[9]

14 Understanding Exam Questions

During each semester you will learn much new information in your courses through class lectures and assigned readings. To find out how much you have learned, teachers will ask you questions on examinations. You must pay close attention to the wording of these questions in order to give correct answers. No matter how much you know, if you do not understand and provide what the teacher is asking for, your answer will be off-target.

The two basic kinds of questions are *short-answer* or objective questions and *essay* questions. With short-answer questions, the teacher is testing whether you know specific pieces of information and can therefore solve straightforward problems that have a single answer. With essay questions, the teacher is testing not only whether you know the information but also how well you understand and can apply that specific information.

Advice on how to read and answer both types of questions will follow, but first you need to know how to prepare for exams. If you do not know the material, you may not even be able to understand the questions, let alone answer them.

14a Preparing for Examinations

In the long run, the best way to prepare for examinations is to keep up with class lectures and assigned readings by taking notes, underlining, summarizing, and outlining (see Chapters 12 and 13). But even if you have done the work throughout the semester and have a complete set of notes, your memory will probably be a bit fuzzy by exam time some weeks later. The following steps will help you review the material and focus your studying.

- *Get an overview of the entire course.* Looking over a syllabus, list of lectures, assignment sheet, or any material that the teacher handed out at the beginning of the course will help you see the shape of the entire course. Quickly skimming through your notes and the assigned books will also help you get an overall view of the topics covered. Then, on a single sheet of paper, make an outline or a list of all the major topics covered in class and in the readings. See if you can notice any pattern in what was studied and any major themes that the teacher kept emphasizing throughout the semester. For example, the psychology teacher may have organized her course around different theories of psychology and may have emphasized how each theory would explain abnormal behavior.

- *Think about the overview.* The overview should help you determine what the teacher considers important and what kinds of questions the teacher is likely to ask. The overview will also help you sort out which topics are fairly clear and fresh in your mind and which topics are unclear and fading fast. The fresh topics should require only a little study, whereas the unclear ones may call for a long, thorough review of all your notes.

- *Schedule your remaining time.* Decide how much time you have available to study for the exam. Divide your time for studying according to how important each topic appears to be and how well you know the topic. Do not waste time memorizing minor facts that you will probably not be tested on or studying material that probably was presented only to make the class more lively. Spend your time on the most important material.

- *Study the material topic by topic in an orderly way.* One good technique for studying each major topic is to combine in outline form the key concepts and facts from both class and reading assignments. Not only will you review the material, but you will also see how the parts fit together. The more you see the logical connections among the many facts and concepts, the more you will remember and the better you will understand.

Exercises

1. Make a list of all the major topics covered thus far in a course you are taking this semester. Use your class notes, the textbook, and the course syllabus to help you.

a. Can you find a pattern of organization in the topics and in the order in which they were covered? Rewrite your list as an outline to reflect this organization. Now imagine that you will be examined on all this material in five days; draw up a study schedule.
b. For this same course, write down a list of three to five ideas or concepts that the teacher repeatedly stressed throughout the semester.

2. For a single topic, one that was covered in both class lectures and readings in a course you are now taking, write an outline of key concepts and facts to show how the information fits together.

14b Short-Answer Questions

The first and most important thing to do when taking any examination is to read the directions—all the directions for all the parts. Then you will know right from the beginning what you have to do and how much time you have to complete each part. Reading the directions carefully will help you schedule your time and guide your decisions.

On a short-answer test, read the directions to learn the following pieces of vital information:

- *Discover how many questions you have to answer.* Knowing how much work you have ahead of you will help you plan your time.

- *Find out whether you have any choices.* If you have choices, make sure you understand and follow the directions exactly. If, in the first part of an exam, you are supposed to answer only 10 out of 20 questions, but you answer all 20 anyway, you have wasted time. The last 10 will not count. If in the second part you are supposed to answer 20 out of 25 questions, but you answer only 15, you will lose credit for 5 questions.

- *Pay attention to how much time you have.* You may have one block of time for the whole exam, or you may have smaller blocks for each part. In either case, you should calculate about how much time you have available for each question. In this way you will not waste too much time on a single question and then have to rush through all the remaining questions.

- *Determine how many points each question is worth.* If some questions are worth more than others, you will want to spend more time on the more valuable questions. Also notice whether incorrect answers will count against you. If there is no penalty, you should make your best guess, even if you are not sure of the answer. But if there is a penalty, you may be better off leaving some questions blank rather than making wild guesses.

- *Know beforehand what extra materials you are allowed.* You may be allowed to use the textbook, a calculator, your notes, or scrap paper. Usually the teacher will let you know ahead of time which materials will be permitted so that you can bring them with you. If you do not bring the extra materials allowed, you are putting yourself at a serious disadvantage.

- *Find out where to record your answers.* Sometimes you may be allowed to fill in or circle the answer on the question itself, but more often special places are provided for the answers. If you have to fill in spaces in a machine-scored sheet, be sure to mark the spaces neatly and clearly. If you have to use a special pencil, be sure that you have one and that you use it. If your answer is in the wrong place or cannot be read, it will do you no good.

- Note what type or types of questions are included. Different types of questions require different types of answers. Several different types of questions are described in the following paragraphs.

Fill-in questions require you to write a missing word or phrase in the blank space within a statement. When filling in the blank, try to use the exact term used in class or in your textbooks. But if you cannot remember the exact term, describe your answer as carefully as you can. You may get credit for a partial or an approximate answer.

True–false questions require you to state whether or not a particular statement is true. In true–false questions, words such as *all, most, some, none, always, probably, never, more,* and *less* are very important. Pay close attention to them. In *modified true–false* questions, you may have a third or fourth choice, such as *uncertain* or *not enough data.* Make sure you know all the possible ways of answering before writing down an answer.

Matching questions provide you with two (or more) lists of information, such as a list of dates and a list of events. You must then indicate, next to each item on one list, the related item from the other list. Sometimes one column may contain extra items, so that some will be left over. In answering matching questions, you should fill in the easiest answers first and cross out items as you use them. This will make the remaining choices easier.

Multiple-choice questions usually require you to choose the best single answer out of four or five choices. But be careful: sometimes the directions will tell you to choose the *worst* answer or the one item that does *not* apply. The directions may also give you the choice of *none of these* or *all of these*. In all multiple-choice questions, make sure you read all the possible answers before writing down your choice. The second choice may sound like a possible answer, but the fifth choice may turn out to be the most precise and therefore the correct answer. If you do not spot the correct answer the first time you read through the choices, you may be able to eliminate some clearly wrong answers. This approach will make it easier for you to choose among the remaining answers and will at least improve your odds of being right if you wind up guessing.

Exercises

1. This exercise will test how well you follow directions. Wrong answers will count against you. You have one minute to complete it. Begin at the bottom and work your way up.

——a. Are you confused? Write *yes* or *no* in the blank space.

——b. If you are male, write *7* in space *b* and *5* in space *d*; if you are female, write *5* in space *d* and *7* in space *b*.

——c. Count the letters in answer *a* and put the number in space *f*.

——d. What is today's date? Do not write the answer in space *d*.

——e. What is the number of this course? Write *it* in space *e*.

——f. Write your first name in answer space *a*.

2. The following questions test your ability *to guess* intelligently. Wrong answers will not be held against you. Answer the questions as directed and put your answers in the answer column. You have five minutes to complete the exercise.

——a. Write down the number of the one *incorrect* statement.

    1. The photoelectric effect involves the release of electrons, when metals are hit by photons of light.

    2. The photoelectric effect was discovered by R. A. Millikan.

    3. The photoelectric effect is the reason why you need to put batteries in your camera.

    4. The photoelectric effect is consistent with quantum theory, but it is contrary to the wave theory of light.

———b. Write down the numbers of the best answers.
    Controversial events in the administration of President Harry Truman included
    1. dropping the atom bomb on Japan.
    2. calling for a decrease in unemployment.
    3. having his daughter sing at the White House.
    4. nationalizing the steel mills.
    5. starting the Vietnam War.
———c. Write T if the statement is true, F if it is false.
    Schizophrenia is always caused by a schizophrenogenic parent.
———d. Fill in the blank.
    Gresham's law states that bad money tends to drive

    ————————— out of circulation.
———e. Write down the number of the one best answer.
    In legal terminology, *de jure* means
    1. de facto.
    2. according to a jury.
    3. according to law.
    4. a group of people who decide whether someone is guilty.
    5. handsome.
———f. The first column contains names of music composers; the second column contains the names of pieces of music they wrote. Match the composer with the piece of music by writing the number of the piece of music in front of the name of the composer.

———Ludwig van Beethoven   1. *Imagine*
———John Lennon   2. *Peggy Sue*
———Bela Bartok   3. *Take the A Train*
———Franz Schubert   4. *Messiah*
———Georg Friedrich Handel   5. *The Unfinished Symphony*
———Buddy Holly   *phony*
———Duke Ellington   6. *Hungarian Dances*
                                  7. *Eroica Symphony*

14c Essay Questions

You generally have greater freedom in answering essay questions than you do in answering short-answer questions, because the teacher is testing how well you think as well as how thoroughly you know the material. But you still must follow directions very carefully. If you do not answer the question the teacher asks in the way the teacher wants it answered, the teacher may conclude that you do not understand the material and that you do not know how to think about the question. To get credit, you need to answer the question as written. Therefore, you should take time to read the question carefully and analyze exactly what you have to do to answer it before you begin to write your answer.

In reading the question, you should look for two things in particular: the *subject* and the *task*.

The subject is the object, event, process, concept, or other piece of information that you are asked to discuss. It is frequently the name of something you have studied in the course. For example, look at this question from a history exam.

Discuss Winston Churchill's leadership role during World War II.

The subject of the question is Winston Churchill and, more specifically, his leadership during World War II. You would be wrong if you discussed Franklin Roosevelt's leadership. You would also be wrong if you discussed Churchill's leadership after the war or during World War I. You must stay within the specific limits of the question.

Some questions have two or more subjects; for example, you may be asked to compare or relate two separate things. Look at the following question, also from a history exam:

Compare Winston Churchill's power to inspire the British in the early days of World War II with Franklin Roosevelt's inability to alert America to the dangers of Hitler during the same period.

In this question you are asked to compare two subjects, and you must discuss each one in your answer. If you discuss only one, you are providing only half the information asked for.

The *task* is what you are asked to do with the information. The task is usually contained in a *key question word*, often the first word of the question. In the first example, the task was *to describe*; in the second, the task was *to compare*. These tasks require you to give different kinds of answers. If you are asked to *give the causes* of American isolationism between the two world wars, but you only *list* isolationist policies, you are not answering the question accurately.

The following list of key question words defines and gives examples of the different tasks you may be asked to carry out on an essay examination. Make sure you know what to do to answer questions containing these different key question words.

Here are the key question words you should look for when you first read the question.

agree, disagree comment on, criticize, evaluate	Give your opinion about a book, quotation, or statement. If the question says *agree or disagree,* you must express either a positive or a negative opinion. If the question says *comment on, criticize,* or *evaluate,* you can make both positive and negative points.
	"The first six weeks of a child's life are the most important period in its emotional development." *Agree or disagree.*
analyze	Break down a topic into all its parts. Be sure to include all the parts and to tell what makes each part different from the others.
	Analyze the corporate structure of the college bookstore.
compare	Show how two things are both alike and different. Be sure to discuss each thing and give both likenesses and differences.
	Compare the sculpture of Renaissance Italy to classical Greek sculpture.
contrast	Show only the differences between two things. Be sure to talk about each one.
	Contrast the nervous system of a flatworm with the nervous system of a frog.
define	Give the exact meaning of a word, phrase, or concept. Show how the thing you are defining is different from everything else of its type. Give examples.
	Define Marx's concept of alienated labor.
explain why	Give the main reasons why an event mentioned happened or happens.

Explain why ocean tides are not high at the same time every night and why they are not always the same height.

describe
discuss

Tell what happened, what the subject looks like, or what the subject is.

Describe the conditions on the ships that brought slaves to America. Then *discuss* one rebellion that took place on a slave ship.

illustrate

Give one or more examples of a general statement. Be sure to relate each example to the general statement.

Primitive tribes usually have rigid family systems. *Illustrate* this, using one of the tribes you studied this semester.

interpret

Explain the meaning of facts given in the exam question. The question may specify what method of interpretation you must use. Be sure to do more than just repeat the facts.

In 1910 Farmtown, Kansas, had 502 farm workers, 37 other blue-collar workers, and 13 white-collar workers. In 1975 the same town had 153 farm workers, 289 other blue-collar workers, and 86 white-collar workers. *Interpret* these statistics in light of national labor trends during this period.

justify
prove

Give reasons to show why a statement is true.

The Industrial Revolution allowed some people to accumulate great wealth. *Justify* this statement, using material you studied this semester.

list
state

Make a list of important points. Be sure to include all the items asked for in the question. Do not give examples unless they are requested.

List the five main methods of air-quality control studied this semester.

outline *review* *summarize*	Give all the main points of a quotation, book, or theory. You do not have to bother with unimportant points.

Outline Galileo's major discoveries.

relate	Show how one object has an effect on another. Be sure to show the connection between them.

Relate the evolution of the horse to the changes in its environment.

trace *list the steps* *or stages*	Give a series of important events, starting at one point and leading up to a final one. Be sure not to leave anything out or to include more than the question asks for. This type of exam question may refer to historical events, recall a process, or ask for detailed directions.

Trace the events that led up to the Civil War.

In answering essay questions, you should follow the principles of good writing that you have learned in your writing classes. The following advice should also help you write an essay that answers the question.

- Think about the question. Ask yourself:
    1. How does the question relate to the material of the course?
    2. Can I use any of the important ideas that the teacher emphasized?
    3. What, from the reading or lectures, would make good examples?

- Plan the essay. On scrap paper list the main points you want to make. Next to each main point put at least one supporting example.

- Make your points clear.
    1. In the opening sentence of your answer, use words from the question. If the question says "Agree or disagree with the following quotation by Bertrand Russell," you should begin your answer with "I agree with the quotation by Bertrand Russell because. . . ."
    2. Begin each of the middle paragraphs with a topic sentence that states one of your major points. Within each middle paragraph, support the major point with reasons and examples.

3. In the conclusion of your answer, relate your answer to one important idea taught in the course.

- Read over the essay. Make sure all your sentences make sense. Make sure your meaning is clear. Make sure you did not forget to answer any parts of the question. Make sure your grammar, sentence structure, and spelling are correct.

Exercises

1. In each of the following questions, underline the subject (or subjects) and circle the key question word.
   a. Discuss the influence of African art on the work of Picasso.
   b. Analyze the influence of Garcia Lorca on the poetry of Allen Ginsberg.
   c. List five of the properties of supercooled helium.
   d. Trace the growth of the Republican party in the American west of the 1850s.
   e. Evaluate the problems facing northeastern cities in the 1980s.

2. In your own words, describe the task that each of the following key question words asks you to do.
   a. Discuss the impact of the Cuban missile crisis on the

Kennedy administration. _____

_____

_____

   b. How do you interpret Andy Warhol's remark that

someday everyone will be famous for ten minutes? _____

_____

_____

   c. Do you agree that marijuana use by teen-agers is the

greatest problem facing American education? _____

_____

_____

_____

    d. Compare reggae to disco. _____

_____

_____

    e. List the best ways to housetrain a dog. _____

_____

_____

3. For a course you are now taking, write essay questions using the following key question words.
    a. justify
    b. illustrate
    c. relate
    d. review
    e. agree or disagree

4. Explain why each of the following questions on the same topic requires a different answer.
    a. Compare the Carter administration to the Johnson administration.
    b. Describe the effect that Carter's economic policies had on the wage and price spiral and specifically what impact his policies had in curbing or increasing inflation.
    c. List President Carter's greatest successes in foreign policy.
    d. Summarize Carter's impact on American society between 1976 and 1980.
    e. Illustrate the major problems facing the United States in the Middle East during Jimmy Carter's administration.

Reading Selections

Introduction

The selections on the following pages will allow you to practice all the various reading skills you've learned so far. The accompanying questions are designed to test your understanding of what you read, so answer them carefully. In some cases you will be able to answer without returning to the selection. In other cases you will want to return quickly to specific passages before you choose an answer. You'll have to use your judgment here. Returning to the selection to check *every* response before you write it will slow you down and will make your reading a real chore. Therefore, you should try to retain as much information as you can when you read each piece for the first time. On the other hand, when you are not certain about something, it's best to check by returning to the paragraph that you believe contains the answer.

You'll notice that numbers in parentheses appear at the end of each question. These numbers refer to chapters and sections in the first part of the book where the skill required to answer the question is explained. Thus, if you are still stumped after you've checked back in the selection, you might find it helpful to turn to the appropriate section of the handbook and review your skills.

Each selection offers two approaches to help you learn the vocabulary. The most difficult words appear with definitions in a section called "Word Highlights" right before you read. Study them. The list is alphabetical; when a difficult word appears in the selection, you can look it up easily. Then a vocabulary exercise appears at the end of the questions on each piece. The vocabulary exercises require that you show your knowledge of the words by answering questions about their uses and meanings. To expand your reading skills, you will want to add the new words to your reading, writing, and speaking vocabularies as soon as possible. That means writing the words down, using them in sentences, and following the other guidelines given in Chapter 1. You should also keep a personal list of other words you don't know in each selection. Check their meanings and learn them too.

The works chosen for this part of the book will teach you or will amuse you, and certainly they will make you think. They come from a wide range of college reading materials. You'll find articles, essays, and sections of books, newspapers, and magazines. You'll find selections from textbooks in psychology, history, and chemistry. You'll find short stories, poems, and myths. In short, they are the kinds of readings a varied program of study can require of today's student.

1 Coyote, the Fire Bringer

by Barbara Stanford

Myths are stories that people tell one another to help make sense of the world. Many myths explain things that don't seem to have an explanation. This myth tells how the American Indians explained the discovery of fire and how they explained why certain animals look as they do.

Word Highlights

exhaustion   the state of being completely tired out and close to collapse

treeline   the place on a mountain above which trees cannot grow because it is too cold

At the beginning of time, people had no fire. They were cold and had to eat their salmon raw. The only fire was on top of a high mountain guarded by evil spirits or "skookums." One day the coyote came to visit the people.

"Coyote," the people said, "we are miserable. Could you please get us fire from the mountains?"

"I will see what I can do," said the coyote.

He went up to the mountains to watch the skookums. He saw that one always guarded the fire while the others slept. When her turn was up, the skookum guarding the fire would say, "Sister, come and guard the fire." It usually took a little while for the new guard to come. The coyote thought that he could steal the fire, but he was afraid that the skookums would catch him before he could get to the bottom of the mountain, because the skookums could run very fast. At last he thought of a plan.

The next day, the coyote called all of the animals together and stationed them in a relay up the mountain. Then he went to the top and waited for the guards to change. At last he heard the skookum guarding the fire say, "Sister, come and guard the fire." Without waiting at all, the coyote jumped up and grabbed a piece of wood carrying the fire.

Down the mountain he ran, but the skookums were right behind him. They caught up with him just as he reached the treeline. One of the skookums grabbed his tail and it turned black. But he had reached the cougar, and passed the flaming torch on to him.

The cougar passed the brand on to the fox, who passed it on to the squirrel. The fire burned a black spot on the squirrel's back and made his tail curl. But he reached the edge of the forest in time to give the fire to the antelope.

The antelope was such a swift runner that all the animals were sure the skookums would tire out. But they didn't. At last the antelope collapsed from exhaustion. There was only a coal left, and a small frog grabbed the coal and swallowed it.

The skookums were right behind. One of them caught the frog by the tail. The frog gave a mighty leap and his tail pulled right off, and since that time frogs have had no tails.

But finally, the frog was exhausted, too. Not knowing what to do, he spat out the coal onto some wood. The wood swallowed it. The skookums came up just as the coal disappeared into the wood. They stood a long time staring. But they did not know how to get the fire back out of the wood. At last they left and went back up the mountain.

Then the coyote ran up joyfully. He knew how to get the fire out of the wood. He took two pieces of wood and rubbed them together.

From that day on, people have had fire to heat their homes and to cook their salmon.

Exercises

Understanding What You Have Read

_____1. The main idea of this selection is (4)
   a. that the coyote brought fire to the people to hurt them.
   b. how the coyote brought fire to the people.
   c. that skookums helped the Indians by teaching them how to cook.
   d. that frogs are not very useful friends when a person is in trouble.

_____2. What is the correct order in which the animals bring fire down from the mountain? (6a)
   a. cougar, coyote, fox, squirrel, antelope, frog
   b. coyote, squirrel, antelope, frog, fox, cougar
   c. coyote, cougar, fox, squirrel, antelope, frog
   d. coyote, fox, cougar, squirrel, antelope, frog

_____3. Put a checkmark before each statement that is true in the story. (5a)
   _____a. The coyote could speak to the people.
   _____b. Frogs once had tails.
   _____c. The skookums were brothers.

_____d. The coyote returns to the village carrying a burning torch.

_____e. The skookums get tired and give up.

_____f. The coyote asks the birds to help, but they refuse.

_____g. The fox gets burned carrying the fire.

_____4. This story is told in (**6a**)

    a. time order.

    b. place order.

    c. order of importance.

    d. reverse order.

   5. Write *maj* before each major detail in the story and *min* before each minor detail. (**5b**)

_____a. The coyote knows how to get fire out of the wood.

_____b. The antelope grows tired.

_____c. The skookums are all women.

_____d. The coyote gets other animals to help him.

_____e. The people were cold and had to eat fish raw.

_____f. The skookums run very fast.

_____g. The coyote is very clever.

Interpreting and Evaluating

_____1. We can infer that the reason why the skookums live above the treeline is that (**7**)

    a. otherwise their fire would burn the woods down.

    b. it's the only place the people will let them live.

    c. the animals can't find them there.

    d. both b and c.

_____2. The animals in the story are (**9**)

    a. tricky

    b. friendly

    c. evil

    d. helpful

_____3. What can we infer was the primary way of lighting fires for American Indians? (**7**)

    a. the sun

    b. rubbing sticks together

    c. rubbing a match against a piece of wood

    d. coal

_____4. The story of how coyote brought fire down from the mountain was probably invented to answer what question? (**10**)

a. why do leaves turn brown in the fall?
b. why does wood burn?
c. how did man get fire?
d. both b and c.

Vocabulary

Match the animals in the left-hand column with the correct description in the right-hand column. (2)

——1. coyote   a. an evil spirit
——2. skookum   b. eats flies and swims
——3. fox   c. looks like a deer
——4. frog   d. howls at the moon
——5. antelope   e. is red and is hunted in England

2 After Rush Hour

by John Watson

The events described here took place in a New York subway, but they could happen anywhere that people with authority and people without power come in close contact. This article raises questions about how police relate to the people they watch over.

Word Highlights

adversaries people on the opposite sides of a battle

articulate able to express oneself well

belligerent in a fighting mood

misdemeanor a lesser crime, not so serious as a felony

prudent careful

rampant all over the place, gone wild

rancid tasting or smelling stale or sour

In the West Fourth Street subway station, I notice a black teenage boy waiting for the train, sitting on a railing just in front of a moving escalator. It's a muggy evening, there's no air in this station, and I'm sure we're both hoping for one of those nice air-conditioned F trains.

So this black kid is just sitting there, perched on the railing, facing out toward the track as opposed to in toward the escalator where he would be obstructing the flow of people. And I'm just standing there about 10 feet away looking for the faraway lights of the oncoming train.

Then all of a sudden a white, mustachioed transit cop is curtly asking the kid for identification. I'm within easy earshot, and there is nothing said by either party before that. The kid turns sullen and asks what he's being hassled about. The cop doesn't explain. The kid pulls out some I.D. and hands it to the cop who looks at it and then barks out a demand for something with an address on it, a driver's license.

Defiantly, the kid pulls out a second piece of identification. The officer looks at it and tells the kid to come with him. Nothing I have seen or heard explains the cop's hardline approach or why the kid is being led away.

I go up to the officer and politely ask what this guy did and where was he taking him. He looks at me like I'm armed and crazy and tells me that it's none of my business and to stay out of this.

"Could I please take down your badge number, sir, as I'd like to report all this," I say.

"Take down my badge number and then *you* show me a piece of identification. What are you, some kinda hotshot lawyer?"

I copy down his badge number and then show him my driver's license, asking, "Could you please tell me what this is all for?"

Looking me over and again asking if I'm a lawyer, he tells me he's taking the kid in for obstructing the escalator and me in for "obstructing a police action." Another black man who's heard all this asks what's going on and the cop seems to get very nervous, so I decide to go with him in silence.

The kid and I are led to a poorly lighted, unventilated cavern where three other transit cops are all clustered around a small electric table fan that barely stirs the rancid air, smoking cigarettes and reading newspapers. It's an incredibly oppressive atmosphere, and I feel sorry for the transit cops whose work environment this is.

The cop who brought us in gives his version of what happened, and I politely interrupt to explain that the kid was in no way blocking escalator traffic and that I was in no way "obstructing a police action," not adding that I thought the way the cop handled the situation was racist and unnecessarily belligerent. He writes the kid a summons, needing help from another officer in looking up the exact wording of the offense. The kid is told to leave.

Another transit cop offers me his thoughts on all this: There are two good reasons to keep people from sitting on the escalator railing. First, these escalators are often put out of service not because of heavy use and poor maintenance but rather rampant vandalism, and transit police officers are the first ones blamed by their superiors for not preventing this. Secondly, an escalator or stairway is the best and quickest route of escape for a purse snatcher or pickpocket. Transit-police officers have strict instructions to keep all passageways clear and to issue summonses to any and all offenders. A police officer's job is in no way to *make* the laws or to *interpret* the laws (that's left to a judge who makes $60,000 a year, a salary he mentions twice, with resentment), but only to *enforce* the laws. Did I know that playing a radio or even taking a bicycle on the subway are both misdemeanor offenses?

Then he speaks to my specific situation. Why in God's name did I stick my nose into someone else's business? Without accusing the first cop of shoddy, racist police work, I explain that I saw and heard the whole thing happen, that the kid wasn't blocking the escalator, and that I felt compelled to ask what the charge was. He explains that it's common practice to lead someone away from a crowd to write out a summons, as a cop with a pencil in one hand and a summons book in his other hand is open to someone grabbing his revolver. He gets me to admit that one or two people who openly question an officer's judgment in front of a crowd could easily incite a riot, and that I know nothing about transit officers unfairly taking the blame when vandalism occurs. He cleverly moves away from the particular injustice of what I saw to the general problems of subway crime and vandalism, of interfering with and resisting arrest, of obstruction of justice.

I listen intently and so get off with only the lecture and a better understanding of the pressure and conditions these cops work under.

But questions remain: Is my accusation of racism too strong? Would a well-dressed white man be confronted with a sharp command for identification for sitting on an escalator railing waiting for a train? Why were there three cops sitting in that room and not out patrolling the vast stretches of the West Fourth Street station? The articulate cop himself explained that there was only one transit officer assigned to that station at any given time. If a bystander does want to get involved and inquire about an apparently undeserved arrest, is a cop's only prudent response a second arrest? Will our police officers always be seen by black kids as evil, white-oriented adversaries?

Will the subways ever change?

Exercises

Understanding What You Have Read

_____1. The main idea of this passage is that (**4**)
   a. kids hang around in subways just to make trouble.
   b. white cops are racists.
   c. the pressures on transit police often make them act belligerently toward black teen-agers.
   d. interfering with police action is dangerous.

_____2. According to the passage, police officers feel it is their job to (**5a**)
   a. interpret the law.
   b. enforce the law.
   c. hassle black teen-agers.
   d. do anything they think best.

———3. Place a checkmark next to each statement that can be
supported by the selection. (**5a**)
———a. The teen-ager was not obstructing the escalator.
———b. The author was taken to jail.
———c. The police officer drew his gun on the author.
———d. The teen-ager was waiting to steal a purse.
———e. There are good reasons for people not to block subway escalators.

———4. According to the police officer's own explanation, why was
he so hostile? (**5a**)
a. He was afraid that there would be a riot.
b. He was afraid that the author was a lawyer.
c. He was afraid that the author was getting out of hand.
d. None of these.

Interpreting and Evaluating

1. What can you infer about the author on the basis of the
selection? Put a checkmark before each detail about the
author that is true. (**7**)

———a. He was a racist.
———b. He was black.
———c. He was not afraid to get involved.
———d. He had a sense of justice.
———e. He hated cops.
———f. His father was a police officer.
———g. He frequently rode on the subway.
———h. He was tired of seeing blacks bothered unnecessarily by law enforcement officers.

——— 2. What can we infer from the passage was the author's
reason for interfering? (**7**)
a. He was a hotshot lawyer.
b. He was helping the police.
c. He felt an injustice was being done.
d. He hated teen-agers.

——— 3. On the basis of the selection, we can conclude that the
author feels that (**9**)
a. police officers shouldn't carry guns.
b. judges make too much money.
c. racism may be the hardest cause of misunderstanding
to erase.
d. police officers treat everybody the same.

_____ 4. We can infer that the teen-ager feels (7)
      a. resentful of white cops who pick on him.
      b. resentful because no one pays attention to him.
      c. happy to have a safe subway to ride on.
      d. none of these.

_____ 5. We can infer that the transit police feel (7)
      a. resentful of black teen-agers who torment them.
      b. resentful of judges who make so much money.
      c. afraid of their superiors.
      d. both b and c.

_____ 6. What conclusion does the author draw about the problems
      in the subway? (9)
      a. He draws no conclusion.
      b. Subway cops should have improved working conditions.
      c. Teen-agers should be taught respect for adults.
      d. The problems in the subways can't be solved easily.

_____ 7. On the basis of the selection, which generalization is true?
      (10)
      a. Cops resent judges.
      b. Subway stations are good places to hang out.
      c. Black teen-agers are defiant toward police officers.
      d. Subways will never change.

_____ 8. What is the purpose of the author ending the selection
      with a paragraph made up of questions? (11d)
      a. It shows that he doesn't know very much about anything.
      b. It shows that he doesn't have solutions for this problem.
      c. It shows that he hasn't thought much about this.
      d. Both b and c.

_____ 9. The author's tone in this selection is (11d)
      a. angry.
      b. cautious.
      c. defiant.
      d. boastful.

_____10. The author's purpose in writing this piece was to (11d)
      a. amuse you.
      b. make you angry.

c. make you aware of an unpleasant situation.

d. make you hate cops.

Vocabulary

Match each figurative phrase from this piece of writing with the animal or thing it suggests. (8)

_____ 1. perched on the railing   a. dogs

_____ 2. barks out a demand   b. cats

                                      c. birds

_____ 3. flow of people   d. water

_____ 4. unventilated cavern   e. caves

Identify whether each word below is an *adjective*, describing a thing, or an *adverb*, describing how something was done. Then write the meaning of the word in the space provided. (**3**)

5. curtly (paragraph 3) _____

_____

6. sullen (paragraph 3) _____

_____

7. defiantly (paragraph 4) _____

_____

8. muggy (paragraph 1) _____

_____

9. oppressive (paragraph 10) _____

_____

_____

10. shoddy (paragraph 13) _____

11. intently (paragraph 14) _____

_____

3 Getting High in Mountainside

by Margo Krasnoff

This student's personal account of the drug problem at her high school is both sincere and well expressed.

Word Highlights

espouse   make someone else's idea one's own; adopt a cause

euphoric   based on a feeling of well-being

incidence   range of occurrence of something

integral   an important part of a whole

Mick Jagger   rock singer; lead in group "The Rolling Stones"

Jack Kerouac   an author of the "beat" generation; known best for his book *On the Road* (1957)

literally   without exaggeration; actually

loomed   rose up in one's sight as something very large or threatening

munchies   slang for hunger brought about by use of drugs

wistful   thoughtful; sad

Everyone laughed when the boy walked into the door. I didn't. They were high. I wasn't.

Marijuana is as integral a part of my high school as its doors. My school is literally high. The incidence of staggering students, 11 o'clock munchies, and rolling papers falling out of lockers is commonplace. Dealers operate in the library behind the biography section where few people venture.

The school is divided into two groups: those who smoke and those who don't. Those who do, eat outside, even in 30-degree weather; their hair covers their eyes in Mick Jagger fashion; they absorb and espouse the wisdom of Jack Kerouac; their rock music is the Allman Brothers Band. When they mumble "like—you know," they're speaking the code and when they laugh it is not at all self-conscious, but an extension of the common bond of grass.

The temptation to smoke is strong but it was not always so. As a freshman, I was totally naive about drugs. No one I knew took them; I imagined that those who did were poor, unloved, and stupid. I could not associate what I had studied in science class with anything that I was made up of. Cigarette smoke made me sick. Never, in my wildest dreams, did I imagine myself smoking a crumpled roll of pot until the experience was a reality. I was curious. Having heard how great it was to float down the stream of consciousness, I felt compelled to try it and join the ocean of kids who got high for kicks.

The first time was exciting. I trembled, as the fear of getting caught loomed before me. I felt that I was taking a risk and that a policeman would snatch the evil weed from my innocent hand, and replace it with handcuffs. But no one ever gets busted.

Sometimes I wish they were. I know it's terrible to wish evil upon another, because he or she would lose all opportunity to become perhaps a doctor or a lawyer. But then his parents would be aware that their child exists and that he's trying to express himself. He needs to be listened to.

Marijuana never really appealed to me, because I could feel free, express myself through poetry, and experience music without it. I like to know that all of me is here and that I control my entire body. I know who I am and can accept it without the fantasies of getting stoned.

Many smoke grass to discover where life's at and how they're going or not going to fit into society. High school students with promising futures are smoking their pot with increased fervor. Some scientists tell us that marijuana is not addictive, but when someone puffs on a joint with that wistful look on his or her face, I can see how strong the attraction is. What I fear is that some kids don't know when to stop.

Marijuana is hurting us all. The high school children drift through school in their euphoric state and don't give a damn about their grades. They don't care about politics or sports, only about where their next nickel is coming from and whether the stuff will be potent.

How can we turn kids off this drug? Surely not by legalizing it. Surely not by closing our ears to conversation and by flicking on our televisions. And surely not by denying that a serious problem exists.

Exercises

Understanding What You Have Read

_____ 1. The main idea of this selection is to show (**4b**)
   a. how to get high in high school.
   b. how to turn kids off drugs.
   c. that it is possible to resist smoking pot.
   d. that smoking marijuana is a major problem of high-school students.

____2. In regard to smoking marijuana, the writer (**5a**)
   a. tried it once or twice.
   b. tried it once but got sick.
   c. would never try it.
   d. stopped trying it after she was handcuffed by the police.

____3. To obtain marijuana, students must (**5a**)
   a. buy it from their science teacher.
   b. buy it in the library.
   c. buy it in 30-degree weather.
   d. avoid the undercover police agents.

____4. The details the author presents to describe what students who smoke marijuana are like do *not* include the fact that students (**5b**)
   a. say "like—you know."
   b. all want to be lawyers or doctors.
   c. enjoy reading Jack Kerouac.
   d. laugh as part of the code.

____5. Among the causes for trying marijuana, the writer does *not* suggest (**6d**)
   a. anger at parents.
   b. excitement.
   c. curiosity.
   d. trying to find out how to fit into society.

____6. The writer's main fear about students who smoke pot is that (**5a**)
   a. they will never fit into society.
   b. they will get in trouble with the police.
   c. they will get in trouble with their parents.
   d. they do not know when to stop.

____7. The writer does not find pot appealing, because (**5a**)
   a. she is afraid of the police.
   b. she is afraid of school officials.
   c. she likes to be in full control of herself.
   d. she prefers wine or alcohol.

Interpreting and Evaluating

____ 1. The word *Mountainside* in the title probably refers to (**7**)
   a. the secret area where students buy pot.
   b. an arena for rock concerts.
   c. a large peak.
   d. the town where the writer lives.

_____ 2. The age of the author is probably (7)
   a. eight.
   b. seventeen.
   c. twenty-two.
   d. thirty-two.

_____ 3. Students who eat outside in 30-degree weather probably do it because (7)
   a. they like cold air.
   b. they need to wake up from their high.
   c. it's a good break from the dull school routine.
   d. they can smoke marijuana more freely outdoors.

_____ 4. The author believes that the parents of a child who smokes pot (9)
   a. would approve.
   b. are not even aware that the child exists.
   c. are not aware that students smoke pot.
   d. should punish the child.

_____ 5. According to the writer, if a student were arrested for smoking pot, the student (9)
   a. would be suspended from high school.
   b. might turn to more serious drugs.
   c. should be given another chance.
   d. could never get accepted at medical school.

_____ 6. If students stopped smoking marijuana, they would probably (9)
   a. be more interested in school, athletics, and politics.
   b. turn to alcohol.
   c. get into good law and medical schools.
   d. have closer relationships with their parents.

_____ 7. In general, the writer believes that people who turn to drugs (10)
   a. should get long prison terms.
   b. do not feel free to express themselves in other ways.
   c. do not understand their parents.
   d. do so because of a hate for society.

_____ 8. The writer believes that laws to allow the use of marijuana (9)
   a. should be passed to prevent illegal dealing.
   b. could never get passed.
   c. are too hard to enforce.
   d. will not help teen-agers avoid the drug.

——— 9. In general, the writer believes that the police (**10**)
  a. should take a strong position in enforcing drug laws.
  b. are too busy to enforce drug laws.
  c. should ignore drug laws for all people, because the laws are too harsh.
  d. should ignore drug laws for high-school students.

———10. It is only the writer's opinion that (**11a**)
  a. people on a "high" laughed when a boy walked into a door.
  b. cigarette smoking makes her sick.
  c. legalizing pot will not "turn kids off" marijuana.
  d. scientists say marijuana is not addictive.

———11. The writer's purpose in this selection is (**11d**)
  a. to report facts in a scientific way.
  b. to present an angry view of drug use.
  c. to convince readers to agree with her point of view.
  d. to make readers laugh.

Vocabulary

Explain in your own words the meaning of the figurative expressions in italics. (8)

1. *float down the stream* of consciousness

_____

2. I felt compelled to try it and join the *ocean of kids* who *got high for kicks*. (Can you find other words immediately before *ocean* that work with *ocean* to make a network of figurative language?)

_____

_____

_____

3. without the fantasies of *getting stoned*

_____

4 Space Speaks

by Edward Hall

This selection is from The Silent Language, *a book-length study of non-verbal communication, which you might be assigned in a number of different social science courses.*

Word Highlights

bacteria microscopic organisms

delimit define; draw the limits of

environment surroundings

external outward

mammals warm-blooded animals

phylogenetic evolutionary

trespasser someone who goes onto someone else's land

vertebrates animals that have spines or backbones

Every living thing has a physical boundary that separates it from its external environment. Beginning with the bacteria and the simple cell and ending with man, every organism has a detectable limit which marks where it begins and ends. A short distance up the phylogenetic scale, however, another, non-physical boundary appears that exists outside the physical one. This new boundary is harder to delimit than the first but is just as real. We call this the "organism's territory." The act of laying claim to and defending a territory is termed territoriality. . . . In man, it becomes highly elaborated, as well as being very greatly differentiated from culture to culture.

Anyone who has had experience with dogs, particularly in a rural setting such as on ranches and farms, is familiar with the way in which the dog handles space. In the first place, the dog knows the limits of his master's "yard" and will defend it against encroachment. There are also certain places where he sleeps: a spot next to the fireplace, a spot in the kitchen, or one in the dining room if he is allowed there. In short, a dog has fixed points to which he returns time after time depending upon the occasion. One can also observe that dogs create zones around them. Depending upon his relationship to the dog and the zone he is in, a trespasser can evoke different behavior when he crosses the invisible lines which are meaningful to the dog.

This is particularly noticeable in females with puppies. A mother who has a new litter in a little-used barn will claim the barn

220

as her territory. When the door opens she may make a slight movement or stirring in one corner. Nothing else may happen as the intruder moves ten or fifteen feet into the barn. Then the dog may raise her head or get up, circle about, and lie down as another invisible boundary is crossed. One can tell about where the line is by withdrawing and watching when her head goes down. As additional lines are crossed, there will be other signals, a thumping of the tail, a low moan or a growl.

One can observe comparable behavior in other vertebrates—fish, birds, and mammals. Birds have well-developed territoriality, areas which they defend as their own and which they return to year after year. To those who have seen a robin come back to the same nest each year this will come as no surprise. Seals, dolphin, and whales are known to use the same breeding grounds. Individual seals have been known to come back to the same rock year after year.

Exercises

Understanding What You Have Read

_____ 1. The main idea of this selection is that (**4b**)
    a. a mother dog protects her puppies.
    b. birds have a strong sense of territory.
    c. most animals have a sense of territory.
    d. all cells have a physical boundary.

_____ 2. Every organism has (**5a**)
    a. physical boundaries.
    b. phylogenetic scales.
    c. a mother who protects it.
    d. a place it always returns to.

_____ 3. An "organism's territory" is (**5a**)
    a. a physical boundary.
    b. the actual space an organism takes up.
    c. a nonphysical boundary.
    d. legal ownership.

_____ 4. Female dogs with puppies will usually (**5a**)
    a. bite any intruder who comes near.
    b. growl when they see anyone.
    c. raise their young in barns.
    d. signal when you cross a boundary near them.

5. Put a checkmark next to things that are examples of a dog's territoriality. (**5a**)

  ____a. Dogs have fixed places where they sleep.
  ____b. Dogs bite people who hit them.
  ____c. Dogs run after cars.
  ____d. Dogs know the limits of the master's yard.
  ____e. Dogs sleep in fixed places.
  ____f. Dogs can be trained to attack.
  ____g. Dogs create zones around themselves.

6. In the following list, circle the answers that give the major details. (**5b**)

  a. Dogs sometimes live on ranches.
  b. Robins return to the same nest year after year.
  c. A mother dog stands up and walks around if a stranger gets too near her puppies.
  d. Dogs are sometimes allowed in dining rooms.
  e. Birds defend their territory.

____ 7. Which of the following statements best expresses the main idea of the sentence "In man, it becomes highly elaborated, as well as being very greatly differentiated from culture to culture"? (**4a**)

  a. Cultures are different.
  b. Human beings make up elaborate cultures.
  c. Human territoriality is very complex.
  d. All of the above.

____ 8. Which paragraph presents ideas in order of increasing importance and complexity? (**6a**)

  a. the paragraph beginning, "Every living thing . . ."
  b. the paragraph beginning, "Anyone who . . ."
  c. the paragraph beginning, "This is particularly . . ."
  d. the paragraph beginning, "One can observe . . ."

____ 9. Which paragraph uses both space and time order? (**6a**)

  a. the paragraph beginning, "Every living thing . . ."
  b. the paragraph beginning, "Anyone who . . ."
  c. the paragraph beginning, "This is particularly . . ."
  d. the paragraph beginning, "One can observe . . ."

____ 10. The writer uses a listing of details when he discusses (**6b**)

  a. man's elaborated territoriality.
  b. bacteria.

c. dogs in rural settings.
d. all of these.

Interpreting and Evaluating

1. Put a checkmark before those statements that we may reasonably infer from the selection. **(7)**
    ____a. Seals treat particular rocks as their territory.
    ____b. Human beings walk around when strangers are near.
    ____c. Female dogs want to protect their young.
    ____d. Skunks give off an odor if you get too near them.

2. Put a checkmark next to the valid conclusions that we can draw from information given in this selection. **(9)**
    ____a. More complicated animals have more complex needs for territory.
    ____b. Human beings express their territoriality in many ways.
    ____c. Horses have a sense of territoriality.
    ____d. Territoriality is the only reason why animals fight.

____3. If another dog were to come near the mother dog with her puppies, which of the following would you predict to happen? **(9)**
    a. The mother dog would not pay attention to the other dog.
    b. The mother dog would run up to and bite the other dog.
    c. The mother dog would play with the other dog.
    d. The mother dog would signal to the other dog that it should get out of her territory.

4. Which of the following would you, by generalizing, consider examples of territoriality? Put a checkmark next to those that are. **(10)**
    ____a. Human beings put up fences around their property.
    ____b. Arthur hangs out in the same place every evening.
    ____c. Carmine doesn't like to drink coffee.
    ____d. Birds build their nests from twigs, straw, and mud.
    ____e. Rattlesnakes will bite anybody who gets near them.
    ____f. Salmon swim upstream to return to the place where they were born.
    ____g. Pam keeps her money in the bank.
    ____h. Strangers stand farther apart than friends.

Vocabulary

Next to each of the vocabulary words from the selection in the left-hand column put the letter of the definition of the word that appears in the right-hand column. (2)

＿＿ 1. boundary	a. cause, bring out
＿＿ 2. organism	b. area
＿＿ 3. territoriality	c. line that separates
＿＿ 4. elaborated	d. a group of animal babies
＿＿ 5. differentiated	e. living thing
＿＿ 6. encroachment	f. complex
＿＿ 7. zone	g. moving back
＿＿ 8. evoke	h. varied, made different
＿＿ 9. litter	i. sense of personal space
＿＿10. withdrawing	j. intrusion, a trespassing

5 Momma

by Dick Gregory

In this passage from Nigger, *the autobiography of Dick Gregory, we see (and feel) the influence of the writer's mother on his family.*

Word Highlights

fat back   a strip of fat from the upper part of a side of pork

diabetes   a disease in which the body does not use carbohydrates (sugars) normally because of a lack of *insulin*, a hormone.

Like a lot of Negro kids, we never would have made it without our Momma. When there was no fatback to go with the beans, no socks to go with the shoes, no hope to go with tomorrow, she'd smile and say: "We ain't poor, we're just broke." Poor is a state of mind you never grow out of, but being broke is just a temporary condition. She always had a big smile, even when her legs and feet swelled from high blood pressure and she collapsed across the table with sugar diabetes. You have to smile twenty-four hours a day, Momma would say. If you walk through life showing the aggravation you've gone through, people will feel sorry for you, and they'll never respect you. She taught us that man has two ways out in life—laughing or crying. There's more hope in laughing. A man can fall down the stairs and lie there in such pain and horror that his own wife will collapse and faint at the sight. But if he can just hold back his pain for a minute she might be able to collect herself and call the doctor. It might mean the difference between his living to laugh again or dying there on the spot.

So you laugh, so you smile. Once a month the big gray relief truck would pull up in front of our house and Momma would flash that big smile and stretch out her hands. "Who else you know in this neighborhood gets this kind of service?" And we could all feel proud when the neighbors, folks who weren't on relief, folks who had Daddies in their houses, would come by the back porch for some of those hundred pounds of potatoes, for some sugar and flour and salty fish. We'd stand out there on the back porch and hand out the food like we were in charge of helping poor people, and then we'd take the food they brought us in return.

And Momma came home one hot summer day and found we'd been evicted, thrown out into the streetcar zone with all our orange-crate chairs and secondhand lamps. She flashed that big smile and dried our tears and bought some penny Kool-Aid. We stood out there and sold drinks to thirsty people coming off the streetcar, and we thought nobody knew we were kicked out— figured they thought we *wanted* to be there. And Momma went off to talk the landlord into letting us back in on credit.

But I wonder about my Momma sometimes, and all the other Negro mothers who got up at 6 A.M. to go to the white man's house with sacks over their shoes because it was so wet and cold. I wonder how they made it. They worked very hard for the man, they made his breakfast and they scrubbed his floors and they diapered his babies. They didn't have too much time for us.

I wonder about my Momma, who walked out of a white woman's clean house at midnight and came back to her own where the lights had been out for three months, and the pipes were frozen and the wind came in through the cracks. She'd have to make deals with the rats: leave some food out for them so they wouldn't gnaw on the doors or bite the babies. The roaches, they were just like part of the family.

I wonder how she felt telling those white kids she took care of to brush their teeth after they ate, to wash their hands after they peed. She could never tell her own kids because there wasn't soap or water back home.

I wonder how Momma felt when we came home from school with a list of vitamins and pills and cod liver oils the school nurse said we had to have. Momma would cry all night, and then go out and spend most of the rent money for pills. A week later, the white man would come for his eighteen dollars rent and Momma would plead with him to wait until tomorrow. She had lost her pocketbook. The relief check was coming. The white folks had some money for her. Tomorrow. I'd be hiding in the coal closet because there was only supposed to be two kids in the flat, and I could hear the rent man curse my Momma and call her a liar. And when he finally went away, Momma put the sacks on her shoes and went off to the rich white folks' house to dress the rich white kids so their mother could take them to a special baby doctor.

Momma had to take us to Homer G. Phillips, the free hospital for Negroes. We'd stand on line and wait for hours, smiling and Uncle Tomming every time a doctor or a nurse passed by. We'd feel good when one of them smiled back and didn't look at us as though we were dirty and had no right coming down there. All the doctors and nurses at Homer G. Phillips were Negro, too.

I remember one time when a doctor in white walked up and said: "What's wrong with him?" as if he didn't believe that anything was.

Momma looked at me and looked at him and shook her head. "I sure don't know, Doctor, but he cried all night long. Held his stomach."

"Bring him in and get his damned clothes off."

I was so mad at the way he was talking to my Momma that I bit down hard on the thermometer. It broke in my mouth. The doctor slapped me across the face.

"Both of you go and stand in the back of the line and wait your turn."

My Momma had to say: "I'm sorry, Doctor," and go to the back of the line. She had five other kids at home and she never knew when she'd have to bring another down to the City Hospital.

And those rich white folks Momma was so proud of. She'd sit around with the other women and they'd talk about how good their white folks were. They'd lie about how rich they were, what nice parties they gave, what good clothes they wore. And how they were going to be remembered in their white folks' wills. The next morning the white lady would say, "We're going on vacation for two months, Lucille, we won't be needing you until we get back." Damn. Two-month vacation without pay.

I wonder how my Momma stayed so good and beautiful in her soul when she worked seven days a week on swollen legs and feet, how she kept teaching us to smile and laugh when the house was dark and cold and she never knew when one of her hungry kids was going to ask about Daddy.

I wonder how she kept from teaching us hate when the social worker came around. She was a nasty bitch with a pinched face who said: "We have reason to suspect you are working, Miss Gregory, and you can be sure I'm going to check on you. We don't stand for welfare cheaters."

Momma, a welfare cheater. A criminal who couldn't stand to see her kids go hungry, or grow up in slums and end up mugging people in dark corners. I guess the system didn't want her to get off relief, the way it kept sending social workers around to be sure Momma wasn't trying to make things better.

I remember how that social worker would poke around the house, wrinkling her nose at the coal dust on the chilly linoleum floor, shaking her head at the bugs crawling over the dirty dishes in the sink. My Momma would have to stand there and make like she was too lazy to keep her own house clean. She could never let on that she spent all day cleaning another woman's house for two dollars and carfare. She would have to follow that nasty bitch around those drafty three rooms, keeping her fingers crossed that the telephone hidden in the closet wouldn't ring. Welfare cases weren't supposed to have telephones.

But Momma figured that some day the Gregory kids were going to get off North Taylor Street and into a world where they would have to compete with kids who grew up with telephones in their houses. She didn't want us to be at a disadvantage. She couldn't explain that to the social worker. And she couldn't explain that while she was out spoon-feeding somebody else's kids, she was worrying about her own kids, that she could rest her mind by picking up the telephone and calling us—to find out if we had bread for our baloney or baloney for our bread, to see if any of us had gotten run over by the streetcar while we played in the gutter, to make sure the house hadn't burnt down from the papers and magazines we stuffed in the stove when the coal ran out.

But sometimes when she called there would be no answer. Home was a place to be only when all other places were closed.

Exercises

Understanding What You Have Read

_____1. The main idea of this selection is (**4b**)
   a. to give a complete picture of the writer's mother.
   b. to tell the problems the family had with welfare.
   c. to show how much the writer owes to his mother.
   d. to tell how hard his mother worked.

_____2. The writer's mother was (**5a**)
   a. ashamed of being poor.
   b. concerned about how her children grew up.
   c. not sure about how to earn money.
   d. hot tempered.

_____3. The mother showed she was cheerful (**5a**)
   a. when they visited the doctor.
   b. when she went to work.
   c. when the social worker came around.
   d. when she explained to the children about the relief delivery.

____4. The mother showed concern for the children's future (5a)
    a. when they were evicted.
    b. when they traded food with neighbors.
    c. when she had a telephone put in.
    d. when she made the children laugh.

____5. The mother was polite and patient (5a)
    a. with the doctor.
    b. with the children.
    c. at the drugstore.
    d. with the schoolteacher.

____6. Which paragraph uses listing of details? (6b)
    a. the paragraph beginning, "So you laugh . . ."
    b. the paragraph beginning, "Like a lot of Negro kids . . ."
    c. the paragraph beginning, "And those rich white folks . . ."
    d. the paragraph beginning, "I wonder how she kept us from hate . . ."

____7. Which paragraph uses time order? (6a)
    a. the paragraph beginning, "Like a lot of Negro kids . . ."
    b. the paragraph beginning, "And those rich white folks . . ."
    c. the paragraph beginning, "I remember how that social worker would poke . . ."
    d. the paragraph beginning, "Momma, a welfare cheater . . ."

____8. Which two things are compared several times in the selection? (6a)
    a. the games the writer's family played and the games the white family played
    b. the doctors the white people went to and the doctors the black people went to
    c. the school the young children went to and the school the older children went to
    d. the time the mother spends on the white children and the time she spends caring for her own

9. Put a *T* in front of those statements that are true; put an *F* in front of those that are false. (5a)
    ____a. Sometimes the mother worked until midnight.
    ____b. Sometimes she phoned her own children from work.

_____c. The white people would always tell her about their plans a long time in advance.

_____d. She worked seven days a week.

_____e. She earned two dollars an hour.

_____f. The welfare department knew about her work.

_____g. She boasted about the people she worked for.

_____h. Her only job was to take care of the children.

Interpreting and Evaluating

_____ 1. From the story about how the mother handled the relief delivery, you can infer that (7)
   a. the mother taught the children how to be proud despite their problems.
   b. the neighbors wouldn't touch welfare food.
   c. she tried to keep the fact that they were on relief a secret from the children.
   d. the relief agency tried not to embarrass the people on relief.

_____ 2. What "lesson" can you infer from the story in the first paragraph about the man falling down the stairs? (7)
   a. Be careful walking down stairs.
   b. Falling down the stairs can be funny.
   c. If you show some strength, people help you more.
   d. None of these.

3. Put a checkmark next to those statements that you can infer from the selection. (7)
   _____a. The mother would have liked to spend more time with her own children.
   _____b. The social worker trusted the mother.
   _____c. The writer's father did not live with the family.
   _____d. The women would boast about the white people because the white people were so nice to them.
   _____e. The women boasted about the white people because the women didn't have much to boast about in their own lives.
   _____f. The white people took the mother's needs and feelings into consideration.

_____ 4. Uncle Tom is a kindly, old slave in Harriet Beecher Stowe's novel *Uncle Tom's Cabin*. In this selection, in the description of visits to the hospital, the phrase *Uncle Tomming* is used figuratively to mean (8)

    a. being kind.

    b. acting very old and sickly.

    c. begging.

    d. pretending you are grateful to the people who treat you badly.

_____ 5. In the second sentence, when the writer writes, "no fatback to go with the beans, no socks to go with the shoes, no hope to go with tomorrow," he is trying to show that (8)

    a. hope is as important as food and clothing.

    b. beans taste better with fatback.

    c. shoes without socks give you blisters.

    d. he didn't know the difference between things and feelings.

_____ 6. The writer uses phrases like "I wonder how Momma . . ." over and over again to show that (**11d**)

    a. his mother was a very confusing person.

    b. he is amazed by her strength in hard situations.

    c. he likes to spend hours wondering about her.

    d. the phrase sounds nice to him.

_____ 7. The mother's tone is cheerful when she says (**11d**)

    a. "Who else you know in this neighborhood gets this kind of service?"

    b. "Don't you worry about those roaches. They're just part of the family."

    c. "I'm sorry, Doctor."

    d. "Bring him in and get his damned clothes off."

_____ 8. The tone of "Momma, a welfare cheater" is (**11d**)

    a. factual and serious.

    b. cruel and nasty.

    c. ironic and angry.

    d. sad but hopeful.

_____ 9. You can conclude that the writer feels that the welfare system (9)

    a. does its best to help people in trouble.

    b. costs the government a lot of money.

    c. should give out more money to help people.

    d. keeps people from helping themselves.

___10. Put a checkmark next to the generalizations that you can
make about the whole selection. (10)

    ___a. The writer is deeply grateful to his mother.

    ___b. The writer feels his childhood was very unhappy.

    ___c. The writer had problems at school.

    ___d. The writer sees his mother as strong and coura-
geous.

    ___e. The writer sees no weaknesses in his mother.

    ___f. The writer was close to his brothers.

    ___g. The writer believes in the importance of good par-
ents.

    ___h. The writer thinks everyone should have a family.

Vocabulary

In each of the sentences below, fill in the word from the following
list that best fits the sentence's meaning. (2a)

fatback	aggravation
temporary	thermometer
linoleum	vitamin
diabetes	

1. People with _____ usually should not eat much
sugar.

2. _____ is made by drying and salting fat from a
hog.

3. I am going to get an ulcer from all this _____.

the _____.

4. The doctor wanted to take my temperature, but he broke

the _____.

5. The job was only _____; soon I had to find another.

6 Easy Job, Good Wages

by Jesus Colon

Through his personal experience, the writer lets us know that work is not always a positive experience.

Word Highlights

depreciating   decreasing the value of

galvanized   made of sheet metal coated with zinc

intermittent   on and off; now and then

mucilage   a type of glue for paper

tenaciously   stubbornly

This happened early in 1919. We were both out of work, my brother and I. He got up earlier to look for a job. When I woke up, he was already gone. So I dressed, went out and bought a copy of the *New York World* and turned its pages until I got to the "Help Wanted Unskilled" section of the paper. After much reading and re-reading the same columns, my attention was held by a small advertisement. It read: "Easy job. Good wages. No experience necessary." This was followed by a number and street on the west side of lower Manhattan. It sounded like the job I was looking for. Easy job. Good wages. Those four words revolved in my brain as I was travelling toward the address indicated in the advertisement. Easy job. Good wages. Easy job. Good wages. Easy . . .

The place consisted of a small front office and a large loft on the floor of which I noticed a series of large galvanized tubs half filled with water out of which I noticed protruding the necks of many bottles of various sizes and shapes. Around these tubs there were a number of workers, male and female, sitting on small wooden benches. All had their hands in the water of the tub, the left hand holding a bottle and with the thumb nail of the right hand scratching the labels.

The foreman found a vacant stool for me around one of the tubs of water. I asked why a penknife or a small safety razor could not be used instead of the thumb nail to take off the old labels from the bottles. I was expertly informed that knives or razors would scratch the glass thus depreciating the value of the bottles when they were to be sold.

I sat down and started to use my thumb nail on one bottle. The water had somewhat softened the transparent mucilage used to attach the label to the bottle. But the softening did not work out uniformly somehow. There were always pieces of label that for some obscure reason remained affixed to the bottles. It was on those pieces of labels tenaciously fastened to the bottles that my right hand thumb nail had to work overtime. As the minutes passed I noticed that the coldness of the water started to pass from my hand to my body giving me intermittent body shivers that I tried to conceal with the greatest of effort from those sitting beside me. My hands became deadly clean and tiny little wrinkles started to show especially at the tip of my fingers. Sometimes I stopped a few seconds from scratching the bottles, to open and close my fists in rapid movements in order to bring blood to my hands. But almost as soon as I placed them in the water they became deathly pale again.

But these were minor details compared with what was happening to the thumb of my right hand. For a delicate, boyish thumb, it was growing by the minute into a full blown tomato colored finger. It was the only part of my right hand remaining blood red. I started to look at the workers' thumbs. I noticed that these particular fingers on their right hands were unusually developed with a thick layer of corn-like surface at the top of their right thumb. The nails on their thumbs looked coarser and smaller than on the other fingers—thumb and nail having become one and the same thing—a primitive unnatural human instrument especially developed to detach hard pieces of labels from wet bottles immersed in galvanized tubs.

After a couple of hours I had a feeling that my thumb nail was going to leave my finger and jump into the cold water in the tub. A numb pain imperceptibly began to be felt coming from my right thumb. Then I began to feel such pain as if coming from a finger bigger than all of my body.

After three hours of this I decided to quit fast. I told the foreman so, showing him my swollen finger. He figured I had earned 69 cents at 23 cents an hour.

Early in the evening I met my brother in our furnished room. We started to exchange experiences of our job hunting for the day. "You know what?" my brother started, "early in the morning I went to work where they take labels off old bottles—with your right hand thumb nail. . . . Somewhere on the West Side of Lower Manhattan. I only stayed a couple of hours. 'Easy job . . . Good wages' . . . they said. The person who wrote that ad must have had a great sense of humor." And we both had a hearty laugh that evening when I told my brother that I also went to work at that same place later in the day.

Now when I see ads reading, "Easy job. Good wages," I just smile an ancient, tired, knowing smile.

Exercises

Understanding What You Have Read

___1. The main idea of the selection is that (**4b**)
  a. the work at the bottle cleaning company was too unpleasant to be worth the money.
  b. the people who worked at the bottle cleaning company all had misshapen fingers.
  c. the foreman was a cruel man.
  d. want ads don't always tell the truth.

2. Write *maj* next to major details and *min* next to minor details. (**5b**)
  ___a. The writer, Jesus Colon, lived with his brother.
  ___b. The factory was on the west side of Manhattan.
  ___c. The ad was in the *New York World.*
  ___d. The ad said, "Easy job. Good wages. No experience necessary."
  ___e. The water did not soften all the glue.
  ___f. The writer had to scrape off the glue with his thumb nail.
  ___g. His thumb swelled and turned red.
  ___h. The tubs were galvanized.
  ___i. He earned 69 cents for three hours work.
  ___j. The brother was in the furnished room.
  ___k. The brother tried and quit the same job.

3. Put a *T* next to the statements that are true and an *F* next to the ones that are false. (**5a**)
  ___a. The writer looked at the "Help Wanted Skilled" column.
  ___b. The bottles were covered all the way over the top with water.
  ___c. Jesus Colon sat on a stool.
  ___d. Scratched bottles are worth less than bottles without scratches.
  ___e. The water made his hands wrinkle.
  ___f. Other people were able to do the work with no problems.

——g. All of his fingers except the right thumb turned pale.

——h. The foreman didn't believe that the writer's thumb was hurting.

——i. The foreman cheated the writer on his pay.

——4. The incident is told in (**6a**)

a. time order.

b. space order.

c. order of importance.

d. no real order.

——5. Which paragraph makes a comparison? (**6c**)

a. the paragraph beginning, "The place consisted of . . ."

b. the paragraph beginning, "The foreman found a . . ."

c. the paragraph beginning, "But these were minor details . . ."

d. the paragraph beginning, "After three hours . . ."

Interpreting and Evaluating

—— 1. From the brother's words, "The person who wrote that ad must have had a great sense of humor," you can infer that the brother (**7**)

a. found the work funny.

b. found the job as hard and underpaid as the writer did.

c. knew a lot about ad writing.

d. liked the person who wrote the ad.

—— 2. Now that you have read the whole selection, what can you infer from the sentence, "I was expertly informed that knives or razors would scratch the glass thus depreciating the value of the bottles when they were to be sold"? (**7**)

a. Glass bottles are very valuable.

b. The experts understand how to do the best job for everyone.

c. The company cared more what happened to the bottles than what happened to the workers.

d. Cleaning bottles is a complex job.

—— 3. The tone of the sentence quoted in question 2 is (**11d**)

a. comic.

b. bitter.

c. friendly.

d. violent.

_____ 4. The title "Easy Job, Good Wages" is (**11d**)
   a. ironic.
   b. accurate.
   c. confusing.
   d. frightening.

5. Put a checkmark next to the conclusions you can safely reach from the selection. (**9**)
   _____a. The writer now believes everything he reads in the paper.
   _____b. The writer distrusts ads that sound too good to be true.
   _____c. He thought the bottle-cleaning job was a fair job.
   _____d. He thought the bottle-cleaning company took unfair advantage of its workers.
   _____e. He thought the pay was good.
   _____f. He and his brother were fooled because they were innocent.
   _____g. He knows better than to be fooled by an ad again.

_____ 6. In building up the details of what was happening to his hands and right thumb, the writer (**11d**)
   a. makes you stop reading.
   b. makes you wonder whether he will survive.
   c. shows you how hard and painful the work was.
   d. is trying to make you scared.

_____ 7. The fact that the brother was fooled into trying the same job helps you make the generalization that (**10**)
   a. the writer's family is not very clever.
   b. the brothers told each other about the job before.
   c. many other innocent people were probably fooled by the ad.
   d. the bottle company was the only company hiring workers in the city.

_____ 8. The writer's overall technique is (**11d**)
   a. to argue for his ideas directly.
   b. to use a personal example to get at his ideas indirectly.
   c. to use gory details to frighten the readers.
   d. to tell a personal story to entertain the readers.

_____ 9. What general attitude does the writer have about the whole experience? (**11d**)
   a. Get the bosses before they get you.
   b. I was really stupid to get involved with this.

2

8 Jesus Colon

c. You have to make a living somehow.
d. Live and learn.

10. Put a checkmark next to those generalizations you can safely make on the basis of the selection. (**10**)
——a. Want ads sometimes lie.
——b. All bosses are cruel to their workers.
——c. There is no way to earn an honest living.
——d. It pays to think twice before you take a job.
——e. Some jobs can be very unpleasant.
——f. Not all companies care what happens to their workers.
——g. Some workers stay at unpleasant jobs, and some workers quit.

11. Generalizing, you can assume that the writer is in favor of which of the following? Put a checkmark next to the laws and proposed laws you think he would support. (**10**)
——a. truth in advertising
——b. minimum wages
——c. lower taxes for businesses
——d. compensation for on-the-job injuries
——e. the right to form labor unions
——f. getting rid of all safety precautions
——g. outlawing glass bottles
——h. improved work conditions

Vocabulary

Put the letter of the definition in the right-hand column next to the appropriate word in the left-hand column. (**2**)

——1. immersed   a. sticking out
——2. imperceptibly b. sold
——3. loft   c. turned around
——4. protruding   d. a part of a factory building
——5. revolved   e. clear, so that you can see through
——6. transparent   f. evenly
——7. uniformly   g. covered with liquid
                    h. so slowly that you can't notice it

© 1981 Houghton Mifflin Company.

7 Apartment B

by Shirley Lim

In cities we live very close to our neighbors—perhaps closer than we would like. This poem discusses the ways in which we keep our distance.

Word Highlights

inaudible   not possible to hear

We hear the others moving
Night after night. One sneezes,
Another answers, a phone rings,
But we do not wish to know
How they live. Having them so close
Is painful enough. We do not want
To hear them speak: only hear
Their inaudible voices,
Like their music and company,
Contained in boxes; hear only
Evening sounds of barks and sirens
To remind us we are human.
Any other speech may break
The bond which keeps us apart.

Exercises

Understanding What You Have Read

_____1. The main idea of this poem is that (**4b**)
  a. when you live close to your neighbors, you learn all their secrets.
  b. neighbors want to talk with the writer, but she does not want to answer.
  c. the writer has to cut herself off emotionally from her neighbors because she and they live too close together.
  d. living in an apartment can be too noisy for someone to fall asleep.

_____2. The main idea of the poem is (**4b**)
  a. stated directly in the first sentence.
  b. stated directly in the last sentence.

    c. stated directly in the middle.

    d. implied by the whole poem.

——3. Why does the writer say, "we do not wish to know how they live"? (**5a**)

    a. She already knows too much about them.

    b. She thinks the neighbors are too noisy and not polite.

    c. She does not like the things they talk about.

    d. None of these.

  4. Put a checkmark next to the things the writer knows that the people in the other apartment do. (**5a**)

    ——a. eat dinner

    ——b. talk

    ——c. play music

    ——d. have big parties

    ——e. have guests

    ——f. watch television

    ——g. own a dog

    ——h. sneeze

    ——i. walk around

——5. In lines 6 through 11, in what order are the details of sound arranged? (**6a**)

    a. space order, moving away from the neighbors

    b. time order, starting with what happens when the neighbor speaks

    c. order of importance, toward what the writer would prefer to hear

    d. both a and c

——6. The last sentence of the poem (lines 13 and 14)

    a. sums up the poem by giving the effect of everything before.

    b. gives the writer's opinion of her neighbors.

    c. changes the subject of the poem.

    d. states the main idea of the poem.

Interpreting and Evaluating

  1. The *others* mentioned in the first line clearly means the neighbors. What clues let us infer this? (**7**)

_____

_____

_____2. We may safely infer that the writer lives (7)
     a. in a private house in the country.
     b. in a private house in the city.
     c. in an apartment building in the city.
     d. in a resort hotel in the country.

_____3. We may conclude that the writer feels that (9)
     a. the neighbors are unpleasant people.
     b. living in an apartment goes against the need for privacy.
     c. if you live in an apartment, you should get to know your neighbors.
     d. the people next door do not want to get to know her.

_____4. We may predict that, if she meets her neighbors on the street, the writer will (9)
     a. invite the neighbors over for dinner.
     b. have a long conversation.
     c. turn her back to them or cross to the other side of the street to avoid them.
     d. say hello politely and move on.

_____5. Why does the writer use the word *we* instead of *I*? (11d)
     a. There are two people living in her apartment.
     b. She is too modest to talk directly about herself.
     c. She wants to suggest that many people share her experience.
     d. She has a split personality.

6. Put a check next to the statements that accurately represent the writer's *opinion.* (11a)
     _____a. "A phone rings."
     _____b. "We do not wish to know how they live."
     _____c. "Having them so close is painful enough."
     _____d. We "hear only evening sounds of barks and sirens."
     _____e. "Any other speech may break the bond which keeps us apart."

7. Have you ever had the experience the writer is talking about? Do you think she describes a good way to respond to neighbors? Write a journal entry on your opinion about the emotions described in the poem. (11c)

_____

_____

_____

_____

_____

_____

_____

_____

_____

Vocabulary

——1. The word *bond* has several meanings. Which meaning is
     used in the phrase "the bond which keeps us apart"? (**2a**)
     a. money paid as bail
     b. a written promise to pay back a loan
     c. something drawing two things together
     d. a glue or cement

——2. In what way is there a bond between neighbors? (**2a**)
     a. They live close together.
     b. They have emotional ties.
     c. They share social contacts.
     d. They share political and economic interests.

——3. In what way does the bond keep them apart? (**2a**)
     a. They refuse to go to each other's parties.
     b. They complain to the landlord about each other's noise.
     c. They get into quarrels over noise.
     d. They keep their emotional distance.

——4. When the writer says that we "only hear their inaudible
     voices, like their music and their company, contained in a
     box," she uses the word *box* (**2c**)
     a. to show that the neighbor's apartment is like a box.
     b. to suggest that she makes a tape recording of the sounds
        and puts the tape in a box.
     c. to suggest that, emotionally, she keeps the neighbors
        distant by putting them in a mental box.
     d. both a and c

——5. In the poem, the word *others* denotes neighbors. What additional connotation might the word *others* have in the poem? (**2c**)

  a. many, many neighbors
  b. people threatening to reach the mind and emotions of the writer herself
  c. shadowy people, almost like ghosts to the writer
  d. b and c

8 The Perennial Lover

by Jovita González

This short story presents an amusing view of why a man writes love letters.

Word Highlights

barometer an instrument used to predict weather changes

dejected low in spirit; downhearted

immensity largeness; hugeness of size

rejection refusal

sentiments feelings

splay spread out; spread wide

unkempt sloppy

Las hijas de las madres que amé tanto
me besan ya como se besa un santo.

The daughters of the mothers I loved so well
They kiss me now as they would kiss a saint.

Carlitos had made love to two generations of girls. As one crop of girls grew up to maidenhood, Carlitos declared his sentiments to each in turn. One by one they outgrew him, married, and had girls of their own. As the second crop came on, he remained ever-ready to offer his heart and hand to anyone who would listen to him.

He was not bad-looking. He was tall and lanky, and had it not been for his coconut head, pivoted on some eight inches of neck, his triangular ears, and big hands and splay feet, he would have been handsome. His moustache was the barometer for his emotions. When he was not in love, it hung limp and unkempt, but in the spring, when the world was aglow with prairie flowers and all Nature invited him to love, it was waxed and triumphant. I remember his coming to the ranch one day and calling my uncle aside most mysteriously.

"Look, Francisco," he said, displaying a package of ruled paper with carnations on one corner, "beautiful, isn't it? This year the carnations are bound to work. Last year I used violets and did not get a single answer. That's because violets do not inspire love; but wait until they see these carnations. I will get so many replies that it will be difficult for me to decide which girl I want. And look! This is what I am going to say."

Then he showed my uncle the circular which he sent every year, his declaration of love, for he always used the same, whether he sent it by mail or uttered it, one hand over his heart and eyes looking up to heaven for inspiration: "I can no longer bear the pain which devours my heart, and I would like to know whether my love is returned or not. Should I be so unfortunate as to be rejected, then I will put between us the immensity of the sea." But in spite of many rejections and more ignorings, he never left on his threatened voyages. He might for a few days go about in a mood suitable to a rejected lover, but he soon forgot.

One May, not long ago, I was back at the ranch and in the store when Carlitos entered. He was the most dejected-looking figure imaginable; his once beautiful moustache was the most melancholy part about him. Between sighs he told the clerk what he wanted. With another sigh he left the store.

"What's the matter with him?" I asked my uncle.

"Caught at last," he answered with a laugh. "Last spring, as usual, he distributed his love letters, and much to his astonishment, he was accepted by Lola, Tio Felipe's thirty-year-old daughter. When he opened the letter, I thought he had received a death notice. He turned as pale as a ghost, and I had to hold him up. When he had somewhat recovered, he said to me in a choking voice, 'Look, look.' I looked and read, 'I am greatly honored by your offer, which I am happy to accept with my father's consent.'

" 'I must congratulate you upon your good fortune,' I said, offering my hand.

" 'But you do not understand,' he said between sobs. 'I never meant to marry at all. I merely sent those letters because it gave me pleasure. Whatever shall I do in the spring now?' "

And this was spring, and his first year of married life.

Exercises

Understanding What You Have Read

_____ 1. The main point of this selection is that (**4b**)
   a. a man who offers to love many women may have his offer returned in an unexpected way.
   b. love is filled with disappointments.
   c. nature invites us to love and we respond with all our hearts.
   d. writing letters can get a man in trouble!

2. In the blank spaces for each statement below, write *maj* if the detail is major and *min* if the detail is minor. (**5b**)

      ___a. Carlitos made love to two generations of girls.

      ___b. He was tall and lanky.

      ___c. His moustache hung limp when he was not in love but was waxed and fine when he was in love.

      ___d. A clerk served Carlitos in the store.

      ___e. Lola accepted Carlitos' offer.

      ___f. Violets do not inspire love as carnations do.

3. Put *T* before each true statement and *F* before each statement that is false. (**5a**)

      ___a. Carlitos likes Mexican women only.

      ___b. He speaks or writes his offers of love.

      ___c. He is very handsome.

      ___d. He gets many replies to his offers.

      ___e. If his love is not returned, he runs away.

      ___f. He makes love in the spring only because it gives him pleasure.

      ___g. Carlitos is a saint.

___4. The key idea of the two lines from the song at the beginning of the selection is (**4a**)

    a. "I am now religious because of love."

    b. "I love the mothers' daughters."

    c. "I loved the mothers and now the daughters worship me too."

    d. "I am a saint about love."

___5. When Carlitos says or writes to a woman that, if she rejects him, he will put between them the immensity of the sea, he probably means that (**4a**)

    a. he will drown himself.

    b. he will take her for a day at the seashore.

    c. he will go away to a country across the ocean.

    d. both a and c are possible.

Interpreting and Evaluating

___ 1. We may infer from Carlitos' appearance at the store that he is (**7**)

    a. delighted at his luck.

    b. tired.

    c. hungry.

    d. unhappy.

_____ 2. We may infer about Lola, Tio Felipe's daughter, that she is (**7**)
   a. attractive and charming.
   b. deeply in love with Carlitos.
   c. not married at thirty for good reason.
   d. drawn to Carlitos by his appearance.

_____ 3. Carlitos believes that the kind of stationery he uses to write his love letters (**7, 10**)
   a. is very important.
   b. is less important than the ink he uses.
   c. is less important than the words he writes on it.
   d. must be bought at a local store.

_____ 4. Next spring Carlitos will probably (**9**)
   a. make love again to all the local girls.
   b. change his declaration of love.
   c. ignore Lola.
   d. none of these.

_____ 5. We may conclude that Carlitos (**10**)
   a. did not marry Lola because her father disapproved.
   b. married Lola because he was a man of honor.
   c. remained a bachelor for the rest of his life.
   d. none of these.

_____ 6. A generalization we can safely draw from this passage is that (**10**)
   a. if you are old, don't make love to someone younger.
   b. if you offer to love anyone, be prepared for results you might not have expected.
   c. unmarried women of thirty accept whatever offers of love they can get.
   d. men who love without being sincere deserve whatever punishment they get.

_____ 7. In regard to the lines from the song, Carlitos' experiences (**9, 10**)
   a. are exactly what the lines suggest.
   b. are quite different from what the lines suggest.
   c. have nothing to do with the lines.
   d. show that songwriters know about love.

_____ 8. In general, we may say about Carlitos that (**10**)
   a. he was eager to get married.
   b. he was not eager for responsibilities.

    c. he hated women.
    d. he was crazy.

___ 9. If Carlitos could have his way, he would probably (9)
    a. marry more than one woman.
    b. have many children.
    c. leave the ranch for the big city.
    d. never have married.

___ 10. The writer treats Carlitos (11d)
    a. in a kind but slightly humorous way.
    b. in a nasty way.
    c. as a suffering victim of a rigid society.
    d. with no respect.

11. Explain the meaning of the following figurative expressions. (8)
    a. "As the second crop came on . . ." (paragraph 1)

_____

_____

    b. "coconut head" (paragraph 2) _____

_____

    c. "His moustache was the barometer . . ." (paragraph 2)

_____

    d. ". . . had received a death notice." (paragraph 7) ____

_____

_____

    e. "as pale as a ghost . . ." (paragraph 7) _____

_____

    f. "a choking voice . . ." (paragraph 7) _____

_____

Vocabulary

For each word in italics, write a definition in your own words on the blank line. Use whatever clues you can find to figure out the meaning. Return to the paragraphs if necessary.

1. grew up to *maidenhood* _____

2. *declared* his sentiments _____

3. it hung *limp* _____

4. world was *aglow* _____

5. *displaying* a package _____

6. violets do not *inspire* love _____

7. showed my uncle the *circular* _____

8. *uttered* it _____

9. more *ignorings* _____

10. threatened *voyages* _____

11. *suitable* to a rejected lover _____

12. the most *melancholy* _____

13. much to his *astonishment* _____

14. my father's *consent* _____

15. *offering* my hand _____

9 The Paleolithic Age

by John P. McKay, Bennett D. Hill, and
John Buckler

This article gives us a picture of what life was like for the forerunners of human beings a long time ago. The lives of cave dwellers may have been more interesting than you imagine.

Word Highlights

aggressive starting fights or attacks

depicted drawn, portrayed

ferocious savage, fierce

grimmest most horrible

Homo sapiens the scientific name for human beings; literally, "wise men"

lore teaching

mammoth an ancient relative of the elephant, having long tusks and a hairy body

Neanderthaler an ancient relative of modern humans, but shorter, hairier, and less intelligent

Paleolithic the era during which people began using stone tools

predators animals that hunt

preyed hunted in order to eat

symbolic logic thinking through the use of signs and symbols

Life in the Paleolithic Age was perilous and uncertain at best. Survival depended on the success of the hunt, but the hunt often brought sudden and violent death. In some instances, Paleolithic peoples were their own worst enemies. At times they fought each other for control of hunting grounds, and some early hunters played an important part in wiping out less aggressive peoples. On occasion Paleolithic peoples seem to have preyed on one another. One of the grimmest indications that Neanderthal Man was at times cannibalistic comes from a cave in Yugoslavia, where investigators found human bones burned and split open.

On the other hand, the peoples of the Paleolithic Age were responsible for some striking accomplishments. Most obvious is the use of the stone implements that gave the period its name. The ability to make and use tools gave Paleolithic peoples the means to change their environment. They could compete with larger and stronger animals and could hunt animals faster and more ferocious than themselves. In the frozen wastes of the north, they hunted

© 1981 Houghton Mifflin Company.

the mammoth, the woolly rhinoceros, and the reindeer. In milder southern climates, they hunted deer, badgers, squirrels, and rabbits. The demands of the hunt sharpened their wits. They supplemented their diet by collecting fruits, nuts, and seeds, and in the process they discovered the plant world around them. Paleolithic peoples learned to control fire and to make clothes from the skins of their prey.

Paleolithic peoples were also world travelers. Before the dawn of history bands of *Homo sapiens* flourished in Europe, Africa, and Asia, and they had crossed into the continents of North America and South America and had landed in Australia. By the end of the Paleolithic Age, there were very few "undiscovered" areas in the world.

The most striking accomplishments of Paleolithic peoples were intellectual. The development of the human brain made possible thought and symbolic logic. An invisible world opened up to *Homo sapiens*. Unlike animals, whose behavior is the result of instinct, Paleolithic peoples used reason to govern their actions. Thought and language permitted the lore and experience of the old to be passed on to the young. The Neanderthalers developed the custom of burying their dead and of placing offerings with the dead, perhaps in the belief that in some way life continued after death.

Paleolithic peoples produced the first art. They decorated the walls of their caves with paintings of animals and scenes of the hunt. They also began to fashion clay models of pregnant women and of animals. These first examples of art illustrate the way in which early men and women communicated to others their experience of the past and hope for the future. Many of the paintings, such as those at Altamira in Spain and Lascaux in France, are found deep in the caves, in areas not easily accessible. These areas were probably places of ritual and initiation, where young men were taken when they joined the ranks of the hunters. They were also places of magic. The animals depicted on the walls were either those hunted for food or those feared as predators. Many are shown wounded by spears or arrows; others are pregnant. The early artists may have been expressing the hope that the hunt would be successful and game plentiful. By portraying the animals as realistically as possible, the artists and hunters may have hoped to gain power over them.

Exercises

Understanding What You Have Read

___1. The main idea of this selection is that (**4**)
    a. Neanderthalers were very much like us.
    b. life in the Paleolithic Age was always very pleasant.
    c. Paleolithic people did some remarkable things.
    d. both b and c.

    2. Put a *T* before those statements that are true according to the selection. Put an *F* before those statements that are false. Put an *X* before those statements that can't be affirmed or denied on the basis of the passage. (**5a**)
    ___a. Paleolithic people collected fruit.
    ___b. Paleolithic people rode horses.
    ___c. Humans have always known how to use tools.
    ___d. Paleolithic people produced the first art.
    ___e. America remained undiscovered until modern times.
    ___f. Neanderthalers ate dead people instead of burying them.
    ___g. Hunters are smarter than other people.
    ___h. Stone tools made humans faster and more aggressive.
    ___i. *Homo sapiens* can see things that are invisible to us.

    3. Put a checkmark next to each thing or activity that the Paleolithic people were the first to discover. (**5a**)
    ___a. how to control fire
    ___b. reading and writing
    ___c. hunting
    ___d. painting
    ___e. sculpture
    ___f. tools
    ___g. magic
    ___h. death
    ___i. North America
    ___j. seeds

___4. What climate did Paleolithic people inhabit? (**5a**)
    a. cold, frozen wastes
    b. hot jungles

    c. damp caves

    d. all climates

Interpreting and Evaluating

_____1. The authors believe that the most striking accomplishments of Paleolithic people were (**7**)

    a. artistic.

    b. intellectual.

    c. religious.

    d. physical.

_____2. We can infer that the Paleolithic people's ability to reason and use symbolic logic enabled them to (**7**)

    a. discover caves.

    b. imagine things that they had not actually seen.

    c. find good-tasting foods.

    d. kill other people.

_____3. Cave paintings were designed for what purpose?

    a. to decorate the drab walls of a Neanderthaler's home

    b. to control magically the outcome of future hunts

    c. to record great hunts for future generations

    d. both b and c.

_____4. A possible generalization about the Paleolithic person's belief in an afterlife is that it came about as a result of (**10**)

    a. seeing what happened to dead people.

    b. seeing a person's knowledge survive him or her.

    c. thinking about existence and reasoning symbolically.

    d. magic.

_____5. It is the author's belief that (**11a**)

    a. caves were part of early religious ceremonies.

    b. Neanderthalers invented the wheel.

    c. Paleolithic people invented the bow and arrow.

    d. cannibalism by early humans was necessary.

_____6. The authors contrast the hardship of life in Paleolithic times with (**6c**)

    a. the remarkable progress these people made.

    b. the incredible brutality of Neanderthalers.

    c. the beauty of paintings found in Lascaux.

    d. none of these.

___7. The authors' tone in this passage is (**11a**)
   a. humorous.
   b. angry.
   c. factual.
   d. sentimental.

Vocabulary

For each word in italics in the left-hand column, select the best meaning from the right-hand column.

___1. *supplemented* their diets
___2. life was *perilous*
___3. not easily *accessible*
___4. using stone *implements*
___5. animals depicted *realistically*
___6. man was *cannibalistic*
___7. *investigators* found
___8. places of *ritual*

a. ate other people
b. people who examine systematically
c. added to
d. true to life
e. dangerous
f. tools
g. gotten to; reached
h. religious ceremonies
i. food gathering
j. groups

10 My Life with R. H. Macy

by Shirley Jackson

The writer, best-known for her horror stories, tells us humorously about the horrors of working for a large department store.

Word Highlights

dividend a bonus

frock a dress

lingerie women's undergarments

segregate to place apart; to isolate

And the first thing they did was segregate me. They segregated me from the only person in the place I had even a speaking acquaintance with; that was a girl I had met going down the hall who said to me: "Are you as scared as I am?" And when I said, "Yes," she said, "I'm in lingerie, what are you in?" and I thought for a while and then said, "Spun glass," which was as good an answer as I could think of, and she said, "Oh. Well, I'll meet you here in a sec." And she went away and was segregated and I never saw her again.

Then they kept calling my name and I kept trotting over to wherever they called it and they would say ("They" all this time being startlingly beautiful young women in tailored suits and with short-clipped hair), "Go with Miss Cooper, here. She'll tell you what to do." All the women I met my first day were named Miss Cooper. And Miss Cooper would say to me: "What are you in?" and I had learned by that time to say, "Books," and she would say, "Oh, well, then, you belong with Miss Cooper here," and then she would call "Miss Cooper?" and another young woman would come and the first one would say, "13-3138 here belongs with you," and Miss Cooper would say, "What is she in?" and Miss Cooper would answer, "Books," and I would go away and be segregated again.

Then they taught me. They finally got me segregated into a classroom, and I sat there for a while all by myself (that's how far segregated I was) and then a few other girls came in, all wearing tailored suits (I was wearing a red velvet afternoon frock) and we sat down and they taught us. They gave us each a big book with R. H. Macy written on it, and inside this book were pads of little sheets saying (from left to right): "Comp. keep for ref. cust. d.a.

no. or c.t. no. salesbook no. salescheck no. clerk no. dept. date M."
After M there was a long line for Mr. or Mrs. and the name, and
then it began again with "No. item. class. at price. total." And
down at the bottom was written ORIGINAL and then again, "Comp.
keep for ref.," and "Paste yellow gift stamp here." I read all this
very carefully. Pretty soon a Miss Cooper came, who talked for a
little while on the advantages we had in working at Macy's, and she
talked about the salesbooks, which it seems came apart into a sort
of road map and carbons and things. I listened for a while, and
when Miss Cooper wanted us to write on the little pieces of paper,
I copied from the girl next to me. That was training.

Finally someone said we were going on the floor, and we de-
scended from the sixteenth floor to the first. We were in groups of
six by then, all following Miss Cooper doggedly and wearing little
tags saying BOOK INFORMATION. I never did find out what that
meant. Miss Cooper said I had to work on the special sale counter,
and showed me a little book called *The Stage-Struck Seal*, which it
seemed I would be selling. I had gotten about halfway through it
before she came back to tell me I had to stay with my unit.

I enjoyed meeting the time clock, and spent a pleasant half-
hour punching various cards standing around, and then someone
came in and said I couldn't punch the clock with my hat on. So I had
to leave, bowing timidly at the time clock and its prophet, and I
went and found out my locker number, which was 1773, and my
time-clock number, which was 712, and my cash-box number,
which was 1336, and my cash-register number, which was 253, and
my cash-register-drawer number, which was K, and my cash-
register-drawer-key number, which was 872, and my department
number, which was 13. I wrote all these numbers down. And that
was my first day.

My second day was better. I was officially on the floor. I stood
in a corner of a counter, with one hand possessively on *The Stage-
Struck Seal*, waiting for customers. The counter head was named
13-2246, and she was very kind to me. She sent me to lunch three
times, because she got me confused with 13-6454 and 13-3141. It
was after lunch that a customer came. She came over and took one
of my stage-struck seals, and said "How much is this?" I opened
my mouth and the customer said "I have a D.A. and I will have this
sent to my aunt in Ohio. Part of that D.A. I will pay for with a book
dividend of 32 cents, and the rest of course will be on my account.
Is this book price-fixed?" That's as near as I can remember what
she said. I smiled confidently, and said "Certainly; will you wait
just one moment?" I found a little piece of paper in a drawer under

the counter: it had "Duplicate Triplicate" printed across the front in big letters. I took down the customer's name and address, her aunt's name and address, and wrote carefully across the front of the duplicate triplicate "1 Stg. Strk. Sl." Then I smiled at the customer again and said carelessly: "That will be seventy-five cents." She said "But I have a D.A." I told her that all D.A.'s were suspended for the Christmas rush, and she gave me seventy-five cents, which I kept. Then I rang up a "No Sale" on the cash register and I tore up the duplicate triplicate because I didn't know what else to do with it.

Later on another customer came and said "Where would I find a copy of Ann Rutherford Gwynn's *He Came Like Thunder*?" and I said "In medical books, right across the way," but 13-2246 said "Right down this aisle, in dictionaries." The customer went away and I said to 13-2246 that her guess was as good as mine, anyway, and she stared at me and explained that philosophy, social sciences and Bertrand Russell were all kept in dictionaries.

So far I haven't been back to Macy's for my third day, because that night when I started to leave the store, I fell down the stairs and tore my stockings and the doorman said that if I went to my department head Macy's would give me a new pair of stockings and I went back and I found Miss Cooper and she said, "Go to the adjuster on the seventh floor and give him this," and she handed me a little slip of pink paper and on the bottom of it was printed "Comp. keep for ref. cust. d.a. no. or c.t. no. salesbook no. salescheck no. clerk no. dept. date M." And after M, instead of a name, she had written 13-3138. I took the little pink slip and threw it away and went to the fourth floor and bought myself a pair of stockings for $.69 and then I came down and went out the customers' entrance.

I wrote Macy's a long letter, and I signed it with all my numbers added together and divided by 11,700, which is the number of employees in Macy's. I wonder if they miss me.

Exercises

Understanding What You Have Read

_____ 1. The writer's main sense of her experience wtih R. H. Macy is one of (**4b**)
   a. confidence and success.
   b. friendliness and joy.

    c. loneliness and confusion.

    d. understanding and acceptance.

_____2. The main idea of the first paragraph is that (**4b**)

    a. she met a friend who worked in lingerie.

    b. they segregated her.

    c. she went to work for a department store.

    d. she and her friend were both scared.

_____3. The main idea of the second paragraph is that (**4b**)

    a. she worked in books.

    b. many women were named Miss Cooper.

    c. they kept calling her.

    d. she kept going wherever they told her to.

   4. In the third paragraph, one sentence clearly states the main idea of the paragraph. Copy that sentence here. (**4b**)

_____

_____5. Among the examples the writer lists to illustrate how numbers control her life, which one is *not* included in the selection? (**5, 6b**)

    a. her checkbook balance

    b. the cash-register-drawer-key number

    c. the time clock

    d. all of these

_____6. What is a *D.A.*? (**5a**)

    a. a departmental assistant

    b. a debt account

    c. a daily average

    d. We never find out what a *D.A.* is.

_____7. The next-to-last paragraph uses which paragraph pattern? (**6**)

    a. comparison and contrast

    b. listing of details

    c. cause and effect

    d. order of importance

_____8. According to the next-to-last paragraph, why did the woman quit? (**6d**)

    a. The work was too hard.

    b. She didn't like working with books.

    c. She didn't need the money.

d. She got tired of all the numbers, papers, and regulations.

Interpreting and Evaluating

1. Put a checkmark next to those statements you can infer from the selection. (7)
   ____a. The woman understood how to use the sales book.
   ____b. Her training did not tell her everything she needed to know.
   ____c. She didn't understand how the books were arranged.
   ____d. She lied when she said D.A.'s were suspended.

____ 2. When the woman wrote up the sale on the second day, you can infer that she (7)
   a. did it correctly.
   b. made two small mistakes.
   c. asked someone to help her.
   d. was bluffing entirely.

____ 3. Why do you think that the woman wrote "1 Stg. Strk. Sl." instead of spelling out the name completely? (7)
   a. It was easier to abbreviate.
   b. That's the way it was written on the book.
   c. Since other things had silly abbreviations in the sales book, she thought that was how to do it.
   d. She wasn't thinking.

____ 4. Why, in her letter to Macy's, did she add all her numbers together and divide by 11,700? (7)
   a. She made a mistake.
   b. She was trying to figure out her pay.
   c. That made as much sense to her as anything else people there did with the numbers.
   d. She liked mathematics.

____ 5. You can conclude that she found the system at Macy's (9)
   a. simple.
   b. frustrating.
   c. manageable.
   d. costly.

6. Put a checkmark next to those statements you could predict with some certainty on the basis of the selection. (9)

——a. She will never work at Macy's again.

——b. She will never work in a small store.

——c. She will receive a sensible reply to her letter.

——d. She will never find out who that girl was who worked in lingerie.

7. Put a checkmark next to the generalizations you can make about this selection. (**10**)

——a. All stores are confusing.

——b. The writer feels that Macy's is big and impersonal.

——c. Workers tend to get lost in big companies.

——d. The girl who works in lingerie probably had as bad an experience as the writer.

——e. The prices in department stores are cheaper than those in small stores.

—— 8. The tone of the last sentence, "I wonder if they'll miss me," is (**11d**)

a. serious.

b. emotional.

c. nostalgic.

d. ironic.

—— 9. Why does the writer call all the women Miss Cooper? (**11d**)

a. They were all sisters.

b. It was a coincidence.

c. They all looked and acted so alike that you couldn't tell them apart.

d. It was a company rule that everybody who worked at the store had to change her name to Miss Cooper.

——10. Why does the writer call the person who tells her about the time clock a prophet? (8)

a. That person treats the clock like a god and preaches its rules.

b. The writer is just being silly.

c. That person acts very wisely.

d. Time is money and money is profit.

——11. Why does she bow to "the time clock and its prophet"? (8)

a. She was told to.

b. She wants to show that she too treats the clock as a god.

c. She is going crazy.
d. It is a company rule.

_____ 12. Why does the writer repeat the word *segregated* so often? (**11d**)
a. It is a common word.
b. She is trying to build up a sense of isolation.
c. She wants to see if the reader knows the word.
d. The word has racial connotations.

_____ 13. This story probably is (**11d**)
a. told exactly the way it happened to the writer.
b. better than things usually are.
c. totally made up.
d. exaggerated to make it funnier.

Vocabulary

1. In the selection, the writer makes a joke about the confusing paperwork by calling one sales form a "duplicate triplicate." Both *duplicate* and *triplicate* have several meanings. Select the meaning for each that best fits the joke. (**3**)
_____ *duplicate*
a. to make copies of something
b. two identical copies of a form
c. a second copy
_____ *triplicate*
a. to make three copies of something
b. three identical copies of a form
c. a third copy

2. Each of these words from the story contains a word part clue. Underline the word part clue and then define the entire word. (*Hint*: Items *c* and *e* are figurative.) (**2b**)

a. acquaintance _____

b. adjuster _____

c. doggedly _____

d. possessively _____

e. stage-struck _____

11 Businesses Owned by Blacks

by Andrew F. Brimmer

This essay by the president of a firm of financial consultants discusses problems facing black businesses in the past, now, and in the future.

Word Highlights

appreciably noticeably

Census Bureau a branch of government charged with collecting data about how many Americans there are, where they live, how much money they have, how much they spend, which racial groups they belong to, and other important pieces of information

deficit a falling short

divergence branching off

gross receipts the amount of money taken in by a company before anything is subtracted

intensify make stronger

perversely stubbornly, contrarily

venturesomeness willingness to take risks

Businesses owned by Blacks are expanding slightly their relative position in the nation's economy, and further modest improvement can be anticipated during the coming decade. However, several underlying trends may intensify the problems which Black enterprises already face. These include the changing pattern of income distribution within the Black community and the varying rates of growth among different industry groups.

As always, the mainspring of economic growth will be the rise in the nation's population. By 1990 (according to the Census Bureau), the population of the United States may be in the neighborhood of 243.5 million, about 13.7 percent above the 214.2 million at the beginning of 1978. The Black population is projected to rise from 24.8 million to 29.8 million, a gain of 20.2 percent. So Blacks would represent around 12.2 percent of the total in 1990, compared with 11.6 percent in 1978.

Income Deficit

By 1990, the Black community might receive about $431 billion in money income, equal to 9.3 percent of the $4,633 billion which the country at large may receive. I estimate that Blacks had $113 billion in money income in 1979, or 7.3 percent of the $1,542 billion total. Thus, over the next decade, Blacks may expand slightly their share of the nation's purchasing power. Yet, they would still face a large income deficit—given their share of the total population.

Black-owned businesses are selling to the community at large an increasing proportion of the goods and services which they market. Yet, they still make most of their sales within the Black community, and the pattern will most likely continue through the 1980s. Unfortunately, over the same period, a noticeable divergence may occur between the geographic distribution of Black consumers and the location of Black-owned businesses.

For instance, Black families (to a much greater degree than Whites) are still concentrated heavily in central cities of metropolitan areas—and to a lesser extent in the suburbs. Black businesses are also found predominantly in central cities. However, during the 1970s, the central cities' share of all Black families declined somewhat, but core cities' share of the total income of Black families declined appreciably. Thus, the demand for goods and services by Blacks in the suburbs was expanding faster than the market left behind in the central city.

Black Business Forecast

Consequently, Black entrepreneurs—who are still heavily concentrated in the older neighborhoods of central cities—are witnessing a gradual (but steady) out-migration of better-paid potential Black customers from their traditional market area.

As is generally recognized, most Black-owned businesses grew up behind a wall of racial segregation and discrimination. Most of them catered to Blacks in segregated neighborhoods and provided services which Blacks could not purchase from venders at large. As a result, Black-owned firms remain heavily concentrated in retail trade. This line still accounts for more than one-quarter of the number and for over two-fifths of the gross receipts of all Black businesses. These fractions are more than twice the proportion of receipts and 1½ times the proportion of firms registered for all American industry.

On the opposite side of the canvas, Blacks are grossly underrepresented in those lines of business where the perversely protective cloak of racial segregation and discrimination was not so evident. For instance, they have only a modest participation in wholesale trade, finance, insurance, and real estate, and construction. The same is true of manufacturing. But, in the last few years, the range of manufacturing activities by Black firms has become somewhat broader (particularly in fabricated metal products and in electrical and electronic equipment).

New Opportunities

But, despite some diversification, a disproportion of Black firms remains concentrated in those lines of business for which long-term growth prospects are below-average. The U.S. Bureau of Labor Statistics has estimated the average growth rate for all industry at 3.3 percent for the years 1980 through 1985. Among broad industry divisions, growth rates are projected to range from a low of 1.7 percent for construction to a high of 4.2 percent for transportation and public utilities. Manufacturing is projected to grow at an average rate of 3.1 percent, compared with only 2.4 percent for retail trade. Again, it is in retail trade that the vast majority of Black-owned businesses are found.

The trends traced above pose a serious challenge to Black businessmen, but they also open up a number of opportunities. The latter are likely to be found in fields such as radio and television broadcasting, metal fabrication, electric and electronic assembly, computer programming and related services, printing and reproduction, and economic and financial consulting.

To take advantage of these opportunities will require imagination, venturesomeness, and cooperation—among Black businessmen as well as with their White counterparts.

Exercises

Understanding What You Have Read

_____1. The main idea of this section is to show that (**4**)
    a. blacks will do well in business, but only if they stay in retail.
    b. although problems will not go away, the enormous opportunities for business in the 1980s will make these problems unimportant.
    c. traditional areas for business among blacks seem to be shrinking.
    d. knowing the many current problems for black business can help blacks develop strategies for the future.

  2. Write *T* next to each statement that is true, write *F* if the statement is false, and write *X* if no support for the statement can be found in the selection. (**5**)
    _____a. Blacks today earn more than their share of the total national income.

_____b. The number of blacks in America will decline during the 1980s.

_____c. More blacks than ever before will go to medical school in the 1980s.

_____d. Blacks will continue to do most of their business in the black community.

_____e. White families will replace black families in most cities.

_____f. In the 1980s there will be more blacks living in the suburbs than ever before.

_____g. The long-term prospects for the kind of businesses now owned by blacks are below average.

_____h. Fewer blacks will bother to compete in sports during the 1980s.

_____i. New opportunities for blacks will open up in broadcasting and computers.

_____j. Blacks will continue to dominate wholesale trades.

_____3. Which industry division will grow fastest between 1980 and 1985? (5)
   a. retail
   b. transportation
   c. construction
   d. computers

_____4. The reason given for the absence of blacks from higher-paying markets is that (5)
   a. black business grew up in traditionally poorer areas.
   b. black businesses were often started to serve needs that blacks could not satisfy through other vendors.
   c. blacks who owned businesses were subject to segregation, just like the customers they served.
   d. all of these.

Interpreting and Evaluating

_____ 1. We can infer that the reason why blacks are now better able to get into new areas of business is that (7)
   a. blacks are themselves investing in black businesses.
   b. blacks today are more willing to enter new fields and better able to get support from investors.
   c. whites are giving up business as a field, leaving it open to blacks.

d. the government is encouraging blacks to take businesses away from whites.

—— 2. Based on this selection, a valid generalization about black businesses would be that (10)
   a. blacks will still need to be lucky and work very hard to succeed in business.
   b. blacks don't have anything more to worry about in the business world.
   c. white business owners regret their former treatment of black-owned businesses.
   d. blacks shouldn't forget that the first law of business is "Every man for himself."

—— 3. In the statement "black-owned businesses grew up behind a wall of racial segregation," the writer is (8)
   a. making a comparison.
   b. referring to the construction industry.
   c. angering blacks and whites.
   d. telling readers of the inner city where black businesses grew.

—— 4. We can conclude that the move by black families away from central cities will do what to black businesses? (9)
   a. wipe them out
   b. improve their income by expanding their markets
   c. improve their business by bringing new customers
   d. force them to follow their customers away from cities

—— 5. For a young person going into business, how much meaning does this article have? (7)
   a. Much, because only businesses owned by blacks are likely to hire blacks.
   b. Some, in terms of where new employment opportunities will be.
   c. Some, because clearly the cities are no place for a young black to begin a business career.
   d. None, because young blacks are more urgently needed in professions such as medicine and law than in business.

—— 6. A conclusion we can safely draw from this article is that (9)
   a. segregationist policies of the past actually helped in the development of black businesses.

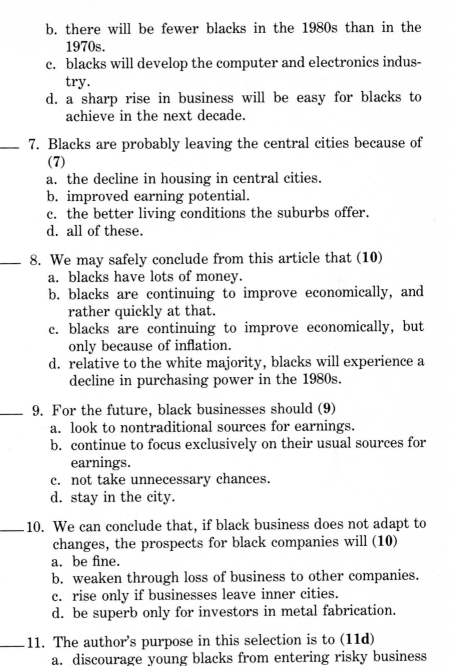

    b. there will be fewer blacks in the 1980s than in the 1970s.

    c. blacks will develop the computer and electronics industry.

    d. a sharp rise in business will be easy for blacks to achieve in the next decade.

_____ 7. Blacks are probably leaving the central cities because of **(7)**

    a. the decline in housing in central cities.

    b. improved earning potential.

    c. the better living conditions the suburbs offer.

    d. all of these.

_____ 8. We may safely conclude from this article that **(10)**

    a. blacks have lots of money.

    b. blacks are continuing to improve economically, and rather quickly at that.

    c. blacks are continuing to improve economically, but only because of inflation.

    d. relative to the white majority, blacks will experience a decline in purchasing power in the 1980s.

_____ 9. For the future, black businesses should **(9)**

    a. look to nontraditional sources for earnings.

    b. continue to focus exclusively on their usual sources for earnings.

    c. not take unnecessary chances.

    d. stay in the city.

_____10. We can conclude that, if black business does not adapt to changes, the prospects for black companies will **(10)**

    a. be fine.

    b. weaken through loss of business to other companies.

    c. rise only if businesses leave inner cities.

    d. be superb only for investors in metal fabrication.

_____11. The author's purpose in this selection is to **(11d)**

    a. discourage young blacks from entering risky business careers.

    b. predict future trends on the basis of current conditions.

    c. get whites interested in investing in black businesses.

    d. make you take action.

_____ 12. The information contained in this article is (**11a**)
   a. all fact.
   b. all opinion.
   c. many facts and some opinions.
   d. many opinions and some facts.

_____ 13. The author's main readers here are (**11d**)
   a. black students.
   b. black and white middle-class Americans.
   c. black middle-class Americans.
   d. the international black community.

Vocabulary

Check a dictionary for the meaning of each of the following words. In the blank spaces, write definitions in your own words. Then, on separate paper, write an original sentence in which you use the word correctly. (**3**)

1. out-migration _____

2. underlying _____

3. intensify _____

4. mainspring _____

5. predominantly _____

6. fabricate _____

7. appreciably _____

8. disproportion _____

9. projected _____

10. entrepreneurs _____

12 The Struggle to Be an All American Girl

by Elizabeth Wong

A woman looks back on her childhood and on the way the culture into which she was born seemed to disturb her efforts to be an American.

Word Highlights

Cinco de Mayo Mexican Independence Day

fragile frail

kowtow A Chinese greeting in which one touches the forehead to the ground to express respect

phonetic representing speech sounds with symbols, each of which stands for a separate sound

pidgin a mixture of two or more languages

raunchy slang for indecent or obscene

repressed held back, secret

smatterings fragmented, superficial knowledge; bits of information

stern severe in appearance; inflexible

stoically in a manner unaffected by joy, grief, pleasure, or pain

---

It's still there, the Chinese school on Yale Street where my brother and I used to go. Despite the new coat of paint and the high wire fence, the school I knew 10 years ago remains remarkably, stoically the same.

Every day at 5 P.M., instead of playing with our fourth- and fifth-grade friends or sneaking out to the empty lot to hunt ghosts and animal bones, my brother and I had to go to Chinese school. No amount of kicking, screaming, or pleading could dissuade my mother, who was solidly determined to have us learn the language of our heritage.

Forcibly, she walked us the seven long, hilly blocks from our home to school, depositing our defiant tearful faces before the stern principal. My only memory of him is that he swayed on his heels like a palm tree, and he always clasped his impatient twitching hands behind his back. I recognized him as a repressed maniacal child killer, and knew that if we ever saw his hands we'd be in big trouble.

We all sat in little chairs in an empty auditorium. The room smelled like Chinese medicine, an imported faraway mustiness. Like ancient mothballs or dirty closets. I hated that smell. I fa-

269

vored crisp new scents. Like the soft French perfume that my American teacher wore in public school.

There was a stage far to the right, flanked by an American flag and the flag of the Nationalist Republic of China, which was also red, white and blue but not as pretty.

Although the emphasis at the school was mainly language—speaking, reading, writing—the lessons always began with an exercise in politeness. With the entrance of the teacher, the best student would tap a bell and everyone would get up, kowtow, and chant, "Sing san ho," the phonetic for "How are you, teacher?"

Being ten years old, I had better things to learn than ideographs copied painstakingly in lines that ran right to left from the tip of a *moc but*, a real ink pen that had to be held in an awkward way if blotches were to be avoided. After all, I could do the multiplication tables, name the satellites of Mars, and write reports on "Little Women" and "Black Beauty." Nancy Drew, my favorite book heroine, never spoke Chinese.

The language was a source of embarrassment. More times than not, I had tried to disassociate myself from the nagging loud voice that followed me wherever I wandered in the nearby American supermarket outside Chinatown. The voice belonged to my grandmother, a fragile woman in her seventies who could outshout the best of the street vendors. Her humor was raunchy, her Chinese rhythmless, patternless. It was quick, it was loud, it was unbeautiful. It was not like the quiet, lilting romance of French or the gentle refinement of the American South. Chinese sounded pedestrian. Public.

In Chinatown, the comings and goings of hundreds of Chinese on their daily tasks sounded chaotic and frenzied. I did not want to be thought of as mad, as talking gibberish. When I spoke English, people nodded at me, smiled sweetly, said encouraging words. Even the people in my culture would cluck and say that I'd do well in life. "My, doesn't she move her lips fast," they would say, meaning that I'd be able to keep up with the world outside Chinatown.

My brother was even more fanatical than I about speaking English. He was especially hard on my mother, criticizing her, often cruelly, for her pidgin speech—smatterings of Chinese scattered like chop suey in her conversation. "It's not 'What it is,' Mom," he'd say in exasperation. "It's 'What *is* it, what *is* it, what *is* it!" Sometimes Mom might leave out an occasional "the" or "a," or perhaps a verb of being. He would stop her in mid-sentence: "Say it again, Mom. Say it right." When he tripped over his own tongue, he'd blame it on her: "See, Mom, it's all your fault. You set a bad example."

What infuriated my mother most was when my brother cornered her on her consonants, especially "r." My father had played a cruel joke on Mom by assigning her an American name that her tongue wouldn't allow her to say. No matter how hard she tried, "Ruth" always ended up "Luth" or "Roof."

After two years of writing with a *moc but* and reciting words with multiples of meanings, I finally was granted a cultural divorce. I was permitted to stop Chinese school.

I thought of myself as multicultural. I preferred tacos to egg rolls; I enjoyed Cinco de Mayo more than Chinese New Year.

At last, I was one of you; I wasn't one of them.

Sadly, I still am.

Exercises

Understanding What You Have Read

____1. The main idea of this selection is to show (**4**)
   a. the course of study at a Chinese school in America.
   b. how Chinese families fight about the correct pronunciation of words.
   c. the pressures on Nationalist Chinese who emigrate to America.
   d. how a Chinese girl's desire to be an American won out over her family's interest in her remaining Chinese.

____2. The children kicked and screamed because (**5**)
   a. they did not want to go to Chinese school at all.
   b. they did not like going to Chinese school so late in the day.
   c. they didn't like the long walk to the schoolhouse.
   d. they were scared of the ghosts in the empty lot.

____3. A *moc but* is (**2a**)
   a. a phonetic sentence for "How are you, teacher?"
   b. an ideograph.
   c. a pen that blotched easily.
   d. a copy pad.

———4. In Chinese school the children learned (5)
    a. reading and speaking skills.
    b. how to use a special pen for ideographs.
    c. lessons in politeness.
    d. all of these.

———5. The school the author attended ten years ago (5)
    a. is exactly the same now as it was then.
    b. is pretty much the same now as it was then.
    c. is no longer standing.
    d. was moved to Yale Street.

———6. By a "cultural divorce" the author means that she (2)
    a. separated from her American husband.
    b. left her Chinese family.
    c. no longer visited Chinatown.
    d. ceased taking instruction in Chinese culture.

———7. The author did not like the sound of the Chinese language, because it (5)
    a. was spoken too softly.
    b. sounded too much like French.
    c. was too rhythmical.
    d. was not slow, soft, or beautiful.

Interpreting and Evaluating

——— 1. An example of a figurative expression is (8)
    a. ". . . he swayed on his heels like a palm tree."
    b. "The room smelled like Chinese medicine, an imported mustiness."
    c. ". . . smatterings of Chinese scattered like chop suey in her conversation."
    d. all of these.

——— 2. We may safely infer that the empty lot was (7)
    a. in part, a Chinese graveyard.
    b. just outside the high wire fence beyond the school.
    c. a fenced-in area that the writer's parents encouraged the children to visit.
    d. a place where the children liked to play after school.

——— 3. We may conclude that the writer believed the American flag was more attractive than the flag of the Nationalist Republic of China because (9)

    a. the Chinese flag needed more color.

    b. the American flag stood taller on the stage.

    c. she simply preferred American things to Chinese things.

    d. the principal preferred the Chinese flag.

_____ 4. We may infer that the child who tapped the bell at the teacher's arrival received the job (7)

    a. as a punishment.

    b. as a reward for excellence.

    c. because she or he was the principal's pet.

    d. because she or he made the best ideographs.

_____ 5. In all probability, the writer's grandmother was an embarrassment because (7)

    a. she spoke no French.

    b. she did not know how to deal with the street vendors.

    c. she spoke Chinese.

    d. she had no sense of humor.

_____ 6. We may safely infer that the writer's mother (7)

    a. hated her own American name.

    b. had no say in the choice of her American name.

    c. joked about her American name.

    d. was infuriated at her husband for choosing a name like Ruth.

_____ 7. From the last two lines, we may conclude that the writer (9)

    a. now hates American ways.

    b. wishes she were really one of us.

    c. has some regrets about becoming so completely Americanized.

    d. now prefers the Chinese New Year to Cinco de Mayo.

_____ 8. If she had a child of her own, we can safely assume that the writer (9)

    a. definitely would not send the child to Chinese school.

    b. definitely would not send the child to American school.

    c. might not send the child to American school.

    d. might send the child to Chinese school.

_____ 9. A generalization with which the writer would probably agree is that (10)

    a. to become completely a part of another person's culture is an important goal.

b. a person should not try to become part of another culture.
c. intermarriages between Chinese Americans and Americans who are not Chinese are not a good idea.
d. becoming part of another culture should not mean giving up one's own culture completely.

____ 10. A generalization with which the writer would probably *not* agree is that (**10**)
a. children's wishes should not be observed fully in regard to educational choices.
b. a wrong choice made in childhood is easy to correct in adulthood.
c. children often put pressure on their parents to make choices that are not always in the children's best interests.
d. children of Chinese parents like to play the way other children play.

Vocabulary

Using sentence clues from the selection, determine the meanings of the words in italics in the following groups. Then select the most appropriate choice given below the words and write your answer in the space provided. (**2a**)

____ 1. the language of our *heritage*
a. parents
b. friends and neighbors
c. tradition and legacy
d. old folks

____ 2. could *dissuade* my mother
a. discourage
b. encourage
c. anger
d. help

____ 3. our *defiant* tearful faces
a. dirty
b. resistant to authority
c. pleading
d. silly

—— 4. ideographs copied *painstakingly*
   a. with extreme care
   b. with great suffering
   c. full of complaints
   d. weakly

—— 5. the quiet *lilting* romance of French
   a. loving
   b. full of gentle melody
   c. loud
   d. adventurous

—— 6. Chinese sounded *pedestrian*
   a. a person traveling on foot
   b. boring
   c. terrible
   d. ordinary

—— 7. chaotic and *frenzied*
   a. lazy
   b. frantic
   c. friendly
   d. fearful

—— 8. as talking *gibberish*
   a. too loud
   b. insanely
   c. childishly
   d. rapid nonsense

—— 9. more *fanatical* than I about speaking English
   a. interested
   b. uninterested
   c. overly enthusiastic
   d. unsure

——10. What *infuriated* my mother
   a. interested
   b. angered
   c. impressed
   d. amused

Use word part clues to determine the meanings of the following words. Write your definitions in the space provided. (**2b**)

   1. maniacal _____

2. mustiness _____

3. ideograph _____

4. chaotic _____

5. forcibly _____

13 Dining in A.D. 2001

by Emily and Per Ola D'Aulaire

The authors predict what we may be eating in the future. The prediction is based on work scientists are doing now.

Word Highlights

automated run by machines

bon appétit French for "have a good meal"

carbohydrates foods containing sugars or starches

cholesterol a substance in the blood resulting from eating fatty foods

comestibles things to eat

discarded thrown away

ecological relating to how plants and animals depend on one another in nature

exotic strange or from far away

fabricated put together by humans

nutrient a food that gives your body something important

ruminants animals that chew a cud, such as the cow

presto Italian for "fast," used often by magicians

scrutiny a close look

seepage liquid that drains through

sterile without germs

The year is 2001, and it's dinner-time at the Smiths'. The menu is pot roast, peas and potatoes, with wine for Mr. and Mrs. Smith, and milk for Junior.

Nothing unusual in this, except that the roast isn't meat; it's made from high-protein soybean meal almost indistinguishable in taste from the real thing. Even though the season is midwinter, with snow on the ground, the Smiths' vegetables are locally grown and fresh; they come from a nearby "factory"—a huge, automated greenhouse where light, temperature and nutrient-bearing water sprays are computer-controlled for growing produce year-round. The wine, round and mellow, has never seen a grape; it's manufactured from whey, a dairy by-product formerly discarded by cheese makers. Finally, Junior's milk has been drawn from the latest biological marvel, a "polyunsaturated cow"; although it tastes like old-fashioned milk, it has much lower quantities of the saturated fats people have been trying to avoid.

Sound far out? Not at all. Every one of these "future foods" is already here. In fact, total sales for fabricated foods should reach $11 *billion* in 1980. And more exotic developments are on the comestibles horizon. "We'll be seeing many more changes in the way food is produced, processed and sold," says Howard Mattson of Chicago's Institute of Food Technologists. "But the basic shape of things we now have on the table won't change. We won't be downing little pink pills and calling it supper."

What *does* lie ahead? More meatless meats, for one thing. Already off and running are such fabricated foods as "ham," "bacon," "steak" and "sausage," all made from soybeans. Jean Mayer, former professor of nutrition at Harvard University and current president of Tufts University, estimates that direct meat substitutes, or extenders, which can be added to real meats like hamburger, will compose about ten percent of total meat consumed in the United States by 1985, with a much higher level reached in the early 21st century.

Why the dramatic increase? Economy, for one thing. It is cheaper—and more ecologically sound—to utilize the high-protein content of a pound of soybeans directly than to cycle it first through cattle, which need up to about nine pounds of vegetable-protein feed to produce a single pound of meat. It is probably more healthful, too. Vegetable products in the right combination contain all the proteins, carbohydrates, fats, vitamins and trace elements needed for good health, without the potentially harmful saturated fats and cholesterol contained in animal products.

What about taste? So far, at least, no one has been able to match the mouth-watering flavor of a charcoal-grilled T-bone steak—though they're getting closer all the time. However, hamburger extended with 25-percent soybean protein already tastes as good as 100-percent ground beef.

Fabricated (which does not necessarily mean artificial) foods are by no means new. Bread, after all, is not found in nature; it took man to arrange the raw ingredients. Ice cream and yogurt are other fabricated standbys. Imitation cheese, made with corn oil, has been on the market for some time, as have non-dairy creamers of polyunsaturated soy oil, bologna made from turkey or chicken, simulated fruit based on seaweed and gelatin, and grapeless wine.

Even some of our most traditional fare, while remaining essentially unchanged in appearance, is headed for technological change. At the U.S. Department of Agriculture's Animal Research Center in Beltsville, Md., scientists have raised cattle whose meat and milk contain reduced amounts of saturated fats—ingredients that are suspected of contributing to heart disease.

The secret of this biological sleight-of-hand is to feed the animals drops of polyunsaturated safflower oil coated with a layer of protein that has been treated with formaldehyde to prevent it from breaking down and converting into saturated fat in the ruminants' digestive systems. Instead, the vegetable oils reach the animals' tissue and milk intact, where they replace saturated fats and— *presto!*—create polyunsaturated cows.

Not even the chicken has escaped the scientists' scrutiny. With the increased emphasis on body weight in poultry—it costs less to produce a small number of large birds than a large number of small ones—the 21st century could see chickens as big as turkeys and, conceivably, turkeys the size of ostriches!

No less revolutionary are the so-called vegetable "factories." Situated near their markets and programmed for year-round growth, these giant greenhouses—adaptable to climates from arctic cold to desert heat—could turn out many times the amounts of greens presently grown in natural surroundings.

On an experimental level, they are already here. The Environmental Research Laboratory (ERL) at the University of Arizona maintains several "controlled-environment-agriculture" greenhouses covering more than three acres under one roof. No fertile soil is needed, only sand—one of the earth's most abundant materials. Temperature, light, water with dissolved plant nutrients, and atmosphere are all computer-controlled.

Since the environment is sterile and self-contained, only a bare minimum of pesticides and fungicides is needed. A plastic liner underlying the sand prevents seepage, reducing water consumption by 90 percent over what is needed in an open field. In a yield comparison of tomatoes and cucumbers grown in a controlled-environment facility in the desert of Abu Dhabi and in fields in the United States, ERL scientists found the desert yields, with year-round harvesting, dozens of times greater.

As for shopping, with gas prices on a one-way trip up, we may someday be ordering our food from home, perhaps via computer terminals tied by telephone circuits to robotized warehouses. Just program in your favorite meals for the week; all the necessary ingredients, in exactly the right amounts as determined by a central computer, will be delivered to your home, much like the daily mail.

Meanwhile, pass the soybean pot roast, toss the vegetable-factory salad, pour the whey-out wine and let's toast the 21st century. *Bon appétit!*

Exercises

Understanding What You Have Read

_____1. The main idea of this selection is to show (**4**)
  a. good ways to make dinner.
  b. the dangers of eating fatty food.
  c. how scientific advances will change what we eat.
  d. how high food prices are ruining proper nutrition.

  2. In the space provided, put a *T* for true statements, an *F* for false statements, and an *X* for statements that are not found at all in the selection. (**5a**)
    _____a. Someday chickens will be as big as turkeys.
    _____b. Someday tomatoes will be as big as pumpkins.
    _____c. Soybeans taste just like hamburgers.
    _____d. Milk is bad for people with heart disease.
    _____e. Fabricated food has never been a part of the human diet.
    _____f. Vegetables will be grown in factories someday.
    _____g. Someday people will shop by computer.
    _____h. Scientists have made artificial cows.
    _____i. Meat will remain an important part of our diet.

_____3. The main point in favor of new foods is that they are (**5a**)
  a. more fun to eat.
  b. cheaper to produce.
  c. healthier.
  d. both b and c.

_____4. How many pounds of feed does the article say a cow needs to produce one pound of beef? (**5a**)
  a. one
  b. four
  c. seven
  d. nine

Interpreting and Evaluating

_____1. We can infer that one benefit of the new process of growing food in sand will be that (**7**)
  a. more food can be grown in desert countries.
  b. more food can be grown in outer space.
  c. more food can be grown in Nebraska.

    d. food already grown in sand, such as spinach, will be cheaper.

___2. A valid generalization about the coming food revolution is that (**10**)
    a. people will eat a lot more chickens than turkeys.
    b. poor people will still eat the same old things.
    c. people will not enjoy the taste of new foods so much.
    d. people will have a better diet than ever before.

   3. Put a checkmark in front of those statements that we can conclude represent some of the major changes to come in the future of food. (**9**)
    ___a. Food will be more plentiful in countries where it is now scarce.
    ___b. More land will be needed for producing food.
    ___c. Computers will eliminate farmers.
    ___d. People will eat little tablets instead of meals.
    ___e. There will be no fat people.
    ___f. We won't eat any junk food.
    ___g. Scientists will invent new animals.
    ___h. Vegetarians will start eating meat.
    ___i. People will eat a lot of yogurt and bread.
    ___j. Bologna will be made from turkey.
    ___k. People will drink more wine than ever before.
    ___l. Vegetables will be grown in February.

___4. The authors' purpose in this selection is to (**11d**)
    a. discuss their opinions.
    b. present all the facts.
    c. make you angry.
    d. make fun of crazy ideas.

___5. What generalization would it *not* be safe to make? (**10**)
    a. More foods will be fabricated.
    b. The small farmer will be driven out of business.
    c. The world will be better off because more food will be available.
    d. People who eat the new foods will run fewer health risks.

___6. What can we conclude is the authors' feeling about the food of the future (**9**)
    a. strongly in favor
    b. mildly amused and slightly in favor

c. disgusted and alarmed

d. no opinion

Vocabulary

_____ 1. The suffix *cide* means "to kill." What would pesticides kill? (**2b**)

a. pets

b. annoying people

c. ruminants

d. pests

_____ 2. Using the definition of the suffix, determine what fungicides would do to a fungus? (**2b**)

a. kill it

b. make it grow faster

c. annoy it

d. control it

_____ 3. Using your dictionary skills, break the word *indistinguishable* into prefix, root word, and suffix. (**3, 2b**)

_____

_____

4. Write a definition of indistinguishable (**3**) _____

_____

14 The Making of a Surgeon

by William Nolen, M.D.

By discussing honestly his thoughts and feelings about his work, a surgeon helps us understand what his job is really all about.

Word Highlights

abdomen belly

anticipate to see ahead of time

competently with the necessary skill

compound having a number of parts

conceit thinking you are better than you actually are

considered thought out

dexterity skill in using the hands

equanimity calm, undisturbed feeling

fracture a break in a bone

penance paying for doing something wrong

recurring happening over and over; repeating

residency the last stage of a doctor's training at a hospital

resident a physician who takes advanced training in a medical specialty

---

How does a doctor recognize the point in time when he is finally a "surgeon"? As my year as chief resident drew to a close I asked myself this question on more than one occasion.

The answer, I concluded, was self-confidence. When you can say to yourself, "There is no surgical patient I cannot treat competently, treat just as well or better than any other surgeon"—then, and not until then, you are indeed a surgeon. I was nearing that point.

Take, for example, the emergency situations that we encountered almost every night. The first few months of the year I had dreaded the ringing of the telephone. I knew it meant another critical decision to be made. Often, after I had told Walt or Larry what to do in a particular situation, I'd have trouble getting back to sleep. I'd review all the facts of the case and, not infrequently, wonder if I hadn't made a poor decision. More than once at two or three in the morning, after lying awake for an hour, I'd get out of bed, dress and drive to the hospital to see the patient myself. It was the only way I could find the peace of mind I needed to relax.

Now, in the last month of my residency, sleeping was no longer a problem. There were still situations in which I couldn't be certain my decision had been the right one, but I had learned to accept this as a permanently recurring problem for a surgeon, one that could never be completely resolved—and I could live with it. So, once I had made a considered decision, I no longer dwelt on it. Reviewing it wasn't going to help and I knew that with my knowledge and experience, any decision I'd made was bound to be a sound one. It was a nice feeling.

In the operating room I was equally confident. I knew I had the knowledge, the technical dexterity, the experience to handle any surgical situation I'd ever encounter in practice. There were no more butterflies in my stomach when I opened up an abdomen—a chest—an extremity. I knew that even if the case was one in which it was impossible to anticipate the problem in advance, I could handle whatever I found. I'd sweated through my share of stab wounds of the belly, of punctured lungs, of compound fractures. I had sweated over them for five years. I didn't need to sweat any more.

Nor was I afraid of making mistakes. I knew that when I was out in practice I would inevitably err at one time or another and operate on someone who didn't need surgery or sit on someone who did. Five years earlier—even one year earlier—I wouldn't have been able to live with myself if I had had to take sole responsibility for a mistake in judgment. Now I could. I still dreaded errors—would do my damnedest to avoid them—but I knew they were part of the penance a surgeon recurrently had to pay. I could accept this fact with equanimity because I knew that if I wasn't able to avoid a mistake, chances were that no other surgeon could have, either.

This all sounds conceited and I guess it is—but a surgeon needs conceit. He needs it to sustain him in trying moments when he's battered by the doubts and uncertainties that are part of the practice of medicine. He has to feel that he's as good as and probably better than any other surgeon in the world. Call it conceit—call it self-confidence; whatever it was, I had it.

Exercises

Understanding What You Have Read

——1. The main idea of this selection is that (**4b**)
   a. young surgeons lose a lot of sleep.
   b. when you get self-confidence, you are really a surgeon.
   c. the writer no longer became nervous before an operation.
   d. he still makes mistakes.

_____2. Which situation does Doctor Nolen *not* mention as being
     helped by self-confidence. **(5b)**
     a. talking to patients
     b. making a decision
     c. doing an operation
     d. making an occasional mistake

    3. In the selection, two things are compared several times.

Those two things are   _____

and _____. **(6c)**

    4. Put a *T* next to the statements that are true according to
     the selection and an *F* next to statements that are false.
     (5a)
     _____a. When he first began, Dr. Nolen would drive to the
        hospital in the middle of the night to visit patients.
     _____b. He often apologized to patients.
     _____c. He no longer makes mistakes.
     _____d. He still dreads errors.
     _____e. He operated on people with punctured lungs.

_____5. According to Doctor Nolen, a surgeon needs conceit **(4b)**
     a. to answer patients' questions.
     b. just to start an operation.
     c. to keep him going through times of doubt and uncer-
        tainty.
     d. to get through medical school.

_____6. The paragraph beginning, "In the operating room . . ."
     uses mainly **(6)**
     a. place order.
     b. listing of details.
     c. comparison and contrast.
     d. time order.

Interpreting and Evaluating

_____1. You can infer that, when the doctor began, he had trouble
     sleeping because **(7)**
     a. he was not confident that he had made the right deci-
        sion.
     b. he was going over all the things he had learned in medi-
        cal school.

     c. he was nervous about what would happen to Walt and
       Larry.
     d. his work would give him nightmares.

____2. You can safely conclude from the selection that (9)
     a. Doctor Nolen no longer finds his work exciting.
     b. he was impatient to leave the hospital.
     c. he didn't learn as much as he should have when he was
       still in medical school.
     d. now he felt ready to handle any surgical case.

____3. You can generalize that the doctor probably believes that
    (10)
     a. older doctors get overconfident and careless.
     b. doctors need a period of residency in order to gain self-
       confidence.
     c. all conceited people would do well as doctors.
     d. you shouldn't become a surgeon if you ever get nervous.

    4. Write the word *fact* next to those statements that, on the
    basis of the essay, are facts. Write *opin.* next to those
    statements that reflect Doctor Nolen's opinions. (11a)
     ____a. Doctor Nolen spent a year as chief resident.
     ____b. There is no patient he could not treat competently.
     ____c. He drove to the hospital at three in the morning.
     ____d. He made a bad decision.
     ____e. Reviewing his decisions would not help.
     ____f. Now he could live with his mistakes.
     ____g. He operated on people with compound fractures.
     ____h. He's probably better than any other surgeon in the
       world.

____5. Which of the following phrases does the writer use most
    often? (11d)
     a. "I'd have trouble . . ."
     b. "I asked myself . . ."
     c. "A doctor must decide . . ."
     d. "I knew . . ."

____6. The tone of the writer is one of (11d)
     a. objective distance.
     b. self-doubt.
     c. friendly openness.
     d. great confidence.

Vocabulary

1. The words *surgeon, surgery,* and *surgical* all appear in the selection. Write a definition of your own for each. (Check a dictionary if you have to.) Then, on another piece of paper, use each word in a sentence of your own. (**2b, 3**)

_____

_____

_____

_____

_____

____2. Which of the meanings of the word *practice* is meant in the phrase "when I was out in practice"? (**2**)
   a. to do over and over in order to improve
   b. the normal way of doing things
   c. the opposite of theory
   d. a doctor's business

3. Complete the following sentences, using words from this list. (**2a**)

critical	infrequently
dread	punctured
err	resolved
extremity	self-confidence
inevitably	technical

   a. The conceited doctor thought he was so perfect that he

      could never _____ .

   b. Who pulled the nail out of the _____ tire?

   c. The decision was _____; if we made a mistake, the business would go bankrupt.

   d. Burglaries happened so _____ in the town that nobody had a lock on the door.

e. Fixing a color television requires much _____ knowledge.

f. I was so rude to Diana that I _____ having to face her.

g. The garbage collectors' strike _____ led to the garbage rotting in the street.

h. Each hand and each foot is an _____ of the body.

i. The argument was never _____; the two families still hate each other.

15 My Mother Who Came from China Where She Never Saw Snow

by Laureen Mar

This poem about a life spent working in a factory pointedly shows the struggles that many women have endured trying to make a life in America.

Word Highlights

fluorescent lights electric lights shaped like tubes and used in factories and office buildings

scrub a short, stunted tree or bush

In the huge, rectangular room, the ceiling
a machinery of pipes and fluorescent lights,
ten rows of women hunch over machines,
their knees pressing against pedals
and hands pushing the shiny fabric thick as tongues
through metal and thread.
My mother bends her head to one of these machines.
Her hair is coarse and wiry, black as burnt scrub.
She wears glasses to shield her intense eyes.
A cone of orange thread spins. Around her,
talk flutters harshly in Toisan wah.
Chemical stings. She pushes cloth
through a pounding needle, under, around, and out,
breaks thread with a snap against fingerbone, tooth.
Sleeve after sleeve, sleeve.
It is easy. The same piece.
For eight or nine hours, sixteen bundles maybe,
250 sleeves to ski coats, all the same.
It is easy, only once she's run the needle
through her hand. She earns money
by each piece, on a good day,
thirty dollars. Twenty-four years.
It is frightening how fast she works.
She and the women who were taught sewing
terms in English as Second Language.
Dull thunder passes through their fingers.

Exercises

Understanding What You Have Read

_____ 1. The main idea of the poem is to show that (**4b**)
   a. the woman in the poem has led a heroic life of struggle.
   b. women factory workers do not see the opportunity in America for people who aren't afraid of a little hard work.
   c. a factory worker faces dull, difficult work every day.
   d. Chinese women are very good at sewing.

2. Put the following main details in the order in which they occurred by writing a *1* next to the thing that happened first, a *2* next to the thing that happened second, and so on. (**6a**)
   _____a. The thread was broken.
   _____b. The mother pushed shiny fabric through the machine.
   _____c. The mother finished 250 sleeves.
   _____d. The mother was paid for the number of sleeves she finished.

_____ 3. The key idea of the line "breaks thread with a snap against fingerbone, tooth" is that (**4a**)
   a. women often broke their teeth or fingers doing this kind of work.
   b. the thread was so brittle that sometimes it simply snapped off.
   c. women often broke the thread with their hands and teeth.
   d. Women often snapped their fingers to make the day go faster.

4. Put a *T* next to those statements that are true in the poem and an *F* next to those statements whose truth cannot be determined from the poem. (**5**)
   _____a. The mother often put a needle through her hand.
   _____b. Women spoke Chinese on the job.
   _____c. The mother used many colors of thread at work.
   _____d. The mother needed glasses on the job.
   _____e. Chemicals were used in the making of coats.
   _____f. The mother did not really work very fast.
   _____g. The fabric the mother used was thick.

_____5. The mother in the poem was sewing (**5b**)
   a. ski masks.
   b. ski pants.
   c. ski coats.
   d. all kinds of coats.

_____6. How many years had the mother in the poem been working
       when this poem was written? (**5b**)
   a. 30 years
   b. 10 years
   c. 8 or 9 years
   d. 24 years

Interpreting and Evaluating

_____1. We can infer from this poem that the women were taught
       sewing terms in English because (**7**)
   a. their employers were Americans with little knowledge
       of Chinese.
   b. every native speaker of English sews as a hobby.
   c. these were words the women needed to know on the
       job.
   d. both a and c.

_____2. When the poet says her mother's hair was "burnt black as
       scrub" she probably means that (**8**)
   a. her hair was often burned by chemicals at work.
   b. her hair was very short.
   c. her hair was worn tied up to keep it out of the spinning
       machines.
   d. her hair was black and stiff and looked like a burned
       bush.

_____3. From the tone of this poem, what can you conclude about
       how the poet views the experience of working in a factory?
       (**11d**)
   a. It is challenging work.
   b. It is always the same.
   c. It offers a chance for someone to earn a reasonable
       working wage.
   d. It enables the women who work there to get better jobs.

_____4. The writer uses the basic technique of letting one day at
       work stand for many years, because (**11d**)

a. this was a special day at work.

b. this was the mother's twenty-fourth anniversary.

c. one day at work is much like any other.

d. one day at work was enough for the daughter.

5. Put a checkmark next to those statements that you can safely infer from the poem. (7)

———a. The mother was good at her job.

———b. The mother hated her job.

———c. The American bosses resented the women speaking Chinese.

———d. The mother frequently worked overtime.

———e. Chinese women enjoy sewing.

———f. The machines made a good deal of noise.

———g. The women did not belong to a union.

———6. In the poem, the mood is one of

a. cheerfulness.

b. unhappiness.

c. admiration.

d. repetition.

———7. A generalization the author would agree with is that (10)

a. full automation is preferable to people's having to work in factories.

b. immigrants can get trapped in hard, meaningless jobs.

c. sewing machines are dangerous enough to be outlawed for home use.

d. all of these.

———8. The reason why the author tells us, in the title, that her mother never saw snow is (7)

a. to show even more vividly how meaningless is the mother's job of making sleeves for jackets used in the snow.

b. to give some background about China's geography.

c. to prove that it does not snow anywhere in China.

d. to show how strange life is in America.

———9. Figurative expressions in this poem may be found in lines (8)

a. 5, 6, 7, and 8.

b. 5, 11, 12, and 13.

c. 1, 3, 4, and 10.

d. 2, 5, 10, and 25.

Vocabulary

_____1. From its use in the line "talk flutters harshly in Toisan wah" we can figure out that Toisan wah is (**2**)
   a. the place where the mother worked.
   b. the name of the mother in the poem.
   c. a dialect of Chinese.
   d. the Chinese word for sewing machine.

_____2. The effect of repeating "it is easy" is meant to show that (**2**)
   a. it *is* easy.
   b. it is exactly the opposite of easy.
   c. the author thinks her mother is stupid.
   d. the author hates the Americans her mother works for.

_____3. Which answer *best* explains the meaning of the line "Dull thunder passes through their fingers?" (**4**)
   a. The job is dull.
   b. The women radiate a power like electricity.
   c. The noise and the vibrations of the machines sound like the rumbling of thunder.
   d. All of these.

_____4. When the poet says "it is frightening," she means the word *frightening* in what sense? (**2**)
   a. The mother scares the poet.
   b. The mother's ability to stand her job scares the poet.
   c. The mother looks scary when she works so fast.
   d. The mother's work is so dangerous that it scares the poet.

16   The Chaser

by John Collier

In this short story, Alan Austen goes to buy a love potion to win his beloved Diana. But there is more to dealing with the old man on Pell Street than meets the eye.

Word Highlights

au revoir   (French) until we meet again

autopsy   a medical search to find out why someone died

draught (*draft*, American spelling)   breeze

laxatives   drugs to relieve constipation

siren   a pretty woman who leads men on

phial   (*vial*, American spelling)   a small bottle

Alan Austen, as nervous as a kitten, went up certain dark and creaky stairs in the neighborhood of Pell Street, and peered about for a long time on the dim landing before he found the name he wanted written obscurely on one of the doors.

He pushed open this door, as he had been told to do, and found himself in a tiny room, which contained no furniture but a plain kitchen table, a rocking-chair, and an ordinary chair. On one of the dirty buff-coloured walls were a couple of shelves, containing in all perhaps a dozen bottles and jars.

An old man sat in the rocking-chair, reading a newspaper. Alan, without a word, handed him the card he had been given. "Sit down, Mr. Austen," said the old man very politely. "I am glad to make your acquaintance."

"Is it true," asked Alan, "that you have a certain mixture that has—er—quite extraordinary effects?"

"My dear sir," replied the old man, "my stock in trade is not very large—I don't deal in laxatives and teething mixtures—but such as it is, it is varied. I think nothing I sell has effects which could be precisely described as ordinary."

"Well, the fact is . . ." began Alan.

"Here, for example," interrupted the old man, reaching for a bottle from the shelf. "Here is a liquid as colourless as water, almost tasteless, quite imperceptible in coffee, wine, or any other beverage. It is also quite imperceptible to any known method of autopsy."

"Do you mean it is a poison?" cried Alan, very much horrified.

"Call it a glove-cleaner if you like," said the old man indifferently. "Maybe it will clean gloves. I have never tried. One might call it a life-cleaner. Lives need cleaning sometimes."

"I want nothing of that sort," said Alan.

"Probably it is just as well," said the old man. "Do you know the price of this? For one teaspoonful, which is sufficient, I ask five thousand dollars. Never less. Not a penny less."

"I hope all your mixtures are not as expensive," said Alan apprehensively.

"Oh dear, no," said the old man. "It would be no good charging that sort of price for a love potion, for example. Young people who need a love potion very seldom have five thousand dollars. Otherwise they would not need a love potion."

"I am glad to hear that," said Alan.

"I look at it like this," said the old man. "Please a customer with one article, and he will come back when he needs another. Even if it *is* more costly. He will save up for it, if necessary."

"So," said Alan, "you really do sell love potions?"

"If I did not sell love potions," said the old man, reaching for another bottle, "I should not have mentioned the other matter to you. It is only when one is in a position to oblige that one can afford to be so confidential."

"And these potions," said Alan. "They are not just—just—er—"

"Oh, no," said the old man. "Their effects are permanent, and extend far beyond the mere casual impulse. But they include it. Oh, yes, they include it. Bountifully, insistently. Everlastingly."

"Dear me!" said Alan, attempting a look of scientific detachment. "How very interesting!"

"But consider the spiritual side," said the old man.

"I do, indeed," said Alan.

"For indifference," said the old man, "they substitute devotion. For scorn, adoration. Give one tiny measure of this to the young lady—its flavour is imperceptible in orange juice, soup, or cocktails—and however gay and giddy she is, she will change altogether. She will want nothing but solitude and you."

"I can hardly believe it," said Alan. "She is so fond of parties."

"She will not like them any more," said the old man. "She will be afraid of the pretty girls you may meet."

"She will actually be jealous?" cried Alan in a rapture. "Of me?"

"Yes, she will want to be everything to you."

"She is, already. Only she doesn't care about it."

"She will, when she has taken this. She will care intensely. You will be her sole interest in life."

"Wonderful!" cried Alan.

"She will want to know all you do," said the old man. "All that has happened to you during the day. Every word of it. She will want to know what you are thinking about, why you smile suddenly, why you are looking sad."

"That is love!" cried Alan.

"Yes," said the old man. "How carefully she will look after you! She will never allow you to be tired, to sit in a draught, to neglect your food. If you are an hour late, she will be terrified. She will think you are killed, or that some siren has caught you."

"I can hardly imagine Diana like that!" cried Alan, overwhelmed with joy.

"You will not have to use your imagination," said the old man. "And, by the way, since there are always sirens, if by any chance you *should*, later on, slip a little, you need not worry. She will forgive you, in the end. She will be terribly hurt, of course, but she will forgive you—in the end."

"That will not happen," said Alan fervently.

"Of course not," said the old man. "But, if it did, you need not worry. She would never divorce you. Oh, no! And, of course, she will never give you the least, the very least, grounds for— uneasiness."

"And how much," said Alan, "is this wonderful mixture?"

"It is not as dear," said the old man, "as the glove-cleaner, or life-cleaner, as I sometimes call it. No. That is five thousand dollars, never a penny less. One has to be older than you are, to indulge in that sort of thing. One has to save up for it."

"But the love potion?" said Alan.

"Oh, that," said the old man, opening the drawer in the kitchen table, and taking out a tiny, rather dirty-looking phial. "That is just a dollar."

"I can't tell you how grateful I am," said Alan, watching him fill it.

"I like to oblige," said the old man. "Then customers come back, later in life, when they are better off, and want more expensive things. Here you are. You will find it very effective."

"Thank you again," said Alan. "Good-bye."

"Au revoir," said the old man.

Exercises

Understanding What You Have Read

____1. The main thing that happens in the story is that (**4b**)
   a. an old man talks about his wife.
   b. a young man marries a woman.
   c. a young man buys a love potion.
   d. a young man falls in love.

____2. While the young man buys a love potion (**5a**),
   a. the old man tells him he will hate his wife.
   b. the old man tells about a poison he sells.
   c. the old man finds out how rich the young man is.
   d. the old man predicts happiness for the young couple.

3. Put a *T* next to the statements that are true and an *F* next to those that are false. (**5a**)
   ____a. The young man needs poison now.
   ____b. The young man loves Diana.
   ____c. Diana loves the young man.
   ____d. The poison costs ten dollars.
   ____e. The love potion costs ten dollars.
   ____f. A young man can afford the poison.
   ____g. The old man believes the love potion will work.
   ____h. The young man looks forward to how much Diana will love him after she drinks the love potion.
   ____i. The poison has a strong taste.
   ____j. The love potion is almost tasteless.

4. Put a checkmark next to the effects the love potion will have on Diana. (**5a**)
   ____a. She will care very much about Alan.
   ____b. She will want to know everything Alan does.
   ____c. She will dream about Alan.
   ____d. She won't want to go to parties.

Interpreting and Evaluating

____ 1. What do you infer about the old man's attitudes toward Alan and Diana? (**7**)
   a. He thinks Alan and Diana will be happy together.
   b. He thinks Alan will get tired of Diana.

c. He thinks love conquers all.

d. None of these.

2. From which of the following of the old man's actions can you infer this attitude? Put a checkmark next to the answers you think are correct. (**7**)

_____a. his tone of voice

_____b. his sales pitch for the poison

_____c. his description of how much Diana will cling to Alan

_____d. a sign he gives Alan

3. Why do you think that the old man sells the love potion for only a dollar but he charges five thousand dollars for the poison? (**7**)

_____

_____

_____

_____

_____ 4. What can you infer from the fact that the old man's parting remark is *au revoir* and not *goodbye*? (**7**)

a. Alan will probably not see the old man again.

b. Alan will probably return.

c. Alan and the old man may meet again in France.

d. Alan will send other young men to the shop on Pell Street.

5. Put a checkmark next to the generalization you *cannot* make about the writer's attitude toward love and marriage. (**10**)

_____a. He thinks love can get tiring.

_____b. He thinks love is truly exciting.

_____c. He thinks marriage can strangle a person.

_____d. He thinks love can sometimes turn into hate.

_____ 6. Which statement do you think best describes the writer of the story? (**11a**)

a. He thinks the world is worse than it really is.

b. He sees life as it really is.

    c. He looks at the amusing side of life.

    d. Other: _____

____ 7. In the first two paragraphs the scene is described as (**11d**)
    a. cheerful and rich.
    b. adventurous and dangerous.
    c. gloomy and run down.
    d. none of these.

  8. What words in the first two paragraphs give that impression? (**11d**)

    a. _____

    b. _____

    c. _____

    d. _____

    e. _____

    f. _____

    g. _____

    h. _____

  9. The writer chose this kind of scene for the story because

    (**11d**) _____

_____

  10. Check the word that does *not* describe the old man accurately. (**11d**)
    ____a. polite
    ____b. businesslike
    ____c. nasty
    ____d. wise

____11. The mood of the story is (**11b**)
    a. funny.
    b. thoughtful.

   c. cheerful.
   d. scary.

——12. The purpose of the story is to (**11d**)
      a. warn young people about the problems of love.
      b. tell you how to clean up your life.
      c. entertain you.
      d. make you laugh.

——13. This story is written for (**11d**)
      a. children.
      b. people who have just fallen in love for the first time.
      c. people who understand something about life.
      d. people who are too old to appreciate love.

   14. In the first sentence, Alan is said to be "as nervous as a
       kitten." Put a checkmark next to the ideas suggested by
       this comparison. (**8**)
       ——a. jumpy
       ——b. furry
       ——c. not experienced
       ——d. frightened

   15. What does the old man mean when he calls the poison a

       "life-cleaner"? (**8**) _____

       _____

——16. A *chaser*, among other meanings, is a drink to wash down
      the strong taste of whiskey. This story is probably called
      "The Chaser" because (**8**)
      a. In a figurative sense the poison would be used to wash
         down the love potion and get rid of the strong taste.
      b. Alan is chasing after Diana; then Diana will chase Alan
         after she drinks the potion.
      c. When Alan is older, he will chase after the old man to
         get some poison.
      d. All of these.

Vocabulary

Next to each of the words in the left-hand column, write the letter
of the correct definition in the right-hand column. (**2**)

_____ 1. acquaintance   a. in secret
_____ 2. adoration   b. being alone
_____ 3. apprehensively   c. splurge
_____ 4. bountifully   d. personal knowledge
_____ 5. confidential   e. richly
_____ 6. imperceptible   f. hate
_____ 7. indulge   g. poison
_____ 8. landing   h. not clearly
_____ 9. obscurely   i. nervously
_____10. scorn   j. not noticeable
_____11. solitude   k. total love
                   l. a platform at the top of the stairs

17 Language for Chimps

by L. Dodge Fernald and Peter Fernald

In this selection from a college psychology text, the authors describe two now-famous experiments with chimpanzees. These experiments helped scientists understand more about the development of language, but many questions still remain unanswered.

Word Highlights

abstract theoretical; apart from the specific

manipulation the act of operating or controlling something by skilled use of the hands

mechanism process or system of parts that operate or interact like a machine

modeling displaying for someone to copy

neurological relating to studies of the nervous system

operant operating to produce effects

rudiments basics

Even the lowest animals communicate with others of their kind. Many of these communicative acts are essentially reflexive, as when a chirping cricket induces others to chirp, and the croaking of a frog initiates this activity in other frogs. These behaviors for the most part serve to signal dangers, interest in mating, and territorial claims.

At a much higher level, among primates, research has shown some communicative acts which are similar to those employed by human beings. Chimpanzees communicate by bowing, grinning, kissing, touching, and patting. They also have a few vocal signals, such as calls and grunts. The question has been posed, therefore, whether the chimpanzee, our closest relative from the standpoint of evolution, biochemical makeup, and neurological development, has the capacity to acquire language.

Learning a Spoken Language

Some years ago, Winthrop and Luella Kellogg decided to study this and other questions, rearing a chimpanzee in a normal human environment. Gua, a seven-and-one-half-month-old female chimpanzee, was adopted into their household to be treated in the same fashion as their ten-month-old son Donald. The two infants were dressed alike, fed in the same way, and allowed equal play opportunities. In going to the park, going to bed, or being toilet trained, both had essentially similar experiences, and the parents tried hard to give them equal affection.

Shortly after the experiment began, Gua became slightly superior to Donald in word recognition, but Donald's inferiority might be explained on the basis of less physical ability. The chimpanzee was more agile and therefore could respond more readily to such requests as "Get up on the chair." As time passed, however, the child gained rapidly on the chimp, and by the end of the period of investigation he was significantly ahead in word recognition.

In word usage, Gua remained nonverbal throughout the experiment. Her communications included some gestures, such as wriggling her lips when she wanted apples, but no words. Her only vocalizations were sudden barks or cries in moments of excitement, fear, or pain. Donald, on the other hand, passed through the normal cooing and babbling stages and, by the end of the research, uttered his first words. He said "da" meaning "down" and "bow-wow" for the dog, and he used a few other words. But as his parents emphasized, he had not shown language mastery either. At the end of the study, he still had not used words in combination. Unfortunately, this research had to be discontinued after nine months, partly because of the increasing strength and enormous agility of Gua around the house.

Learning a Sign Language

It is possible that Gua's failure to develop words, as well as prior cooing and babbling, was due to her limited speech mechanisms, rather than a deficit in mental ability. No primate, as far as we know, has demonstrated coordination of mouth and throat mechanisms comparable to that displayed by a young child in speaking. To find out whether the chimpanzee is capable of learning human language, it was concluded, a different approach is required.

For this purpose another chimpanzee, named Washoe, was reared entirely apart from human speech 35 years later. This wild-born, twelve-month-old female was exposed only to the gestural language employed by the deaf in North America, called American Sign Language (ASL). During the four years of this experiment, ASL gestures were taught to Washoe by any and all means available, using the best methods known to science. Operant conditioning, modeling, and direct manipulation of the hands were used, and thus Washoe's training differed markedly from that of Gua years earlier.

For example, whenever Washoe imitated a sign that was modeled by one of her experimenters, she was immediately tickled, an experience she obviously enjoyed. Furthermore, when she brought her hands together at the tickled region in a pattern crudely resembling the ASL sign for "more," she was tickled again. Through this operant conditioning, an acceptable sign for "more" was established. The sign for "tree," however, was taught to Washoe by manipulating her arm, bending it at the elbow, and making her grasp the elbow with her free hand. In these ways, Washoe acquired a larger and larger vocabulary, learning at a more rapid rate as the experiment progressed. Like a normal child, rather than becoming more confused as more words were added, she seemed to learn them more easily and had a vocabulary of 160 signs at the end of the four-year experiment.

Months of Training	Total Signs Used
7	4
14	13
27	34
36	85
48	160

More important, Washoe made 294 different two-sign combinations, and comparative studies have shown that 78 percent of these combinations are similar to the earliest two-word combinations of children. This finding suggests that four-year-old Washoe, who began training at age one year, has been using language much like a child approximately 16 to 27 months old. On this basis,

Washoe's attainment is noteworthy, despite the fact that she lags behind a human child. She "speaks" ASL, which may have a slower developmental rate than English, and her teachers were not native signers, which also may have influenced her progress.

After any language user begins using words in combinations, the next task is that of word order. Unfortunately, the evidence for word order has not yet been made available for Washoe. She uses many correct sequences, but she also makes mistakes, such as signing "Drink you" instead of "You drink." Despite their importance, we simply do not know the exact frequencies of Washoe's appropriate and inappropriate word orders or how they compare with those of human babies, especially deaf children using ASL as a first language.

In summary, we can say that Washoe apparently has achieved the early stages of human language development, but just how far she or others like her will progress remains to be observed. Educated human beings use language in highly abstract and complex ways, far in advance of Washoe's level of communication, as illustrated in Franklin Roosevelt's simple wartime slogan, "All we have to fear is fear itself."

Intraspecies Communication

Today perhaps two dozen chimpanzees similar to Washoe are being schooled in one way or another. One is acquiring language on a computer that keeps records of all the conversations. After six months of training, this chimpanzee was able to "read" word symbols corresponding to those on her keyboard. Another, using ASL, has progressed to the point at which she called a radish "food" until she experienced the bitter taste. With no sign for this flavor, she immediately called it "cry hurt food." Still another, acquiring language by using plastic chips as word-symbols, apparently can respond correctly to compound sentences, even those involving two different commands.

Suppose that Washoe or one of these other chimpanzees progresses to much further language development. Better yet, suppose that two or three chimps do so. What then? Has the chimpanzee achieved our level of communication? Not necessarily.

Language learning in chimpanzees will be most impressive not when one or more animals can communicate with human beings through cleverly arranged human systems, but when they use language to cooperate with and instruct each other. Hence, some young male chimpanzees are being prepared for such an experiment. They are being taught a specified and intentionally limited number of ASL signs. Then, when they know the rudiments of this language well and the time is right, they will be exposed to Washoe. With this start, will the more learned chimpanzee be capable of and interested in tutoring the youngsters in a fuller use of language? If so, only then can we say that the species, through language, is perhaps headed towards a cultural evolution—that is, to a significantly higher level of social organization than it now displays.

Exercises

Understanding What You Have Read

____ 1. The main idea of this selection is (**4b**)
   a. to show how chimps talk.
   b. to show the problems chimpanzees have in communicating among themselves.
   c. to describe ASL, American Sign Language.
   d. to show different approaches to the question of whether chimpanzees can learn language.

____ 2. When many crickets chirp together, they may be (**5b**)
   a. responding to the arrival of warm weather.
   b. signaling the mating season.
   c. imitating the croaking of frogs.
   d. searching for water.

____ 3. Winthrop and Luella Kellogg raised Donald and Gua (**5b**)
   a. by paying more attention to Gua.
   b. by paying more attention to Donald.
   c. by raising Donald as if he were a chimpanzee.
   d. so that their experiences were basically alike.

____ 4. Throughout their training in word recognition (**5a**)
   a. Gua was superior to Donald in everything.
   b. Gua was superior at first, but then Donald pulled ahead.
   c. Donald was superior at all times.
   d. Donald and Gua developed at just about the same rate.

____ 5. In regard to word usage, Gua (**5b**)
   a. finally uttered the word "da."
   b. could not vocalize anything at all.

    c. remained completely nonverbal.

    d. showed mastery equal to Donald's.

_____ 6. Washoe's training differed from Gua's in that Washoe (5b)

    a. was not raised along with a human child.

    b. learned sign language, not words.

    c. was taught by means of the best-known scientific methods.

    d. all of these.

_____ 7. An example of *operant conditioning* is (5b)

    a. manipulating Washoe's hands to make signs.

    b. modeling a sign for Washoe to copy.

    c. tickling Washoe after she made an appropriate sign.

    d. none of these.

_____ 8. At the end of the experiment with Washoe (5a)

    a. she had a vocabulary of more than 150 words.

    b. she was becoming more confused as signs were added to her vocabulary.

    c. she was taught speech sounds.

    d. she was more advanced than a typical human child of the same age.

_____ 9. Comparisons between the order of words Washoe used and the order of words used by human babies (5b)

    a. are unimportant.

    b. cannot yet be made.

    c. are the basis for current language theory.

    d. influence instruction for deaf children.

_____10. "Cry hurt food" was the sign one chimpanzee used to name (5b)

    a. a plastic chip.

    b. a keyboard symbol.

    c. a radish.

    d. a compound sentence.

_____11. *Cultural evolution* means (2a)

    a. moving geographically into a different culture.

    b. advancing to a higher social plane or level.

    c. using language appropriately.

    d. learning to communicate in any manner.

Interpreting and Evaluating

____ 1. If the cooing of one pigeon induced surrounding pigeons to coo, this communication would probably (7)
    a. be a reflexive act.
    b. prove that species of birds talk sensibly to each other.
    c. be unimportant.
    d. be a high form of language interaction.

____ 2. We may infer from the photograph on p. 303 that (7)
    a. Gua always had to be pulled along by Donald.
    b. Gua and Donald disliked walking in the leaves.
    c. Gua and Donald found nothing unusual in being together.
    d. all of these.

____ 3. We may infer that, if Gua wanted something very badly, she might (7)
    a. bark.
    b. cry.
    c. move her mouth.
    d. all of these.

____ 4. From the experiment with Gua, we may safely conclude that, after nine months, a chimp and a human child will (9)
    a. communicate reasonably well together.
    b. be cooing and babbling.
    c. not show command over language.
    d. be enormously agile.

____ 5. We can predict from the information in this article that, if the Kelloggs had continued the experiment beyond nine months, Gua would probably have been (9)
    a. able to communicate only with Donald.
    b. too large and active for indoor family life.
    c. using words in combination.
    d. uttering words like "da" and "bow-wow."

____ 6. That Gua's inability to speak may be related to her uncoordinated voice organs more than to her mental abilities is (11b)
    a. only an opinion of the authors.
    b. a proven fact.
    c. still being investigated by the Kelloggs.
    d. none of these.

_____ 7. The generalization "No primate, so far as we know, has demonstrated coordination of mouth and throat mechanisms comparable to that displayed by a young child in speaking" is (**10, 11**)
a. supported by evidence presented in this selection.
b. hearsay.
c. probably based on the authors' knowledge of the field, even though they offer no evidence to support it.
d. none of these.

_____ 8. We may conclude that, compared to Washoe's training, Gua's (**9**)
a. was not so scientific.
b. was performed entirely apart from human speech.
c. was superior.
d. was abnormal.

_____ 9. The authors conclude that four-year-old Washoe lags behind a human child of the same age because (**9**)
a. she cannot speak.
b. she uses language like a two-year-old.
c. she combines words with great difficulty.
d. none of these.

_____10. We may conclude that 22 percent of the two-sign combinations Washoe makes (**9**)
a. are similar to children's early two-word combinations.
b. are not like a child's early two-word combination.
c. have not been studied comparatively.
d. are related to inferior instruction.

_____11. From the table on p. 304, we may infer that the longer Washoe was trained (**7**)
a. the less she learned.
b. the more she wanted to learn.
c. the more two-word combinations she made.
d. the more she learned.

_____12. The authors do not explain why Washoe gives the sign for "Drink you" instead of the sign for "You drink," because (**7**)
a. they do not know.
b. they expect readers to figure this out for themselves.

c. they are not interested in that aspect of her development.

d. none of these.

_____ 13. We may conclude that the authors believe that Roosevelt's slogan "All we have to fear is fear itself" (**9**)
a. is an important political statement.
b. is a statement that researchers will try to teach in sign
language to chimps.
c. is a complicated remark.
d. is a very simple statement to understand.

_____ 14. If chimps learned to communicate with humans, the authors of this selection (**7, 11**)
a. would be unimpressed.
b. would be less impressed than if the chimps taught each
other.
c. would be more impressed than if the chimps taught
each other.
d. would speak to them in American Sign Language.

_____ 15. In general, the most difficult thing to teach monkeys
about language is probably the ability to (**10**)
a. communicate among themselves.
b. communicate with humans.
c. speak in sign language.
d. tutor their young in communication skills.

Vocabulary

1. Look at these words from the selection. Try to determine
their meanings. (Use a dictionary where necessary.) Then
do the crossword puzzle, filling in the words that best suit
the meanings given. You may have to add new endings to
the words in order to make them fit in the spaces in the
puzzle.

acquire	induce
agile	lag
capacity	primate
complex	reflexive
deficit	species

ACROSS

1. related to an involuntary action
5. able to move quickly and easily
6. a category of classification
8. an order of animals including monkeys, apes, and humans
9. shortage

DOWN

2. fall behind
3. complicated
4. persuaded
5. gains possession of
7. ability to receive, hold, or absorb

2. The following words from the selection all have smaller parts that you can recognize. From the word part clues, try to determine the meanings. Write them on the blank lines. Check your definitions in a dictionary. (**2b**)

1. biochemical _____

2. nonverbal _____

3. vocalization _____

4. gestural _____

5. attainment _____

18 A Different Approach to Classroom Testing

by James J. Berry and William M. Leonard, II

The results of this educational experiment may make you wonder how people actually learn and perform in school.

Word Highlights

accumulated added together

adequate fully suitable

anxiety fear caused by feeling of danger about to come

continuous without stopping

recorded set down in writing

significantly in an important way

traditional involving ideas or approaches that have been handed down from generation to generation

---

In two sociology classes at the Illinois State University at Normal, we structured the courses in a traditional fashion except that we tried a different approach to testing in one of the classes. At the beginning of the semester, we assigned students in that group partners with whom to take examinations, all of which were open-book tests. The other class took open-book examinations, too, but students worked independently. In both classes, exams were the same, the book was the same, and the lectures were based on the same materials.

Partners had similar accumulated grade point averages (within one-half a GPA unit). Partnerships could be broken if either party felt the other was not cooperating or not doing adequate preparation for the class. Only three of the 30 pairs eventually broke up.

The result of this matching process was a situation in which each student was able to confer with a partner throughout the examination. They could exchange ideas and make decisions about answers. Then, the students recorded their joint answers on the test paper.

Interaction between pair members was not continuous, and students usually carried on their discussions in an undertone. Occasionally, a student raised a voice in disagreement, but no one complained of the noise level.

What were the results? The paired students performed significantly better than those who took examinations alone. On all three exams, the paired group averaged 6 percent higher scores than the unpaired group. Also, 85 percent of the paired students indicated that pairing reduced their test anxiety, and 60 percent felt that the paired setting was a better learning one than the singles setting.

We would not have been surprised to find that two A students would do better on an exam working together than working alone and that two C students working together would show some improvement. What was not expected, however, was that two C students working together would do as well as or better than two A students working independently. The two students with the lowest grade point averages in the paired group obtained the second highest grade on the first exam and the fifth highest grade on the final. Interestingly, they earned the lowest grades on the second exam, which was taken in singles style.

On the basis of this one small experiment, we believe that—with a relatively small investment of money and/or time—improvements for many students can be made in the classroom. Students respond well to social settings where cooperation in problem solving is possible. They also react well to challenging situations that are not too threatening.

There is no reason to suspect that this approach would not work in any of the traditional teaching–learning situations. High school or junior high school classes might benefit even more than college groups from this method.

Exercises

Understanding What You Have Read

_____1. The main idea of this selection is (**4b**)
   a. to show how to improve students' grade-point averages.
   b. to discuss the results of pairing students on an examination.
   c. to urge a change in the approach to teaching in high schools and junior high schools.
   d. all of these.

_____2. The writers compare and contrast (**6c**)
   a. paired students and unpaired students.
   b. high schools and colleges.
   c. state universities and private colleges.
   d. paired students and noise levels.

3. For each of the following, write T if the sentence is true, F if the sentence is false, and X if there is no way to answer the question on the basis of information in the reading.
    ——a. Paired students earned higher grade-point averages.
    ——b. Twenty-seven pairs remained in partnership throughout the semester.
    ——c. Two C students working together did not do as well as two A students working alone.
    ——d. Two C students working together did as well as two A students working together.
    ——e. Unpaired groups averaged 6 percent lower than paired groups.
    ——f. Students could break up their partnerships if they felt a lack of cooperation.
    ——g. Students were suspicious of the new plan.
    ——h. Although students talked during exams, there was not too much noise.
    ——i. Students were encouraged to enter separate answers on the exam sheets.
    ——j. A majority of the students preferred the paired setting to the singles setting.

——4. The authors do not offer evidence to support the idea that (**11b**)
    a. some pairs broke up.
    b. high school classes could benefit more from pairing than could college classes.
    c. paired students did better on exams than unpaired students.
    d. students preferred the paired setting to the unpaired setting.

Interpreting and Evaluating

—— 1. We may infer that the two authors are (**7**)
    a. college students.
    b. professional examiners.
    c. college professors.
    d. high school teachers.

—— 2. We may infer that the instructor in front of the class of paired students taking exams (**7**)
    a. watched carefully to prevent cheating.

   b. reminded the students often to keep their voices down.
   c. sent many students to the dean for loud dis-
      agreements.
   d. none of these.

_____ 3. We can infer that the students in the classes (7)
   a. were all remedial college students.
   b. were all advanced college students.
   c. were high school and college students.
   d. were of mixed ability.

_____ 4. The authors believe that taking exams in paired groups is
   (7)
   a. noisy.
   b. threatening.
   c. threatening and challenging.
   d. challenging but not threatening.

_____ 5. The authors conclude that (9)
   a. their idea needs further study.
   b. students can do better in school if they take exams
      under paired conditions.
   c. students with very low grade-point averages should
      not have to take traditional courses.
   d. independent student work should not be encouraged.

_____ 6. If two C students working together were compared to
   two B students working separately, those who would
   probably do better are (9)
   a. the B students.
   b. the C students.
   c. no way to tell.
   d. the C students, if they studied very hard.

_____ 7. In general, the authors believe that (10)
   a. people working together do a better job than people
      working separately.
   b. people working separately do a better job than people
      working together.
   c. grade-point averages do not show students' true
      abilities.
   d. small experiments are the most valuable for finding
      facts.

_____ 8. In general, these authors would approve of education that
   (10)

    a. stressed new ideas and approaches.

    b. combined tradition and new ideas.

    c. relied mostly on tradition without introducing many new ideas.

    d. none of these.

____ 9. It is only the authors' opinion that (**11a**)

    a. paired groups on exams averaged higher than unpaired groups.

    b. two paired students with the lowest grade-point averages received the second-highest grade on the first exam.

    c. partners had similar averages.

    d. the pairing approach would probably work in any traditional teaching–learning situation.

____10. The authors' tone (**11d**) is

    a. angry.

    b. factual.

    c. humorous.

    d. sentimental.

Vocabulary

For each word in italics in the left-hand column select the best meaning from the right-hand column.

____ 1. *structured* the course	a. alone
____ 2. worked *independently*	b. lowered
____ 3. *eventually* broke up	c. pointed out
____ 4. *confer* with a partner	d. shared
____ 5. their *joint* answers	e. low voice
____ 6. in an *undertone*	f. consult
____ 7. students *indicated*	g. wanted
____ 8. *reduced* their test anxiety	h. dangerous
____ 9. *challenging* situation	i. demanding skill
____10. not too *threatening*	j. finally
	k. organized

19 What's Being Done About Dropouts

Reprinted from U.S. News & World Report, June 2, 1980

The growing number of students dropping out of high school in the 1980s and some of the ways in which educators are fighting to keep students in school are the subject of this selection from a popular weekly news magazine.

Word Highlights

alternate a substitute

discipline controlled behavior expected to produce mental or moral improvement

pilot program a program set up to act as a model for others

stratum a layer, in this case a layer of society

Graduation ceremonies are being held in schools all around the country, but tens of thousands of youngsters face the prospect of never getting diplomas.

They are the dropouts who continue to leave the nation's schools, despite aggressive efforts in many places to keep them in the classrooms. This school year, as in the past decade, there was an average of 26 dropouts for every 100 graduates.

So widespread is the problem that at any time 2.4 million school-age American youths are not in school, according to latest Census Bureau figures.

"It's one of the nation's greatest educational problems," says Ernest Boyer, former U.S. commissioner of education.

Up Here, Down There

For reasons not entirely clear, the dropout rate varies widely from city to city and is falling in some areas while rising in others. In Denver, the dropout rate declined from 11.5 percent in 1978 to 9.9 percent in the past year, while in Kansas City, Mo., the rate rose slightly from 6.2 percent in 1977–78 to 6.3 last year.

Problems are much worse in New York and Chicago, where recent studies indicate that about half the students drop out. However, that estimate also includes students who transfer out of a school district and may complete their education elsewhere.

There are a number of reasons why so many American youngsters continue to leave schools. Many girls drop out because of pregnancy. Boys get bored with classes and leave to take jobs. Foreign-born students become discouraged with language problems. Others run into troubles with teachers or other students. Some are failing and cannot face the discipline required to keep up with schoolwork.

A major part of the blame for today's high dropout rate is being placed on the nation's rising divorce rate and the resulting breakup of families. Myra Sampson, principal of Chicago's Community Christian Alternative Academy, puts it this way: "One of the biggest causes goes back to the family. The family today is not what it was years back." Dropouts typically are from broken homes, she adds, where baby-sitting and financial needs conflict with the children's going to school.

Dropouts come from every economic and social stratum, but there is a higher proportion among the poor and minorities. The rate among blacks is about twice that among white youngsters—49.6 dropouts for every 100 black graduates, compared with 23.3 per 100 white graduates, according to the Bureau of Labor Statistics.

To tackle the high dropout rates, which many observers cite as a reason for nagging crime and unemployment among the nation's youths, cities and states are trying a number of programs.

In Philadelphia, some 200 youngsters are enrolled in the Edison Project, aimed at managing potential dropouts ages 15 through 19. Says project manager Walter Spector: "We're dealing with people who almost everybody has forgotten. We recruit them and handle each student on an individual basis, stressing the learning of basic skills." So far, about 30 percent of these high-risk youths have stayed in school.

Operation Far Cry in New York City contacts youngsters by telephone to persuade them to return to a regular or an alternate school or evening classes, or to join a career program. Five outreach centers each handle about 100 youths and involve 10 to 15 teachers, counselors and community workers.

Denver is trying a different approach with its Hold Youth Program, in which potential dropouts at nine high schools and 18 junior highs are identified and counseled. A special teaching program has been set up for those teen-agers who attend school for only half a day and do not rotate classrooms with each subject. A strong student–teacher relationship is stressed, and teachers communicate frequently with parents to seek their cooperation.

Says Bettye Emerson, program manager for Denver's junior high schools: "The Hold Youth classroom is an intensive-care center for the student who needs motivation and encouragement."

Flexible Schedules

Chicago's Community Christian Alternative Academy on the city's West Side is trying small classes and individual attention to lure dropouts back into a school environment. In Milwaukee, a new work–study specialty school is being planned for 300 students, with classes to be conducted at odd hours in order not to conflict with work schedules.

Several state projects also are being tried. For example, the Illinois State Board of Education has established 13 new alternative-education programs, serving about 1,500 teen-agers in both public and private schools. Colorado has set up pilot programs at six state schools to study the effect of school environment on behavior and learning. Explains William Van Buskirk, senior consultant to the Colorado project: "While we can't change the home or neighborhood environment, we can alter the school environment to reduce the rate of dropping out."

The most effective remedy, as some officials see it, may be what dropouts find on the outside. Says Marc Bassin, director of one New York dropout program: "One of the best motivations for youths to return to school is the education they pick up from being in the streets. They find there are no worthwhile jobs out there for people without high school diplomas."

Exercises

Understanding What You Have Read

_____ 1. The main idea of this selection is that (**4**)
   a. nothing can be done about dropouts.
   b. the reasons why students drop out are too complicated to understand.
   c. new and varied approaches at schools are addressing the serious problem of students dropping out.
   d. Philadelphia's efforts to keep students in school are a model.

2. According to the selection, which methods are being used for fighting the dropout problem? Put a checkmark next to each one you choose. (**5**)

_____a. stressing strong student-teacher relationships
_____b. identifying potential dropouts early
_____c. calling dropouts on the phone.
_____d. encouraging potential dropouts to leave school early
_____e. working to keep students interested
_____f. being very strict with students
_____g. sending dropouts to minimum-security hotels or communes
_____h. making school more responsive to students

_____3. For every 100 students who enroll in high school, how many drop out? (5)
a. 9.9
b. 52
c. 30
d. 26

_____4. In Denver the dropout rate (5)
a. declined 1.6 percent.
b. rose 1.6 percent.
c. rose 9.9 percent.
d. declined 11.5 percent.

_____5. Of the following reasons for students dropping out, which does the article *not* suggest? (5)
a. teen-age pregnancies
b. boredom
c. trouble with teachers, students, or school work
d. poor religious training

_____6. For every two black students who drop out of school (5)
a. one black student graduates.
b. one white student drops out.
c. 23.3 white students drop out.
d. none of these.

_____7. The Edison Project in Philadelphia stresses (5)
a. on-the-job training.
b. basic skills and individual counseling.
c. telephone calls to convince dropouts to return.
d. all of these.

_____8. New York's Operation Outreach serves about how many dropouts? (5)

a. 500
b. 100
c. 115
d. 18

Interpreting and Evaluating

_____ 1. We can infer that the reason why more urban than rural students drop out is that (**7**)
  a. teachers in cities are inferior to teachers in other parts of the country.
  b. city kids are always getting into trouble with the law.
  c. there simply are more students living in cities than are living in other places.
  d. there are lots of good things for dropouts to do in cities.

_____ 2. Which generalization can correctly be made from the article? (**10**)
  a. Only poor and minority students drop out.
  b. Dropouts earn more money than high school graduates.
  c. Few dropouts regret their decision.
  d. Dropouts come from every class and group.

_____ 3. We can infer that the reason why so many students continue to drop out is that (**7**)
  a. school is pretty boring to most students.
  b. educators have not yet addressed the real causes for students dropping out.
  c. educators are too busy doing important things to worry about a few dropouts.
  d. educators need dropouts to keep the schools from getting overcrowded.

_____ 4. What conclusion does the article draw about the alternative education programs? (**9**)
  a. Most of them don't work at all.
  b. Many of them are good.
  c. They are not necessary.
  d. They are less effective than the experiences dropouts have on the streets.

_____ 5. We may infer from this article that, if dropouts decreased (**7**)

a. schools might not serve their students effectively.
b. the crime rate might also decrease.
c. teachers would not lose their jobs.
d. students' home environments would improve.

____ 6. We may infer that, for dropouts in New York and Chicago, statistics are (**7**)
a. completely accurate.
b. not completely accurate.
c. unreal.
d. unconvincing.

____ 7. We may infer that the reasons why relatively more blacks drop out than whites is that (**7**)
a. blacks have more economic and social problems.
b. whites have more economic and social problems.
c. more whites come from suburban schools where drug use is a big problem.
d. most blacks would rather work than go to school.

____ 8. Which generalization would most educators be likely to agree with? (**9**)
a. Most dropouts are too smart to be bothered with school.
b. Dropouts need encouragement.
c. Dropouts need to move to better neighborhoods.
d. Helping dropouts is a waste of time for schools.

____ 9. We can conclude that the reason why a high dropout rate is a problem for our society is that (**10**)
a. dropouts will get the good jobs before other students can finish school and apply for them.
b. America needs trained people, and everyone's contribution can help society.
c. dropouts will go on welfare.
d. dropouts will become criminals.

____10. The tone of this article is (**11d**)
a. straightforward and factual.
b. depresssed.
c. angry and bitter.
d. boring.

Vocabulary

The words in italics below appear in "What's Being Done About Dropouts." Select from the choices given at the right the letters of the correct definitions for the words *as they are used in the selection*. Write the letters in the spaces provided. There are two more choices than you will need. (**2a**)

___ 1. despite *aggressive* efforts	a. tempt
___ 2. the dropout rate *declined*	b. category
___ 3. social *stratum*	c. alternate;
___ 4. *nagging* crime and unemployment	change
___ 5. we *recruit* them	d. bold; energetic
___ 6. *rotate* classrooms	e. enroll
___ 7. to *lure* dropouts back	f. surroundings
___ 8. effect of the school *environment*	g. stimulation
___ 9. *motivation* for youths to return	h. dropped
___10. managing *potential* dropouts	i. annoying
	j. hostile
	k. possible
	l. spin on an axis

20 The Discovery of the Electron

by Alan Sherman, Sharon Sherman, and Leonard Russikoff

The electron is one of the most important components of the atom, which is itself the basic material from which all things are made. In this passage from Chapter 4 of their text, the authors describe how scientists isolated the electron and discovered some of its properties. The drawings and photographs are designed to illustrate some of the writer's points.

Word Highlights

physicist a scientist who studies matter and energy and how they are related to each other

ultraviolet a kind of electromagnetic radiation just above visible light on the scale of radiations

voltage electromotive force

zinc sulfide a chemical substance

In the mid 1800s scientists wanted to know whether the atom was really indivisible. They also wanted to know why atoms of different elements had different properties.

A major breakthrough came with the invention of the Crookes tube, or *cathode-ray tube* (Figure 4.1 on p. 326). What is a cathode-ray tube and how does it work?

Everybody knows that some substances conduct electric current (that is, they are conductors), while other substances do not. But with enough electrical power, a current can be driven through any substance—solid, liquid, or gas. In the cathode-ray tube, a high voltage electric current is driven through a *vacuum*. The tube contains two pieces of metal, called *electrodes*. Each electrode is attached by a wire to the source of an electric current. The source has two *terminals*, positive and negative. The electrode attached to the positive electric terminal is called the *anode*; the electrode attached to the negative terminal is called the *cathode*. Crookes showed that when the current was turned on, a beam moved from the cathode to the anode; in other words, the beam moved from the negative to the positive terminal. Therefore the beam had to be negative in nature.

What was this beam? Was it made of particles or waves? Did it come from the electricity or from the metal electrodes? Physicists

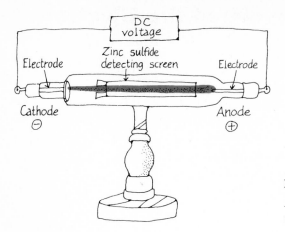

Figure 4.1

A Crookes or cathode-ray tube

in Crookes's time were not sure about the answers to these questions, but they did make guesses. Whatever this beam was, it traveled in straight lines (they knew that because it cast sharp shadows). For lack of a better name, the German physicist Eugen Goldstein called the beams *cathode rays*, since they came from the cathode.

The cathode rays appear as a beam of light as they move through the tube. To help the observer see the beam, there is a screen coated with zinc sulfide in the tube. The cathode rays produce light when they hit the zinc sulfide screen. By the way, if it weren't for the cathode-ray-tube, you'd never be able to watch television. This is because a television tube is a cathode-ray tube, and the face of the picture tube serves the same purpose as that zinc sulfide screen you see in Figure 4.1. Furthermore, most novels and many magazines are set in type by cathode-ray tube equipment.

The German physicists in Crookes's time favored the *wave theory* of cathode rays because the beam traveled in straight lines, like water waves. But the English physicists favored the *particle theory*. They said that the beam was composed of tiny particles which moved very quickly—so quickly that they were hardly influenced by gravity. That was why the particles moved in a straight path. Notice how an experimental observation led to two different theories.

Crookes proposed a method to solve the dilemma. If the beam *was* composed of negative particles, a magnet would deflect them. But if the beam was a wave, a magnet would cause almost no deflection. Particles would also be more easily deflected by an elec-

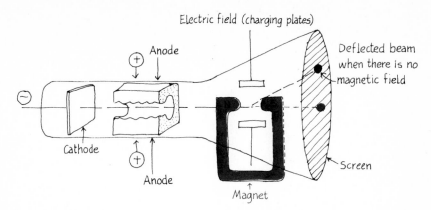

Figure 4.2

*The Thomson experiment:
(1) A beam of electrons
(dashed line) moves from
cathode toward anodes.
(2) Some electrons pass between anodes. (3) Electric
field causes beam of electrons to bend. This is visible
on the screen. (4) But ex-
perimenter can add a mag-*
*net to counteract deflection
caused by electric field, and
make the beam follow a
straight path. (5) One can
then measure the strengths
of the electric and magnetic
fields and calculate the
charge-to-mass ratio (e/m) of
the electron.*

tric field. In 1897, the English physicist J. J. Thomson used both these techniques—magnetic and electric—to show that the rays were composed of particles (Figure 4.2). Today we call these particles *electrons*. (The term *electron* was suggested by the Irish physicist George Stoney, in 1891, to represent the fundamental unit of electricity.) In 1911 a young American physicist named Robert Millikan determined the mass of the electron: 9.11×10^{-28} grams. (To get an idea of how small this is, notice that minus sign up there in the exponent, and think of all the zeros we would have to put before the 9 if we wrote the entire number as a decimal.)

Next someone had to prove that the electrons weren't coming from the electricity, but were being given off by the metal electrodes. Proof that metals do give off electrons came from the laboratories of Philipp Lenard, a German physicist. In 1902 he showed that ultraviolet light directed onto a metal makes it send out, or emit, electrons. This effect, known as the *photoelectric effect*, indicated that metal atoms—and the atoms of other elements—contain electrons.

Exercises

Understanding What You Have Read

_____ 1. The main idea of this selection is (4)
   a. to describe how a cathode tube works.
   b. to show the process scientists used to find the electron and discover its properties.
   c. to show the reader the superiority of German scientists.
   d. to make the reader aware of the contributions of Robert Millikan and to tell a little about him.

_____ 2. Write a *T* next to each true statement and an *F* next to each false statement. (5)
   _____a. Electrons are negatively charged.
   _____b. Typesetters use cathode-ray tubes to set newspapers and magazines in type.
   _____c. The positive terminal of a cathode-ray tube is called the cathode.
   _____d. Eugen Goldstein named the electron.
   _____e. At first scientists thought that electricity was like water.
   _____f. The English scientist J. J. Thomson was right that the electron behaved more like a particle than like a wave.

_____ 3. It is a fact that electricity (5a)
   a. is a weak force.
   b. can be carried through conducting substances only.
   c. can be carried through anything if enough force is used.
   d. was discovered by George Stanley.

_____ 4. A beam that casts shadows that are not sharp could probably travel (5)
   a. from England to Germany but not back again.
   b. very quickly but not as fast as a sharp-shadow beam.
   c. in a curved line.
   d. inside a box at night.

_____ 5. J. J. Thomson decided that cathode rays were particles because (5)
   a. a magnet could deflect a cathode-ray beam moving across it.

      b. cathode-ray particles sometimes become so large that
         scientists can see them with the naked eye.
      c. a magnet could not deflect a beam of cathode rays
         moving across it.
      d. the beam was not deflected by an electric field.

_____ 6. In Figure 4.1, "DC voltage" is (**5b, 5c**)
      a. a vacuum.
      b. the source of an electric current.
      c. the zinc sulfide detecting screen.
      d. an electrode.

_____ 7. In Figure 4.2, the deflected beam would have to be (**5b, 5c**)
      a. positively charged like an anode.
      b. broken by an electric field.
      c. returned to the anode.
      d. negatively charged.

_____ 8. The purpose of the charging plates in Figure 4.2 is to (**5b, 5c**)
      a. create conditions for electron beams to bend.
      b. produce a screen.
      c. stimulate the anode.
      d. charge the magnet.

_____ 9. The pattern of organization in this selection is (**6**)
      a. time order.
      b. cause and effect.
      c. listing of details.
      d. order of importance.

_____10. The scientist who first made study of the electron possible
      was (**5**)
      a. Stoney.
      b. Crookes.
      c. Cooke.
      d. Lenard.

Interpreting and Evaluating

_____1. We can infer from the description of the electron that it is (**7**)
      a. very powerful.
      b. incredibly small.

c. very straight.

d. lighter than air.

_____2. We can infer about the photoelectric effect that it (**7**)

    a. proved that metal does not contain electrons.

    b. was a valuable tool for scientists.

    c. indicated that all elements contain electrons.

    d. helped scientists to invent photography.

3. Put a checkmark next to those statements that can be supported by evidence from the text and an X next to those statements that cannot. (**7, 11**)

    _____a. Cathode rays produce light when they hit a screen made of zinc sulfide.

    _____b. Many scientists were killed by electrical discharge as a result of these cathode-ray experiments.

    _____c. Electrons move too quickly to be influenced by gravity.

    _____d. Atoms of different elements have different properties.

    _____e. With enough electrical power, a current can be driven through anything.

    _____f. The wave/particle dilemma is still a problem facing scientists today.

    _____g. Electrons have magnetic properties.

4. Write a *1* next to the discovery or event that occurred first, a *2* next to the number of the second discovery, and so on. (**5, 6a**)

    _____a. the mass of the electron

    _____b. demonstration of cathode rays as particles

    _____c. the photoelectric effect

    _____d. the naming of the electron

_____5. We may conclude from the paragraph beginning "Crookes proposed" that, in the number 9.11×10^{-28}, the -28 in the exponent tells us to (**9**)

    a. subtract 28 from 9.11

    b. add 28 to 9.11

    c. add zeroes after the number and move the decimal point 28 places to the right.

    d. add zeroes before the number and move the decimal point 28 places to the left.

_____6. We can safely generalize from the paragraph beginning "The German physicists in Crookes's time" that (**10**)

a. German physicists were interested only in the military uses of cathode rays.

b. gravity has no influence on electrons.

.c. English scientists have no influence on electrons.

d. people observing the same experiment can reach different conclusions.

_____7. This selection was probably written for (**11d**)

a. a scientific journal.

b. a children's book about dinosaurs.

c. a college textbook.

d. a medical school text.

Vocabulary

_____1. As used in this selection, *conductors* refers to (**2**)

a. people who collect tickets on trains.

b. people who direct symphony orchestras.

c. things that measure electric current.

d. things that transmit electric current.

_____2. As used here, *terminals* refers to (**2**)

a. fatal disease states.

b. places to await trains.

c. places to await buses.

d. none of these.

_____3. As used here, *vacuum* refers to (**2**)

a. a machine that cleans using suction.

b. a machine that draws blood out of people.

c. a space containing nothing.

d. a space wherein all the air has been purified.

_____4. The beam referred to in this selection is (**2**)

a. a piece of wood.

b. a stringbeam.

c. a stream of water.

d. a stream of electromagnetic particles.

_____5. In the expression "A magnet would deflect them," *deflect them* means (**2**)

a. turn them into iron.

b. cause them to swerve.

c. electrify them.

d. make them photoelectric.

_____6. A *dilemma* is always (2)
  a. a scientific problem.
  b. the basis of most experiments in physics.
  c. a choice between two equal alternatives.
  d. a choice between two alternatives, with one choice clearly preferable to the other.

_____7. A *particle* is (2)
  a. a large part to which a small group belongs.
  b. one of the features of electrons.
  c. a current.
  d. a very small unit of matter.

_____8. As it is used in this selection, the word *current* means (2)
  a. happening at this time.
  b. a raisin.
  c. a flow of electricity.
  d. occurring previously.

_____9. In the first sentence of the selection, the word *indivisible* means (2)
  a. not able to be divided.
  b. easy to break down into parts.
  c. liberated.
  d. advisable.

21 Hemingway in Paris

by Malcolm Cowley

In this essay, a literary critic tells about some of the influences on the development of Ernest Hemingway's skills as a writer. This is the kind of selection a literature teacher might ask you to look at in order to help you understand Hemingway's novels.

Word Highlights

blue pencil   cross out; eliminate

commission   power to carry out an assignment

convoy   a group of military cars and trucks

correspondent   someone employed to send news regularly from a faraway place

decorum   that which is proper in behavior

disciple   faithful follower

dispatched   sent off

doctrine   body of rules

ethics   moral rules of right and wrong

groping   searching blindly with the hands

grudgingly   giving in unhappily and without really wanting to

incendiaries   those who set fires to cause damage

instinctive   referring to a natural gift

persecutions   annoying attacks and punishments

roving   wandering about, moving from place to place

vehemently   eagerly, with great and sometimes violent feeling

---

At the end of December 1921, when Ernest Hemingway was twenty-two years old and newly married, he came to Paris for a second visit. The first, in May 1918, had lasted only until he picked up a Red Cross ambulance, which he drove in convoy to the Italian front. There he had been gravely wounded early in July, and he had spent the following months in and out of military hospitals. After his return to Chicago he had written many stories and poems and had even started a novel, but he had so far published nothing over his own name except in high school papers and in the weekly magazine of *The Toronto Star*. He now planned to finish out his apprenticeship as a writer, and this second visit—interrupted by four unhappy months in Toronto—was to last for nearly seven years. His apprenticeship, however, would end spectacularly in 1926, with the publication of *The Sun Also Rises*.

In days when many things have ended, it is a melancholy pleasure to go back over the records of that era when everything

was starting, for Hemingway and others, and when almost anything seemed possible. He came to Paris with letters of introduction from Sherwood Anderson, whom he had known well in
Chicago, and also with a roving commission from *The Toronto Star*
to write color stories, for which he would be paid at space rates if
the stories were printed. In those days such commissions were
easy to obtain, since they did not obligate a newspaper to spend
money, and usually they led to nothing but a few rejected or
grudgingly printed manuscripts. Hemingway's stories were good
enough to feature, and they quickly led to definite assignments,
with travel expenses.

Suddenly elevated to the position of staff reporter and authorized to send cables—but not too many of them—Hemingway
was dispatched to the Genoa Economic Conference in March 1922,
to the Near East in September for the closing days of the Greco-
Turkish War, and to Lausanne at the end of November for the
peace conference that followed. He also worked for Hearst's International News Service on the last two of these assignments, earning while he learned. In Constantinople he listened to stories about
the burning of Smyrna and studied the Greek retreat—so he afterward said—as if it were a laboratory experiment in warfare. At
Lausanne he studied the mechanics of international relations, with
the help of barside lectures from William Bolitho, already famous
as a correspondent. In both places he studied the curious language
known as cabelese, in which every word had to do the work of six
or seven. At three dollars a word he would put a message something like this on the wires: KEMAL INSWARDS UNBURNED SMYRNA
GUILTY GREEKS. The translation appearing in the Hearst papers
would be: "Mustapha Kemal in an exclusive interview with the
correspondent of the International News Service [KEMAL INS-
WARDS] denied vehemently that the Turkish forces had any part
in the burning of Smyrna [UNBURNED SMYRNA]. The city, Kemal
stated, was fired by incendiaries in the troops of the Greek rear
guard before the first Turkish patrols entered the city [GUILTY
GREEKS]."

Cabelese was an exercise in omitting everything that can be
taken for granted. It contributed to Hemingway's literary method,
just as the newspaper assignments contributed to his subject matter. Going back over the records, one is astonished to find how
much he learned during that first year abroad. He said afterward,
"A great writer seems to be born with knowledge. But he really is
not; he has only been born with the ability to learn in a quicker
ratio to the passage of time than other men and without conscious

application, and with an intelligence to accept or reject what is already presented as knowledge." Hemingway had that gift to such an extent that one thinks of him as an instinctive student who never went to college. His motto through life was not that of Sherwood Anderson's groping adolescent, "I want to know why," but rather, "I want to know *how*"—how to write, first of all, but also how to fish, how to box, how to ski, how to act in the bull ring, how to remember his own sensations, how to nurse his talent, how to live while learning to write, and more broadly how to *live*, in the sense of mastering the rules that must be followed by anyone who wants to respect himself. Many of his stories can be read and have been read by thousands as, essentially, object lessons in practical ethics and professional decorum.

Since Hemingway could find no textbooks in many of his fields, or none that could be trusted, he went straight to the best teachers. Among those under whom he studied during his first Paris years were Gertrude Stein and Ezra Pound, who did not love each other, and a cross-eyed Negro jockey from Cincinnati named Jim Winkfield.

How much he learned from his two older literary friends is the subject of a long-standing argument, but I think he learned a great deal. He listened attentively, and he had too much confidence in himself to fear, as many young writers do, that he would end as somebody's disciple. He could afford to take from others because he gave much in return. What he gave to Miss Stein is partly revealed in his letters to her, now in the Yale Library: he got her work published in *The Transatlantic Review* when he was helping to edit it, and having learned that she had only a bound manuscript of *The Making of Americans*, he typed long sections of it for the printer. One thing he took partly from her was a colloquial—in appearance—American style, full of repeated words, prepositional phrases, and present participles, the style in which he wrote his early published stories. One thing he took from Pound—in return for trying vainly to teach him how to box—was the doctrine of the accurate image, which he applied in the "chapters" printed between the stories that went into *In Our Time*; but Hemingway also learned from him to bluepencil most of his adjectives and adverbs. What he learned from Jim Winkfield was simpler; it was the name of a winning horse.

I heard the story from the late Evan Shipman, poet, trotting-horse columnist, and one of Hemingway's lifelong friends. Winkfield, he told me, had won the Kentucky Derby in 1901, on His Eminence, and again the following year, on Alan-a-Dale. By

1922 black jockeys were not being employed on American tracks, and Winkfield was in France training horses for Pierre Wertheimer, who had a famous stable. There is no outside audience when colts are trained in France, and there are no professional clockers at their time trials; every stable has its own secrets. At Wertheimer's stable the secret was Epinard, a sensationally promising colt with an unfashionable sire. Winkfield, who was seeing a lot of Hemingway, told him that Epinard was going to run his first race at Deauville that summer. Having borrowed all the money he could, Hemingway laid it on Epinard's nose.

That wasn't his one lucky day at the track. In June of the same year—writing from Milan, where he said that most of the races were fixed—he reported to Gertrude Stein that he had picked seventeen winners out of twenty-one starts. Most of his winnings went into the bank, together with proceeds from a small trust fund inherited by his wife, born Hadley Richardson. He was a foresighted young man, and already he planned to stop working for newspapers. Miss Stein encouraged the decision. "If you keep on doing newspaper work," she told him, "you will never see things, you will only see words, and that will not do—that is, of course, if you intend to be a writer."

Hemingway had never intended to be anything else, but writing every day was a luxury he still couldn't afford. *The Star*, impressed by a series of articles he had lately submitted on the French occupation of the Ruhr, offered him a job in the home office at a top reporter's salary, for those days, of $125 a week. In September 1923 he left for Toronto with the intention of working two years and saving enough money to finish a novel. Soon he came into conflict with Harry C. Hindmarsh, then assistant managing editor of *The Star*, who tried to break his spirit with what seems to have been a series of nagging persecutions. Hemingway resigned explosively at the end of December, and the following month he was back in Paris with Hadley and their new baby, born in Toronto. He was resolved to get along as best he could while writing for himself.

Exercises

Understanding What You Have Read

——1. The main idea of this selection is to show (**4b**)
    a. how Hemingway learned to bet on horses.
    b. how Hemingway made friends in Paris.

c. how and what Hemingway learned in Paris.

d. the early life of Ernest Hemingway.

2. For each of the following write *T* if the sentence is true, *F* if the sentence is false, and *X* if there is no way to answer the question on the basis of the information in the reading. (**5a**)

_____a. Hemingway had a mean temper.

_____b. He visited Paris for the first time in 1921.

_____c. He had published many stories and poems before he came to Paris.

_____d. He wrote stories on commission for the *Toronto Star*.

_____e. Hemingway's use of *cabelese* was the best among all the other reporters.

_____f. He was more interested in knowing the *why* than in knowing the *how* about things.

_____g. He disliked Sherwood Anderson.

_____h. His friends in Paris included Gertrude Stein, Ezra Pound, and Jim Winkfield.

_____i. Hemingway wanted to help Gertrude Stein but had no way to do it.

_____j. He learned about accurate images from Ezra Pound.

_____k. Hemingway wrote *The Making of Americans*.

_____l. Books that Hemingway wrote include *The Sun Also Rises* and *In Our Time*.

_____m. He wanted to stop working for the newspapers so he could write.

_____n. He hated newspaper work.

_____o. The *Toronto Star* paid him $125 a week to work in the home office.

3. Skim the first paragraph for the information required, and write it in the space provided. (**5c**)

a. the date *The Sun Also Rises* was published _____

b. the length of time Hemingway spent in Paris _____

c. what he did in 1918 _____

_____4. *Cabelese* is (**2a, 5a**)
   a. slang.
   b. a foreign language, half French, half Turkish.
   c. a funny way the French have of speaking.
   d. a way of writing that leaves out any words that can be taken for granted.

_____5. Hemingway used cabelese when he sent telegrams, because (**5a**)
   a. he liked to joke around with his editor.
   b. he was always interested in language.
   c. he could not speak Turkish.
   d. none of these.

_____6. When the newspaper editors received Hemingway's message in cabelese, they (**5a, 7**)
   a. printed exactly what he sent them.
   b. checked on a special code book.
   c. changed his message into longer and complete sentences.
   d. translated it into English.

_____7. About writers, Hemingway believed that they (**5a**)
   a. definitely had more knowledge than most people.
   b. seemed smarter but in fact only learned more quickly than most people.
   c. were smarter but learned more slowly than most people.
   d. were like everybody else except that they had talent.

_____8. One of the things Hemingway did *not* want to learn how to do was (**5a**)
   a. be somebody's disciple.
   b. perform in the bull ring.
   c. fish.
   d. ski.

_____9. Among Hemingway, Stein, and Pound (**5a**)
   a. they all liked each other.
   b. Hemingway liked Stein but not Pound.
   c. Stein liked Pound but not Hemingway.
   d. Stein and Pound did not like each other.

Interpreting and Evaluating

_____ 1. We may infer that, in regard to betting on horses, Hemingway (7)
   a. knew nothing.
   b. always listened to "hot" tips.
   c. was rather lucky.
   d. none of these.

_____ 2. We may infer that, in regard to sports, Hemingway (7)
   a. was interested in them only if he could make money.
   b. was always interested in watching but never interested in playing.
   c. was a superior athlete.
   d. was deeply interested.

_____ 3. We may infer that the writer believes that Hemingway's years in Paris were (10)
   a. a good way to learn another culture.
   b. important in teaching him French.
   c. disturbing for Hemingway.
   d. valuable in building his talent.

_____ 4. Hemingway was probably elevated to the position of staff reporter because (7, 9)
   a. no one else wanted the job.
   b. it was required that an American hold the job.
   c. his work as a commission reporter was so good that he was promoted.
   d. none of these.

_____ 5. According to the presentation by the writer, we can conclude about Hemingway that (9)
   a. he continued to learn as a writer all through his life.
   b. he learned all he had to in Paris.
   c. he was ungrateful for his friends' help.
   d. none of these.

_____ 6. In the sentence, "Having borrrowed all the money he could, Hemingway *laid it on Epinard's nose*" the expression in italics means (8)
   a. bet money on a race in which the horse ran.
   b. bought the horse, Epinard.
   c. tried to see if the horse could balance dollars on its nose.
   d. paid to mate the horse with an unfashionable sire.

_____ 7. In general, this writer believes that a person who wants to be an author should (**10**)
   a. try to learn whatever possible from anybody.
   b. go to Paris twice.
   c. make friends of writers and jockeys.
   d. work for a newspaper.

_____ 8. We may conclude about Hemingway's life that he lived it (**9**)
   a. very carefully.
   b. very sadly.
   c. very seriously.
   d. none of these.

_____ 9. About the fact that Hemingway did not go to college, the writer of this selection believes (**7**)
   a. it was unfortunate.
   b. it was probably unnecessary.
   c. it would have helped develop Hemingway's talent.
   d. it would have ruined Hemingway's talent.

_____10. About the fact that Hemingway learned a great deal from Gertrude Stein and Ezra Pound, we may conclude that (**9**)
   a. not all students and critics agree.
   b. all students and critics agree strongly.
   c. Hemingway was not grateful.
   d. there is evidence in his letters to Miss Stein.

_____11. It is clear that the writer of this selection believes that Hemingway is (**11**)
   a. a poor writer.
   b. an excellent writer.
   c. a good newsman but a poor writer of fiction.
   d. the inventor of cabelese.

_____12. It is only the writer's opinion that Hemingway (**11a**)
   a. was assigned as a reporter of the Genoa Economic Conference.
   b. had a gift that allowed him to accept or reject what is presented as knowledge.
   c. resigned from *The Star* in December of 1923.
   d. all of these.

Vocabulary

Choose the best meaning for each word in italics.

____ 1. *gravely* wounded
    a. not badly
    b. very seriously
    c. mortally
    d. unfortunately

____ 2. finish out his *apprenticeship*
    a. college work
    b. day's work
    c. period of learning
    d. cooperation

____ 3. did not *obligate* a newspaper
    a. suggest
    b. offer
    c. ask
    d. require

____ 4. suddenly *elevated*
    a. demoted
    b. forced
    c. promoted
    d. lifted up to another floor

____ 5. *authorized* to send cables
    a. requested
    b. compelled
    c. given power
    d. selected

____ 6. *denied* vehemently
    a. said not to be true
    b. told to do
    c. rushed away
    d. lied

____ 7. first year *abroad*
    a. married
    b. on ship
    c. in a foreign country
    d. as a correspondent

_____ 8. groping *adolescent*
    a. infant
    b. adult
    c. hero
    d. youth

_____ 9. listened *attentively*
    a. tiredly
    b. bravely
    c. with little attention
    d. with concentration

_____ 10. trying *vainly*
    a. bloodily
    b. without success
    c. without interest
    d. weakly

_____ 11. doctrine of the *accurate* image
    a. colorful
    b. vivid
    c. beautiful
    d. exact

_____ 12. an unfashionable *sire*
    a. father
    b. friend
    c. trainer
    d. jockey

_____ 13. *foresighted* young man
    a. handsome
    b. willing
    c. looking toward the future
    d. intelligent

_____ 14. *nagging* persecutions
    a. weakening
    b. annoying and persistent
    c. praising
    d. unfair and unequal

_____ 15. resigned *explosively*
    a. criminally
    b. without any reason
    c. after much thought
    d. violently

Index

To The Student:

We want this book to help you and students like you as much as possible. Your answers to the following questions will let us know how to make future editions of this book even more helpful. Please mail your answers to

English Editor
College Division
Houghton Mifflin Company
One Beacon Street
Boston, MA 02108

1. Is the writing style of the book clear? ____yes ____no

Which specific sections could be clearer? _____

_____

_____

_____

2. Circle the chapters in the *Handbook* you found most helpful.

1   2   3   4   5   6   7   8   9   10   11   12   13   14

What was most helpful in these chapters? _____

_____

_____

_____

3. Circle the chapters in the *Handbook* you found least helpful.

1   2   3   4   5   6   7   8   9   10   11   12   13   14

What was the problem with these chapters? _____

_____

_____

_____

4. Are there any reading or study skills you would like to see added to this book? ____yes ____no

If yes, which? _____

5. Were the exercises useful? ____yes ____no

Would you like to have more review exercises? _____

_____

_____

6. Rate each *Reading Selection* in Part 2 for interest and difficulty.

Selection	Read	Degree of Interest (1 = very dull 5 = very interesting)	Level of Difficulty (1 = too easy 5 = too difficult)	Did Not Read
1. Coyote	____	1 2 3 4 5	1 2 3 4 5	____
2. After Rush Hour	____	1 2 3 4 5	1 2 3 4 5	____
3. Getting High	____	1 2 3 4 5	1 2 3 4 5	____
4. Space Speaks	____	1 2 3 4 5	1 2 3 4 5	____
5. Momma	____	1 2 3 4 5	1 2 3 4 5	____
6. Easy Job	____	1 2 3 4 5	1 2 3 4 5	____
7. Apartment B	____	1 2 3 4 5	1 2 3 4 5	____
8. Perennial Lover	____	1 2 3 4 5	1 2 3 4 5	____
9. Paleolithic Age	____	1 2 3 4 5	1 2 3 4 5	____
10. Life with R. H. Macy	____	1 2 3 4 5	1 2 3 4 5	____
11. Businesses Owned by Blacks	____	1 2 3 4 5	1 2 3 4 5	____
12. All American Girl	____	1 2 3 4 5	1 2 3 4 5	____
13. Dining in A.D. 2001	____	1 2 3 4 5	1 2 3 4 5	____
14. Making of a Surgeon	____	1 2 3 4 5	1 2 3 4 5	____
15. Mother Who Came from China	____	1 2 3 4 5	1 2 3 4 5	____
16. Chaser	____	1 2 3 4 5	1 2 3 4 5	____
17. Language for Chimps	____	1 2 3 4 5	1 2 3 4 5	____
18. Classroom Testing	____	1 2 3 4 5	1 2 3 4 5	____
19. Dropouts	____	1 2 3 4 5	1 2 3 4 5	____
20. Discovery of the Electron	____	1 2 3 4 5	1 2 3 4 5	____
21. Hemingway in Paris	____	1 2 3 4 5	1 2 3 4 5	____

ABCDEFGHIJ-A-898765432l